STUDIES IN MUGHAL INDIA

STUDIES IN MUGHAL INDIA

By

JADUNATH SARKAR, M.A.

Being Historical Essays, 2nd Edition, with 12 new Essays added.

GYAN

Published by

GYAN

Gyan Publishing House
5, Ansari Road
Daryaganj, New Delhi-110002
Phone: 011-47034999, 9811692060
E-mail: books@gyanbooks.com

Distribution Network
gyanbooks.com
India, USA, Canada, UK, Australia, France

ISBN : 978-81-212-6822-6 (PB)
First Published, 1919

2nd Impression 2022

Printed at: Gyan Press, Delhi.

STUDIES IN MUGHAL INDIA
Author: JADUNATH SARKAR

STUDIES IN MUGHAL INDIA

JADUNATH SARKAR, M.A.,
Indian Educational Service (Bihar).

Being *Historical Essays*, 2nd Edition, with 12 new Essays added.

1920

WORKS BY PROF. JADUNATH SARKAR.

History of Aurangzib, *based on original sources.*

Vol. I. Reign of Shah Jahan.

,, II. War of Succession.

,, III. Northern India, 1658-1681.

,, IV. Southern India, 1645-1689.

Shivaji and His Times, *an original life based on an exhaustive study of Persian, Marathi and Hindi sources, and English Dutch and Portuguese Records.* 2nd edition, revised and enlarged.

Studies in Mughal India, *22 historical essays.*

Economics of British India,

4th edition, brought up to 1917.

Anecdotes of Aurangzib,

(Persian text of *Ahkam-i-Alamgiri* with English trans., notes, and a life of Aurangzib.)

Mughal Administration,

a study of its machinery, official duties, policy, procedure, achievements and failure.

Chaitanya's Life and Teachings,

translated from the saint's 16th century Bengali biography.

CONTENTS.

[*These were published in the 1st edition of my *Historical Essays*, 1912.]

By the same author.

History of Aurangzib, based on original Persian sources.

Vol. I. Reign of Shah Jahan.
„ II. War of succession.
„ III. Northern India, 1658-1681.
„ IV. Southern India, 1644-1689.

Rs. 3-8 each.

Shivaji and his Times,	... ...	„ 4.
Economics of British India, 4th ed.	...	„ 3.
Chaitanya's Pilgrimages and Teachings,	...	„ 2.
Anecdotes of Aurangzib, (*Ahkam-i-Alamgiri*) Persian text and Eng. translation,	...	„ $1\frac{1}{2}$.

—:o:—

M. C. Sarkar & Sons, 90/2 Harrison Road, Calcutta.
W. Heffer & Sons, Cambridge (England.)

STUDIES IN MUGHAL INDIA.

THE DAILY LIFE OF SHAH JAHAN.

POPULAR VIEW WRONG.

The Mughal palaces at Delhi and Agra every year draw thousands of visitors from far and near. Their beauty and splendour have moved the wonder of the world and the rapture of admiring artists and eloquent writers. The globe-trotter in India gives them the foremost place in his tour programme. Photographs and lantern-slides have made them familiar to far-off lands and home-staying people.

But what is it that the common tourist sees in them? He may feast his eyes on their delicate mosaics and reliefs; he may soothe his spirit in the cool recesses of those pure white domes. But what he looks at is after all stone, bare stone. Does he ever reflect that these halls were once full of life, crowded with all the moving pageants of a Court? Does he try to realise that life of a bygone world, so distant, so unlike his? If so, what is his mental picture of it?

We are afraid that most Europeans still lie under the spell of the popular novelists. With them, all Oriental kings were heartless brainless despots, full of pride and ignorance, surrounded by pimps and sycophants, squeezing the last farthing out of a down-trodden peasantry, and spending their hoards on sensual pleasure or childish show,—who passed their lives in toying with women in the harem, in listening to the fulsome praise of faithless courtiers, or in stupefying themselves with intoxicants,—men whose animal existence was never ennobled by intellectual exercise or spiritual musing, æsthetic culture or the discipline of work. Such is the Sultan (or Rajah) of nearly every English novel, with his jewelled turban, curled up moustaches, bloodshot eyes, nose high up in the air, and a small arsenal thrust into his waist-band. This idea has been impressed on the general public of Europe by popular writers, who sacrifice truth to literary effect, and whose ignorance of Eastern history is only equalled by their pride in everything Western.

But a little reflection will show that this view cannot possibly be true. From Akbar to Aurangzib we had four great rulers, who reigned in unbroken succession for a century and a half (1556—1707), extended their dominion, maintained peace at home and respect abroad, developed an administrative system in all its branches, and carried many arts towards perfection. Could this work have been done by sleepy voluptuaries? The world is not so easily governed. Inefficiency has a very short lease even in the East. An empire like that of the "Great Mughals" in its best days could not have been a dead machine; administration, arts and wealth could not have developed, as they did develop in that period, if we had had only *faineants* on the throne, in the council-chamber, and at the head of armies.

Happily the contemporary Persian histories fully describe the Emperor's daily routine of work and enable us to picture the life of his Court. Let us see how Shah Jahan lived and worked in his beloved palace of Agra. (True, he founded New Delhi and named it after himself, but Agra was the city of his heart.)

EMPEROR'S DAILY ROUTINE.

A.M.

4 ...Wakes—Prayer—Reading.

6-45...Appears at *Darshan* window—elephant combats—review of cavalry.

7-40...Public Darbar *(Diwan-i-am)*.

9-40...Private Audience (*Diwan-i-khas*).

11-40...Secret Consultation in the *Shah Burj*.

12 ...In harem—meal—siesta—charity to women.

P.M.

4 ...Public Audience—Evening prayer.

6-30...Evening assembly in the *Diwan-i-khas*.

8 ...Secret Council in the *Shah Burj*.

8-30 ..In the harem—music.

10 ...Hears books read.

10-30...4 A.M.—Sleeps.

MORNING PRAYER.

The Emperor woke from his sleep about two hours before sunrise, and after his morning toilet spent some time in religious devotions. After saying the customary prayer based on the Prophet's *Traditions*, which is not obligatory on Muslims, he sat with his face towards Mecca, reciting the verses of the *Quran* and meditating on God. Shortly before sunrise, he performed the first obligatory prayer of the day in the palace mosque, and then engaged in his worldly duties.

DARSHAN.

His first work was to show himself to his subjects. In the eastern wall of Agra fort, overlooking the foreshore of the Jumna which stretches like a plain below, there was a window called the *jharokha-i-darshan*, from the Sanskrit word *darshan* meaning the sight of someone high or holy. Vast crowds of expectant people assembled on the bank every morning. The Emperor appeared at the window about 48 minutes after sunrise, and showed his face to his subjects, who at once bowed, while he returned their salute. From two to three quarters of an hour were spent here, not merely in showing himself, but also in business and pleasure. The plain being outside the fort walls, the public had free access to it, and the oppressed could submit their petitions or make their complaints to the Emperor, without having to grease the palms of door-keepers and court-underlings, or going through the tedious and costly process of a law suit. Thus the Emperor daily came in touch with the common people and could freely learn their thoughts and feelings. Often a string was let down from the window, and the petitions tied to it and pulled up by the attendants above for immediate submission to the Emperor. This wise practice was instituted by the great Akbar. Curiously enough, there was a class of Brahmans, called the *Darshanis*, who did not begin their day's work nor eat their breakfast until they had gazed at the auspicious face of the Emperor!

After the public salute and admission of complaints were over, the plain was cleared, and elephant-fights took place there. This was the special prerogative of the Emperor, and not even the princes of the blood could order such a fight for themselves. Shah Jahan was specially fond of this sport, and on some days as many as five pairs of elephants were made to fight single combats in succession for his delight. This spacious plain was a safe place for their wild charges, encounter, and pursuit. In the fort quadrangle hundreds of spectators would have been trampled to death by these moving mountains.

Fierce war-elephants and newly captured ones, which had not been fully tamed, were here shown to the Emperor. It was impossible to take them, like the other elephants, to the court-yard inside the fort. On the river-side, too, war-elephants were trained to charge cavalry, and thus made to lose their natural fear of horses. Here were also paraded the horses of the Imperial army and of the retainers of the nobles.

DIWAN-I-AM.

Next took place the Public Darbar in the *Diwan-i-am* or Hall of Public Audience. Akbar and Jahangir used to hold Court at the very same spot, but under canvas awnings stretched on poles set up for the occasion. In 1628 Shah Jahan built a gilt and decorated wooden pavilion, for the shelter of the courtiers. This was replaced in 1638 by the present *Diwan-i-am*, a stately edifice of red sandstone, painted white with lime, supported on 40 noble pillars, and open on three sides. In the centre of the fourth side or back is a raised alcove of the purest white marble, richly decorated with *pietra dura* work and low reliefs of flowers and foliage. Here sat the Emperor overlooking the hall below.

GRAND DARBAR.

In the Persian histories we have a detailed account of how a grand *darbar* was held in those days. The Emperor sat on his cushioned seat in the alcove. On his right and left were the princes, his sons; these took their seats only when commanded to do so. In the Hall stood the courtiers, officers, nobles, and gentry in due order, with their backs to the three open sides. Those who attended on the Emperor's person were stationed on his right and left near the two pillars close to the alcove, their backs being turned to the wall. Facing the Emperor, stood the chief officers of State, rank behind rank, according to their gradation. The royal standard bearers, holding the golden banners and *tugh* and *qur*,* were drawn up on the Emperor's left with their backs to the wall.

Thus the entire Hall, 201 feet long and 67 feet broad, was filled with men. But it was too small to hold all who deserved or sought audience. Silver railings

* The Turkish standard of balls and the Yak cow's tail fixed on a rod and borne aloft. The Mughal Emperors were Turks of the Chaghtai tribe.

fenced it round on the three sides with only three openings in them. In the court-yard in front a space was enclosed with a railing of painted wood on which velvet canopies richly embroidered with gold were spread. Here stood all men below commanders of two hundred, archers of the guard, musketeers, and some of the retainers of the nobles, when they attended the darbar. At the doors of the Hall and of the two railings (silver and wooden) trustworthy mace-bearers and sergeants-at-arms in their splendid uniforms kept guard, excluding strangers and persons who had no *entree* at Court.

The audience stood ready and expectant, when, at about 7-40 A.M., the Emperor entered the alcove by the back door, took his seat, and the business of the Court began.

The High Bakhshi or Paymaster-General reported to the Emperor the petitions of the military officers or *mansabdars*, and immediately received His Majesty's orders giving promotions to some, new posts to others. Officers who had come to the capital from the provinces had audience. Those who had been newly appointed to some province or post were next presented by the heads of their departments, *viz.*, the Commandant of the Artillery (*Mir-i-atish*), the Paymaster of the mounted musketeers, or the Paymaster of the gentlemen troopers (*ahadis.*) These chiefs recommended every deserving man among them for some royal favour. The presentees bowed and got their *congee*, usually accompanied by a robe of honour and gift in the form of jewellery, orders or arms.

Next came the clerks of the Department of Crown-lands or the Emperor's privy* purse. Through their chiefs,—the *Mir-i-saman* and the *Diwan-i-bayutat*, they submitted their various proposals and got prompt orders from His Majesty.

Then the courtiers who enjoyed the Emperor's confidence placed before him the despatches of the princes, and of the governors, *faujdars*, *diwans* (revenue heads,) *bakhshis* and other officers of the provinces, and also any presents (*peshkash*) sent by them.

The letters of the princes and chief officers were read or heard by the Emperor himself. The purport only of the rest was reported to him. When this work was over, the Chief *Sadr* reported the important points of the despatches of the provincial *Sadrs* sent to him. He also brought to the Emperor's notice cases of needy scholars, Syeds, Shaikhs, and pious men, and got grants of money for each according to his need or deserts.

The work of public charity being over, orders previously passed about *mansabs*, *jagirs*, cash grants, and other financial affairs, were submitted to the Emperor a second time for confirmation. There was a special officer to remind the Emperor of these things, and he bore the title of the *darogha* of *arz-i-mukarrar*.

Next, the officers of the Imperial stables displayed before His Majesty the horses and elephants with their fixed rations. This practice had been started by Akbar in order to punish those officers who stole the Imperial grant and starved the animals. If any horse or elephant looked lean or weak, the money allowed for its feeding was resumed and the officer in charge of it reprimanded. Similarly the retainers of the nobles, whose horses had been recently mustered and branded, were paraded in full equipment in the court-yard within view of the Emperor. The darbar lasted two hours, sometimes more or less according to the amount of the business to be done.

DIWAN-I-KHAS.

Then, a little before 10 A.M., His Majesty went to the Hall of Private Audience* and sat on the throne. Here he wrote with his own hand the answers to the most important letters. Of the other letters a few were read to him by the Court agents of the high grandees, or by the *wazir*, or by the officers appointed to submit the despatches of the provincial viceroys. In reply to them, *farmans* or Imperial letters were drafted by the ministers in the terms of their master's verbal orders. The drafts were afterwards revised and corrected by the Emperor, written out fair, and sent to the harem to be sealed with the Great Seal,† of which the Empress Mumtaz Mahal had charge.

The highest revenue officers now reported on very

* Popularly called the *Ghusal-khanah* because Akbar's bath-room was adjacent to its site..

† *Uzuk*, a small round seal, bearing only the Emperor's name, affixed to *Sahti farmans*. (Blochmann's *Ain*, i. 52 & 260.)

important matters connected with the Crownlands, and the assignments on revenue made in favour of military officers, and learnt the Emperor's pleasure on each point. The Head of the Royal Charity Department brought to the Emperor's notice special cases of needy men; most of them received cash grants, some lands, others daily stipends. A fund was created for this purpose out of the gold, silver and jewels against which the Emperor was weighed (*wazan*) every birthday, and the money which was offered by the nobles and princes as sacrifice (*tasadduq*) in order to avert calamities and bad omens from him.

Then a short time was passed in inspecting the works of skilful artisans, such as jewel-setters, enamellers, &c. Plans of royal buildings were placed in his hands, and he added elements of beauty to them or made alterations where necessary. On the plans finally approved, the prime-minister Asaf Khan wrote an explanation of the Emperor's wishes, for the guidance of the architects. This was an important work, as Shah Jahan was very fond of building noble edifices,—which will remain as his memorial to all time. The Superintendent of the Public Works Department with expert architects attended this private darbar to consult their master.

These works being over, the Emperor occasionally looked at the hunting animals, hawks and leopards, which had been trained for him. Mettled horses, ridden by expert horse-tamers, were made to go through their exercises in the yard of the private palace, under His Majesty's eyes.

SHAH BURJ.

Nearly two hours were thus occupied, and at about half past eleven the Emperor left this Hall and entered the lofty *Shah Burj* or Royal Tower. The most confidential business was done here. None but the princes and a few trusted officers could enter this tower without special permission. Even the servants had to stand outside, till they were sent for.

Secret affairs of State, which it would have been harmful to make public, were discussed with the Grand *Wazir*. A *precis* was made of the important and confidential letters to be sent to noblemen serving in the distant provinces. Such urgent matters about the Crownlands, the payment of the military, &c., as had been submitted in the two previous darbars of the day were now reported by the *wazir* and the Emperor's orders taken on them. Some three quarters of an hour were usually spent here, but the time varied according to the amount of the business to be despatched.

IN THE HAREM AT NOON.

It was now nearly midday and the Emperor entered the harem, where he performed the *zuhar* prayer, ate his meal, and took a nap for an hour. With most kings the harem is a place of pleasure and rest. But work pursued Shah Jahan even there. A crowd of female beggars—poor widows and orphans, maidens of decayed families, daughters of poor scholars, theologians and pious men,—besought the royal charity. Their petitions were put before the Empress by her chief servant Sati-un-nissa, called the Female Nazir; and Her Majesty reported the cases to the Emperor, who gave lands to some, pensions or donations to others, and garments, jewels, and money as the dowries of maidens too poor to marry. Large sums were every day spent in the harem in this work of relief.

AFTERNOON AUDIENCE.

Shortly after 3 P.M. the Emperor performed his *asar* prayer, and sometimes visited the Hall of Public Audience again. The men present bowed. A little State business was gone through in a short time. The palace-guards, called *chawkidars*, were drawn up before him and presented their arms. Then His Majesty joined the congregation of his Court to perform the sunset prayer in the Private Audience Hall.

SOIREE IN THE DIWAN-I-KHAS.

The day was now spent, but the day's work was not yet over. The *Diwan-i-khas* was lit up with fragrant candles set in jewelled candelabra, the Emperor and his choice associates gathered here and spent some two hours, at first in attending to the administration and afterwards in pleasure. But it was pleasure of an elevated and refined character. He heard music, vocal and instrumental, and often deigned to join in it. If we may trust the Court chronicler, Shah Jahan was a past master of Urdu song, and his performances were so sweet and charming that "many pure-souled *Sufis* and holy men with hearts withdrawn from the world, who attended these evening assemblies, lost their senses in the ecstasy produced by his singing."

SECRET COUNCIL AGAIN.

After the *isha* prayer (8 P.M.) he went to the Shah Burj, and if there was any secret business of State still to be done, he summoned the Grand *Wazir* and the *Bakhshis* and despatched it there,—leaving nothing over for the morrow.

MUSIC AND READING IN THE HAREM.

At about 8-30 P.M., he retired to the harem again. Two and sometimes three hours were here spent in listening to songs by women. Then His Majesty retired to bed and was read to sleep. Good readers sat behind a *pardah* which separated them from the royal bed chamber, and read aloud books on travel, lives of saints and prophets, and histories of former kings,—all rich in instruction. Among them the Life of Timur and the Autobiography of Babar were his special favourites.

Finally, after 10 P.M., the Emperor fell asleep and enjoyed a night's repose of six hours.

COURT OF JUSTICE ON WEDNESDAY.

Such was the life of the Mughal Court on ordinary days. But we must remember that Friday is the

Muhammadan Sabbath, when no Court was held. Wednesday, too, was specially set apart for doing justice,—which is one of the most important duties of Oriental kings. On that day no darbar was held in the *Diwan-i-am*, but the Emperor came direct from the *darshan* window to the Private Audience Hall, at about 8 A.M., to sit on the throne of justice. True, he had appointed wise, experienced and God-fearing men to act as judges of Canon law (*qazis*), judges of common law (*adils*), and superintendent of the law-court, but the king himself was the fountain of justice and the highest court of appeal. On Wednesday none had *entree* except the law officers, jurists versed in *fatawa*, pious and upright scholars, and the few nobles who constantly attended on the Emperor's person. The officers of justice presented the plaintiffs one by one, and reported their grievances. His Majesty very gently ascertained the facts by inquiry, took the law from the *ulema* (Canon-lawyers), and pronounced judgment accordingly. Many had come from far-off provinces to get justice from the highest power in the land. Their plaints could not be investigated except locally; and so the Emperor wrote orders to the governors of those places, urging them to find out the truth, and either do justice there or send the parties back to the capital, with their reports.

Such was the settled life of Agra or Delhi, but it was often varied by rides through the city, generally in the afternoon, river trips on the Jumna in the State barges, hunting expeditions, and tours, for the Great Mughals were active rulers and often visited the provinces with their whole Court, performing grand progresses through the country. Thus we see that the royal throne was not exactly a bed of roses even in those days. The king had his duties, and his division of his time showed that he knew the fact. It was a strenuous life that Shah Jahan led, and he gave peace, prosperity and contentment to his people. An old Persian manuscript of the India Office Library, London, after giving Shah Jahan's routine of work, addresses him in the following couplet:—

Khalq sabuk dil ze giran bariyash,
Fitna giran khab ze bidariyash.

"O! king, thy subjects are light-hearted because thou hast taken a heavy load on thy shoulders;
Oppression has fallen into a deep sleep (in thy kingdom) because thou hast banished sleep from thy eyes."

And the praise was right well deserved.*

---

* The materials for this essay have been collected from Abdul Hamid's *Padishah-namah*, I.A. 144-154, 221, I B. 235, and India Off. Pers. Ms. No. 1344, *f7. a & b.*

THE WEALTH OF IND, 1650.

WHEN Milton wrote,

> High on a throne of royal state, which far
> Outshone the wealth of Ormuz and of Ind,
> Or where the gorgeous East with richest hand
> Showers on her kings barbaric pearl and gold,—

could he have been thinking of India under Shah Jáhan, the builder of the Taj and the Peacock Throne? For, the finest example of eastern royal magnificence was afforded by that king's Court. The contemporary history of Abdul Hamid Lahori enables us to estimate accurately the wealth of the Mughal Emperor in 1648. A rupee of that time was worth 2*s*. 3*d*., but its purchasing power was about seven times that of to-day.

The REVENUE was 20 *krores* of rupees (22½ million pounds), of which the newly acquired provinces,—Daulatabad, Telingana, and Baglana,—yielded 1½ *krores*. The Crown-lands supplied the Emperor's privy purse with three *krores* of rupees (3½ million pounds sterling).

In the first twenty years of his reign, Shah Jahan spent 9½ *krores* of rupees in rewards and gifts,—about 4½ *krores* in cash and 5 *krores* in kind. His BUILDINGS absorbed more than three millions sterling, as the following list will show:—

At Agra—

The Pearl Mosque and the palaces and gardens in the fort	... 60 lakhs.
The Taj Mahal...	... 50 ,,

At Delhi—		
Palaces	... 50	lakhs
Jumma Masjid	... 10	"
New wall round Delhi	... 4	"
The *Idgah* outside Delhi	... ½	"
At Lahore—		
Palaces, gardens, and canal ...	... 50	"
At Kabul—		
Mosque, palace, fort, and city-wall ...	... 12	"
In Kashmir—		
Royal buildings and gardens ...	... 8	"
At Qandahar, &c.—		
Forts of Qandahar, Bist, and Zamindawar	... 8	"
At Ajmir, &c.—		
Ajmir, Ahmadabad, &c. (buildings) ...	... 12	"
At Mukhlispur—		
Imperial palaces	... 6	"
Crown Prince Dara Shukoh's palace ...	... 2	"
	272½	"
	=£3,065,625	

The Imperial JEWELLERY was worth 5 *krores* of rupees, besides two *krores'* worth given away to the princes and others. Of the former, the Emperor wore on his head, neck, arms, and waist fully two *krores'* worth; these were kept in the *harem* in charge of the women servants, while the remainder (worth 3 *krores*) was deposited in the outer apartments in the custody of the slaves.

His rosary contained 5 rubies and 30 pearls, and was valued at 8 *lakhs*. There were two other rosaries of 125 large round rubies worthy of kings; between every pair of beads was a coloured *yaqut* (topaz?) The midmost bead in each rosary weighed 32 *ratis* (= 28 carats) and cost Rs. 40,000, and the price of the two strings taken together reached 20 *lakhs*. They had been mostly collected by Akbar.

Only second-rate jewels were, however, put in the Emperor's rosary (the first named one). All the largest and finest rubies were reserved for his *sarpech* (aigrette or jewel worn on the turban). This ornament was tied to his head-dress on the anniversary of the coronation: it had 5 large rubies and 24 pearls set on it;—of these the largest ruby in the centre weighed 288 *ratis* (=252 carats) and was valued at two *lakhs* of rupees, though in the market it would have been considered cheap at 4 *lakhs*. The total price of the *sarpech* was 12 *lakhs*. On 11th November, 1644, a big pear-like pearl costing Rs. 40,000 and weighing 43 *surkhs* (=124 gr. Troy?) was added to it. The largest ruby (or diamond?) in the Imperial treasury was about 430 *ratis* (=378 carats) in weight and worth two *lakhs*, but it had not the flawless lustre of the central gem of the *sarpech*. Yet another ruby, shaped like a pear, and weighing 47 *ratis* (=41 carats) only, cost half a *lakh*.

On 12th March, 1635, Shah Jahan sat for the first time on the newly finished PEACOCK THRONE. "Many gems had been collected by three generations of Emperors,—Akbar, Jahangir, and Shah Jahan. Of what use were they if the people could not gaze at them?" asks the Court annalist, Abdul Hamid Lahori. So, all the jewels in the outer palace (worth 2 *krores*) were ordered to be shown to the Emperor, and out of them he chose the very best, valued at 16 *lakhs*. With one *lakh tolahs* (=3255 lbs. Troy) of pure gold, equivalent to 14 *lakhs* of rupees, the artisans of the Imperial gold-smith department under the superintendence of Bebadal Khan, constructed a throne $3\frac{1}{4}$ yards long, $2\frac{1}{2}$ yards broad, and 5 yards high, and studded it with these jewels. The inner roof was enamelled and had only a few stones set here and there; but the outside was covered with rubies, *yaquts*, and other gems. Twelve pillars of emerald supported this roof. Above it were placed two figures of peacocks ornamented with jewels, and between them a tree set with rubies, diamonds, emeralds, and pearls.

Three jewelled steps led up to the Emperor's seat, which was surrounded on eleven sides with jewelled planks serving as railings; (the twelfth was open, being in front of the Emperor and just above the steps).

Of these eleven panels the most splendid was the middle one, on which the Emperor rested his arm in reclining. It cost 10 *lakhs* of rupees, its central ruby alone being worth one *lakh*. This ruby had been presented by Shah Abbas I., the Persian king, to Jahangir, and had inscribed on it the names of Timur, Mir Shahrukh, Mirza Ulugh Beg, Shah Abbas, Jahangir the son of Akbar, and Shah Jahan! Inside the throne, a poem by Haji Muhammad Jan Qudsi, in 20 couplets, was inscribed in letters of enamel, the last three words (*Aurang-i-shahanshah-i-adil*) giving the date of its construction. Apart from the salary of the craftsmen, the materials alone of the throne cost one *krore* of rupees.

Such vast treasures would naturally tempt spoilers from far-off lands, and required a strong force to safe-guard them. Accordingly, we find that the Imperial ARMY in 1648 comprised—

	200,000	cavalry,
	8,000	*mansabdars* (commanders),
	7,000	*ahadis* (gentlemen troopers) and mounted musketeers,
	40,000	foot musketeers* and artillerymen,
in addition to	185,000	cavalry under the princes and nobles.
TOTAL ...	440,000	

These did not include the local militia posted in the *parganahs* and commanded by the *faujdars*, *kroris* (District Collectors,) and *amlas*,—who must have numbered several *lakhs* more. In a letter written just before his captivity Shah Jahan describes himself as the lord of 900,000 troopers. The total armed strength of the empire, then, approached one million of men, though it did not include all India.†

---

* Of these, 16,000 accompanied the Emperor and the remaining 30,000 were quartered in the various *Subahs*.

† Authorities,—for Revenue (Abdul Hamid's *Padishahnamah*, II. 711-714); Building (*Ibid* and Waris's *Padishahnamah*, Khuda Bakhsh Ms., 101*b*, 116*a*, 122*b*); Jewellery (Abdul Hamid, II. 391-393); Peacock Throne, (*Ibid*, I. B. 77-81); Army (*Ibid*, II. 715).

THE COMPANION OF AN EMPRESS.

THE following biographical sketch gives us a picture of the inner life of the Mughal Court at the height of its glory, introduces to us a learned and accomplished Persian lady, and finally tells the simple and sad tale of a mother's love and grief which has an interest quite apart from its value as a side-light on Indian history.

The Persians, who have been rightly called 'the French of Asia,' supplied many of the most brilliant gems that gathered round the throne of India's Muhammadan rulers. From Persia came Mahmud Gawan, the heaven-born minister of the Bahmani Sultans of the Deccan, Mir Jumla, the right-hand man of Aurangzib, Abul Fath, the physician and friend of Akbar, Ali Mardan Khan, the general and administrator, Ruhullah Khan, the finance minister of Aurangzib, and many other worthies of the field and the council-chamber. From Persia, too, came the highly accomplished lady who is the subject of this memoir.

Sati-un-nissa* (lit. 'the lance-head among women') was the daughter of a respectable native of Mazendran, a province of Persia, and belonged to a family of scholars and physicians. Her brother Taliba Amuli, was unrivalled in his age in he choice of words and the power of clothing fine sense in equally fine phrases, and earned the title of "Prince of Poets" at the Court of Jahangir. When her husband Nasira, a brother of

* *Sati*, a Persian word, means as I have taken it here. But *Sitti*, spelt in exactly the same way, is an Arabic word meaning 'Madam', 'grandmother'.

the great physician Raknai Kashi, died in India, Sati-un-nissa entered the service of Mumtaz Mahal, the renowned Empress of Shah Jahan. Here her ability, charm of speech, perfect mastery of the proper conduct of a dependent, and knowledge of medicine and various kinds of treatment, won her royal mistress's heart, and she was promoted above all the old servants and entrusted with the Empress's seal, the badge of the head of her establishment. She was a good elocutionist and could recite the Quran well and read Persian works in prose and verse properly. For her literary accomplishments she was appointed tutoress to the Princess Royal Jahanara, and very soon taught her to read the Quran and write Persian.

She was also the intermediary of the Emperor's charity to women. Whenever she heard of an honest woman in distress or of a virgin too poor to be married, she reported the case to the Empress, and the latter brought it to the Emperor's ear on his coming to the harem in the evening. Large sums were daily spent in helping these poor women, lands and daily stipends or cash bounties were given to the wives and widows, and ornaments and money paid to the virgins. Sati-un-nissa acted as the Imperial almoneress, and the historian praises her as "attentive, eloquent, expert, and gentle in manner."

When the Empress died (7th June, 1631), Sati-un-nissa, as her chief servant and agent, accompanied the corpse to its last resting-place at Agra (the Taj Mahal).

Shah Jahan, as a loving husband, faithfully cherished her memory and did not marry again, though he survived her by 35 years. The duties of the late Empress, as the female head of the Imperial family, now fell to her eldest daughter Jahanara, and she had to play her mother's part in conducting marriage ceremonies, entertaining female guests, and performing other social functions peculiar to the mistress of a household. In this task she was ably assisted by her former tutor, Sati-un-nissa, to whom she gave her seal and control of her household staff, on her mother's death. Thus the subject of our memoir continued to be the highest lady servant of the Mughal Empire, and was like a mother to the orphan princes and princesses.

At every marriage of a prince of the blood royal, Sati-un-nissa, as a sort of female *major domo*, conveyed the imperial presents to the bride's house. The male officers who accompanied her stayed outside, while she entered the harem and made over the gifts to the bride's mother, from whom she received liberal rewards for her pains. Mumtaz Mahal before her death used to lay aside money, jewels and precious articles, in view of her sons' marriage when they would grow up. Jahanara constantly added to them. At the time of marriage these were spent in offering tribute to the Emperor, gifts to the princes and Begams, and presents and robes to the nobles and courtiers. At the marriage of the Crown Prince Dara Shukoh, (11th November, 1632), these amounted to sixteen lakhs of rupees,—seven lakhs in jewels, one lakh in cash, four lakhs in gold and silver ornaments and rare articles of all countries in the world, and the balance in elephants and horses. By order of Jahanara, Sati-un-nissa arranged all this vast collection for display in the spacious courtyard of Agra Fort in front of the window at which the Emperor used to show his face to his adoring subjects.

At night the whole place was illuminated, forming a sort of exhibition. The courtiers and nobles feasted their eyes on the treasures, and even the Emperor condescended to pay a visit.

So, too, at the marriage of the second prince, Shujah (23rd February, 1633), a display was made of wedding presents worth 10 lakhs of rupees, all supplied by Mumtaz Mahal and Jahanara. Sati-un-nissa's capacity for organisation and artistic taste must have found ample scope for exercise in getting up such exhibitions.

In addition to being the head servant of Jahanara, Sati-un-nissa was also made by the Emperor the *Sadar* or Superintendent of the harem, in reward of her fidelity and obedience. She had also to wait at the Emperor's table and serve him with provisions,—as the most honoured and trusted of women attendants. Thus she was constantly in the Emperor's eyes and was most kindly treated by him.

She had no child of her own, but adopted the two daughters of her late brother, Taliba. On them she lavished all the love and maternal yearnings of a childless widow's heart. The younger of the two, on whom she particularly doted, was married to Hakim Zia-ud-din, a nephew of her late husband. The bridegroom was brought over from Persia and cherished at the Imperial Court through her influence. But this young woman, the centre of all Sati-un-nissa's affection, died of a long illness following childbirth (10th January, 1647). A mother's grief is too strong for any earthly control. Sati-un-nissa, "in spite of her wisdom and philosophy, cast off all patience, and abandoned herself to mourning for eleven days in her house, outside the citadel of Lahore."

But Shah Jahan was the kindest of men, a model husband, father and master of household. He could not neglect an old servant. On 22nd January, hoping that her grief had now somewhat abated, he kindly had her brought to her official residence within the Imperial harem, went there in the company of Jahanara, consoled her in many ways, and took her with himself to the palace.

Next day, as the Emperor went out to hunt, Sati-un-nissa returned to her own house for some necessary works. After eating her meal and saying the evening prayers, she betook herself to reading the *Quran*.

At about 8 P.M. she suddenly cried out, "I feel like being choked," and rapidly grew worse. The Persian doctor Masih-uz-Zaman, a distant relative, was immediately summoned. At his arrival, she bowed to salute him, then raised her head, and at once sank down on her side. The pulse was still beating; the doctor and her son-in-law continued applying remedies for fainting, but to no purpose. When the pulse failed, they knew that she had left the world. Thus she followed her daughter in death by a fortnight only.

Next day (24th January) the news reached Shah Jahan in the hunting camp. He was deeply touched, and ordered all honour to be shown to her mortal remains and Rs. 10,000 to be spent on her funeral. After more than a year the body was taken out and finally buried west of the Taj Mahal, close to the outer quadrangle, in a tomb built by Government at an expense of Rs. 30,000. A village yielding Rs. 3,000 a year was assigned for the pay of its attendants. Thus she was not parted from her beloved master and mistress even in death.

WHO BUILT THE TAJ MAHAL?

MUMTAZ MAHAL'S DEATH.

In 1607 A. D., when Shah Jahan (then Prince Khurram) was 15 years old, his father Jahangir betrothed him to Arjmand Banu Begam (afterwards surnamed Mumtaz Mahal), a daughter of Nur Jahan's brother, Asaf Khan. Five years afterwards (1612), the marriage was celebrated: the bridegroom was then 20 years and 3 months of age, and the bride just 14 months younger. After 19 years of wedded life, in which she bore 14 children to her royal husband, the Begam died of the pain of child-birth, prolonged for 30 hours, at Burhanpur, on Tuesday, 7th June, 1631 (17 Ziqada, 1040 A.H.)

Shah Jahan was so overpowered by grief that for one week he could not bring himself to appear at the window of the Hall of Audience, or to attend to any affair of State. He said that he would have turned *faqir* for the rest of his life, if kingship were not a sacred charge which no one can lay aside at his pleasure. He gave up the use of coloured dress, scents, and jewels; forbade music and song at the annual coronation and birthday ceremonies,—indeed they now sounded strangely like dirges and wailing in his ears. His beard which had not more than 20 grey hairs, now rapidly turned white. At every visit to her tomb, he used to shed "rivers of tears" over her remains, and lament, saying, "Empire has no sweetness, life itself has no relish left for me now!" If he visited the *harem*, he promptly returned weeping and sighing, "Nobody's face can delight me now!" True, Shah Jahan had married two other wives, the daughters of Muzaffar Husain Mirza and Shah Nawaz Khan, 2 years before and 5 years after his union with Mumtaz Mahal; but these were political alliances (*ba iqtiza-e-maslihate*), not love-matches. Mumtaz Mahal so fully occupied his heart that there was no space left there for any other love; and the Emperor in weal and woe, in settled residence and travel, never parted with her company. (*Padishahnamah*, i. 387, and *Muntakhab-ul-Labab*, i. 459).

The following account of her death is given in a rare Persian manuscript (the autobiography of Qasim Ali Afridi, affixed to his *Diwan*), belonging to the Khuda Bakhsh Library. The story seems to be current at Agra, and is also found in a Ms. treatise on the Taj which has been lent by the Khuda Bakhsh Library to the Victoria Memorial Hall.

"Shah Jahan had, besides his four sons, four daughters; Anjuman-ara, Gaiti-ara, Jahan-ara, and Dahar-ara [Gauhar-ara]. It is said that just before the birth of the last, a sound of crying was heard in the womb of Mumtaz Mahal. Immediately on hearing it, the Begam despaired of her life, summoned the Emperor to her side, and said in plaintive accents, 'It is well-known that when the babe cries in the womb, the mother can never survive its birth. Now that it is my lot to leave this mortal sphere for the eternal home, O King! pardon aught that I may have said amiss. Pardon every fault that I may have committed, as I am about to set out on my last journey......Sir King! I shared your lot at the time of your captivity [in your father's reign] and other afflictions. Now that the Lord God has given it to you to rule the world, I have, alas, to depart in sorrow! Promise to keep my two last requests.' The Emperor promised 'on his life and soul,' and asked her to state her wishes. She replied, 'God has given you four sons and four daughters. They are enough to preserve your name and fame. Raise not issue on any other woman, lest her children and mine should come to blows for the succession. My second prayer is that you should build over me such a mausoleum that the like of it may not be seen anywhere else in the world.' Then, a moment after giving birth to Dahar-ara, she died." (Pp. 22*b*-23*a*).

But the above is merely a popular legend. The contemporary historian, Abdul Hamid Lahori (author of the *Padishahnamah*) is silent about it. He describes the death-scene thus:

"When the Begam learnt that her death was certain, she sent the Princess Jahan-ara to call the Emperor to her. He at once arrived in great concern and sorrow. She commended her sons and her mother to his care and then set out on her last journey." (i. 386).

Her body was at first laid in the earth in a building within a garden on the bank of the river Tapti opposite

Burhanpur. On the 1st December following her death, it was taken out and sent to Agra in charge of Prince Shuja, arriving at the latter town on the 20th of the month. (i. 402).

THE TAJ, ITS BUILDERS AND STONES.

A spacious tract of land, south of Agra city, was chosen for the burial place, and purchased from its owner, Rajah Jai Singh, the grandson of Man Singh (*Padishahnamah*, i. 403). Plans for the tomb were submitted by all the master architects of the land. When one of these was approved by the Emperor, a wooden model of it was first made (*Diwan-i-Afridi*, 23*a*).

Begun early in 1632, the Taj was completed in January 1643, under the supervision of MUKARRAMAT KHAN and MIR ABDUL KARIM, at an expense of fifty lakhs of rupees (*Muntakhab-ul-Labab*, i. 596, and *Padishahnamah*, ii. 322 *et seq.*). The *Diwan-i-Afridi* estimates the cost at 9 krores and 17 lakhs of rupees and names the following artisans as employed in the construction:—

(1) Amanat Khan Shirazi, writer of Tughra inscriptions, from Qandahar.

(2) Master (*ustád*) Isa, mason, a citizen of Agra.

(3) Master Pirá, carpenter, a resident of Delhi.

(4-6) Banuhár, Jhat Mal, and Zoráwar, sculptors, from Delhi.

(7) Ismail Khan Rumi, maker of the dome and the scaffolding (*dhola*) supporting it.

(8) Rám Mal Kashmiri, gardener. (P. 23*a* and *b*.)

Other workmen are named in a recent Urdu work on the Taj, but I know not on what authority.

The following twenty kinds of precious stones were set in the Taj, (*Diwan-i-Afridi*, 23*b*):—

(1) Cornelian from Qandahar.

(2) Lapis lazuli from Ceylon.

(3) Onyx from 'the upper world' (?)

(4) *Patunja* from the river Nile.

(5) Gold [stone?] from Basrah and the sea of Ormuz.

(6) *Khatu* from the hill of Jodhpur.

(7) *Ajuba* from the hill-rivers of Kumaon.

(8) Marble from Makrána.

(9) *Mariama* from the city of Basrah.

(10) *Badl*-stone from the river Banas.

(11) *Yamini* from Yemen.

(12) *Mungah* from the Atlantic Ocean.

(13) *Ghori* from Ghor-band.

(14) *Tamrah* from the river Gandak.

(15) Beryl from the hill of Bábá Budhan.

(16) *Musai* (stone of Moses!) from Mount Sinai.

(17) *Gwaliori* from the river of Gwalior.

(18) Red [sand-] stone from all directions.

(19) Jasper from Persia.

(20) *Dalchana* from the river Asan.

ITS ENDOWMENT.

On the 12th anniversary of her death, (27th January, 1643), Shah Jahan visited the Taj Mahal, and bestowed in *waqf* 30 villages of the parganahs of Agra and Nagarchin, yielding a revenue of 1 lakh of rupees, and the serais, and shops adjoining the tomb, producing another lakh of rupees in rent, for the up-keep of the mausoleum and the support of the pious men placed in it. The *Padishahnamah* (ii. 327) gives a list of these villages, (only 29, however, being named.)

[** Qasim Ali Khan Afridi was born in 1771 and died in 1827 A.D. His father was named Burhan Khan, and his grand-father Neknam Khan.]

AURANGZIB.

I.

EARLY LIFE.

Muhiuddin Muhammad Aurangzib, the third son of the Emperor Shah Jahan and his famous consort Mumtaz Mahal, was born on 24th October, 1618, at Dohad, now a town in the Panch Mahal *taluq* of the Bombay Presidency and a station on the Godra-Rutlam railway-line. The most notable incident of his boyhood was his display of cool courage when charged by an infuriated elephant, during an ELEPHANT COMBAT under his father's eyes on the bank of the Jumna outside Agra Fort, (28 May, 1633). The victorious beast, after putting its rival to the flight, turned fiercely on Aurangzib, who firmly kept his horse from running away and struck the elephant on the forehead with his spear. A sweep of the brute's tusk hurled the horse on the ground; but Aurangzib leaped down from the saddle in time and again faced the elephant. Just then aid arrived, the animal ran away, and the prince was saved. The Emperor rewarded the heroic lad with his weight in gold.

On 13th December, 1634, Aurangzib, then 16 years of age, received his first appointment in the imperial army as a commander of ten thousand cavalry (nominal rank), and next September he was sent out to learn the art of war in the campaign against Jhujhar

Singh and his son Vikramajit, the Bundela chiefs of Urchha, who were finally extirpated at the end of the year.

From 14th July, 1636 to 28th May, 1644, Aurangzib served as VICEROY OF THE DECCAN,—paying several visits to Northern India during the period to see the Emperor. This his first governorship of the Deccan, was marked by the conquest of Baglana and the final extinction of the Nizam-Shahi dynasty of Ahmadnagar. He was married, first to Dilras Banu, the daughter of Shah Nawaz Khan Safawi, (8th May, 1637), and at some later but unknown date to Nawab Bai, and began to have children by them, his eldest offspring being Zeb-un-nissa, the gifted poetess, (born 15th February, 1638).

In May, 1644 the prince gave up his duties and took to a life of retirement, as a protest against Dara Shukoh's jealous interference with his work and Shah Jahan's partiality to his eldest son. At this the Emperor was highly displeased, and at once deprived him of his governorship, estates, and allowances. For some months the prince lived at Agra in disgrace. But on 25th November, when Jahanara, the eldest and best-beloved daughter of Shah Jahan, recovered from a terrible burn, her joyful father could refuse her nothing, and at her entreaty Aurangzib was restored to his rank. On 16th February, 1645, the viceroyalty of Gujrat was given to him; his vigorous rule suppressed lawlessness in the province and won rewards from the Emperor.

From Gujrat Aurangzib was recalled two years later and SENT TO CENTRAL ASIA to recover Balkh and Badakhshan, the cradle of the royal house of Timur. Leaving Kabul on 7th April, 1647, he reached Balkh on 25th May, and battled long and arduously with the fierce enemy. The bravest Rajputs shed their blood in the van of the Mughal army in that far-off soil; immense quantities of stores, provisions and treasure were wasted; but the Indian army merely held the ground on which it encamped; the hordes of Central Asia, "more numerous than ants and locusts," and all of them born horsemen,—swarmed on all sides and could not be crushed once for all. The barren and distant conquest could have been retained only at a ruinous cost. So, a truce was patched up: Nazar Muhammad Khan, the ex-king of Balkh, was sought out with as much eagerness as Sir Lepel Griffin displayed in getting hold of the late Amir Abdur Rahman, and coaxed into taking back his throne, and the Indian army beat a hurried retreat to avoid the dreaded winter of that region. Many *krores* of rupees of Indian revenue were thus wasted for absolutely no gain; the abandoned stores alone had cost several *lakhs*, and much property too had to be sacrificed by the rearguard for lack of transport.

During this campaign Aurangzib did an act which made his fame ring throughout the Islamic world. While the Mughal army was fighting desperately with the vast legions of Abdul Aziz Khan, King of Bukhara, the time for the evening prayer (*zuhar*) arrived. Disregarding the prohibitions of his officers, Aurangzib dismounted from his elephant, knelt down on the ground, and deliberately and peacefully went through all the ceremonies of the prayer, in full view of both the armies. Abdul Aziz on hearing of it cried out, 'To fight with such a man is to ruin one's self,' and suspended the battle.

From Balkh, Aurangzib returned to Kabul on 20th October, 1647, and was afterwards appointed Viceroy of Multan (15th March, 1648). This post he held till July, 1652, being twice in the meantime called away from his charge to BESIEGE QANDAHAR (16th May—5th September, 1649, and 2nd May—9th July, 1652). This fort had been wrested from Shah Jahan by the Persians, and these two huge and costly sieges and a third and still greater one under Dara (28th April—27th September, 1653) failed to recover it.

With his SECOND VICEROYALTY OF THE DECCAN (to which his appointment was made on 17th August, 1652), began the most important chapter of Aurangzib's early life. What Gaul was to Julius Cæsar as a training-ground for the coming contest for empire, the Deccan was to Aurangzib. Many hundreds of his letters, preserved in the *Adab-i-Alamgiri*, give us much interesting information about his life and work during the next six years,—how he overcame his recurring financial difficulties, how he gathered a picked band of officers round himself, how ably and strenuously he ruled the country, maintaining order and securing the happiness of the people. By constant inspection and exercise he kept his army in good condition. He must have been often out on tour, as he admits in one of his letters that he was a hard rider and keen sportsman in those days. Thus the year 1658 found him beyond doubt the ablest and best equipped of the sons of Shah Jahan in the ensuing War of Succession.

At this period, too, occurred the only romance of his life, his PASSION FOR HIRA BAI, (surnamed ZAINABADI), whom he took away from the harem of his maternal uncle. It was a case of love at first sight, and Aurangzib's infatuation for the beautiful singer knew no bound: to please her he consented to drink wine! Their union was cut short by her death in the bloom of youth, which plunged her lover in the deepest grief.

After a long intrigue he seduced from the King of Golkonda his *wazir* Mir Jumla, one of the ablest Persians who have ever served in India. At Aurangzib's recommendation Shah Jahan enrolled Mir Jumla among his officers and threw the mantle of imperial protection over him. To force the Golkonda King to give up Mir Jumla's family and property, Aurangzib made a RAID ON HAIDARABAD (Jan.—Apr., 1656); the King fled to Golkonda where he was forced to make a humiliating peace with immense sacrifices. Mir Jumla joined Aurangzib (20th March), was summoned to Delhi and created *wazir* (7th July), and then on 18th January, 1657, returned to the Deccan to reinforce Aurangzib.

A year after this unprovoked attack on Golkonda, on the death of Muhammad Adil Shah, King of BIJAPUR, Aurangzib with his father's sanction INVADED the latter country, (January, 1657), captured the forts of Bidar and Kaliani (29th March and 1st August respectively), and was looking forward to annexing a good deal of the territory, when the whole scene changed in the most unexpected and sudden manner.

The Emperor Shah Jahan had now reached his 66th year, and was evidently declining in health. His eldest son and intended heir-apparent, Dara Shukoh, who lived with him and conducted much of the administration, induced him to recall the additional troops sent to Aurangzib for the Bijapur war, on the very reasonable ground that the Bijapur King had thrown himself on the Emperor's mercy and offered a large indemnity and piece of territory as the price of peace. But this peremptory order to Aurangzib to come to terms with Bijapur gave him a sharp check when flushed with victory and cut short his schemes of aggression. Besides, the depletion of his army left him too weak to hold the Bijapuris to their promises, and thus the fruits of his victory were lost to him.

II.

WAR OF SUCCESSION.

On 6th September, 1657, Shah Jahan at Delhi was taken severely ill. For some time his life was despaired of. Dara attended him day and night with extreme filial piety, but he also took steps to secure his own succession. He stopped the couriers on the roads and prevented his brothers from getting true news of Court affairs. But this only aggravated the evil: the wildest rumours prevailed all over the country; the Emperor was believed to be already dead; the officers in the provinces were distracted by the prospect of an empty throne; lawless men in all parts raised their heads without fear of punishment. Two of the princes, Murad and Shuja, openly crowned themselves in their governments, Gujrat and Bengal respectively. Aurangzib after a short period of gnawing anxiety and depressing uncertainty, decided to play a subtler game. He denounced Dara as an apostate from Islam, proclaimed his own design to be merely to free the old Emperor from Dara's domination and to purge the State from non-Islamic influences, and lastly he made an alliance with Murad Bakhsh swearing on the *Quran* to give him all the Mughal territory from the Panjab westwards.

Meanwhile Dara had despatched two armies, one under his son Sulaiman Shukoh and Mirza Rajah Jai Singh against Shuja who was advancing from Bengal, and the other under Maharajah Jaswant Singh and Qasim Khan against Aurangzib and Murad. The first army surprised and routed Shuja at Bahadurpur, opposite Benares, (14th February, 1658), and pursued him to Mungir. But Aurangzib and Murad effected a junction outside Dipalpur and crushed Jaswant's army after a long and terribly contested BATTLE AT DHARMAT, 14 miles south of Ujjain, (15th April). Dara sent off urgent orders recalling his son from Bengal. But his division of his forces had been a fatal mistake: Sulaiman returned from far-off Bihar too late to help his father or even to save himself. Aurangzib had the immense advantage of crushing his enemies piecemeal, while his own armed strength was doubled by the league with Murad.

From Ujjain the victorious brothers pushed on to the capital. AT SAMUGARH, 10 miles east of Agra, DARA who had issued from the city with a second army, attacked them on a frightfully hot day (29th May), was signally DEFEATED, and fled from Agra towards Delhi and the Panjab. Aurangzib now marched on Agra, compelled his old father to surrender the fort by stopping the supply of drinking water from the Jumna, and kept Shah Jahan strictly confined in the harem for the remainder of his life. Then, at Mathura he treacherously MADE MURAD PRISONER at a banquet (25th June), and advancing to Delhi crowned himself Emperor (21st July, 1658). Dara was chased through the Panjab and Sindh to Tatta, whence he fled to Gujrat over the Rann of Cutch, undergoing terrible hardships on the way. A second army which he raised was destroyed near Ajmir (13th March, 1659), and he was hunted by Aurangzib's generals from place to place, till he reached Dadar, at the Indian mouth of the Bolan Pass, whose chief betrayed him to Aurangzib. The captive DARA was brought to Delhi, paraded with insult through the bazar, and MURDERED by some slaves of Aurangzib, (30th August, 1659), who had got the Mullas to issue a sentence that according to Islamic Law Dara deserved an apostate's death. MURAD BAKHSH was BEHEADED in Gwalior prison as a judicial punishment, on the accusation of a man whose father he had slain in Gujrat, (4th December, 1661). Dara's eldest son, Sulaiman Shukoh, was secretly done to death in the same State-prison.

Meantime SHUJA had gathered together a new army and advanced beyond Allahabad to make a second attempt for the throne. But he was signally DEFEATED at KHAJWAH (5th January, 1659), and driven back to Bengal, whence after a two years' struggle on land and river he was forced to flee miserably to ARRACAN for refuge (6th May, 1660). Here he was MASSACRED with his whole family for a plot against the Burmese King on whose hospitality he was living.

Thus all his rivals being removed from his path, Aurangzib became the undisputed sovereign of India.

III.

AURANGZIB'S REIGN IN NORTHERN INDIA.

The new monarch now enjoyed a long period of comparative peace: he received grand embassies from Persia (22nd May, 1661), Bukhara (17th November, 1661), Mecca, Abyssinia (1665), and Arabia, sent to congratulate him on his accession; and the envoys were treated to a sight of the lavish splendour of the Mughal Court,—a splendour which dazzled the eyes of Bernier, Tavernier and other European travellers of the time. He had a sharp attack of illness (12th May—24th June, 1662), which threatened to shake his newly established throne; but he recovered and paid a visit to Kashmir (1st May—29th September, 1663).

Though peace reigned in the heart of the empire, there was WAR ON THE FRONTIERS: ambitious and enterprising officers tried to extend their master's dominion; Daud Khan, the Governor of Bihar, conquered Palamau (April—December, 1661). Mir Jumla, the Governor of Bengal, overran Kuch Bihar and Assam, capturing their capitals on 19th December, 1661 and 17th March, 1662; but famine and pestilence destroyed his army, and he sank down under disease before reaching Dacca on return (31st March, 1663). Shaista Khan, the next Governor of Bengal, wrested Chatgaon (Chittagong) from the Portuguese and Burmese pirates (26th January, 1666), and also captured the island of Sondip in the Bay of Bengal. An expedition from Kashmir forced the ruler of Greater Tibet to be a feudatory of the Emperor and to "submit to Islam" (November, 1665). To crown all, the able and astute general Jai Singh tamed Shivaji, the daring and hitherto invincible Maratha chief, annexed two-thirds of his forts, (Treaty of Purandar, 11th June, 1665), and induced him to do homage to the Emperor by a visit to Agra (12th May, 1666). Aurangzib's lack of statesmanship in dealing with Shivaji and the latter's romantic escape from prison (19th August) are a familiar tale all over India. True, the Mughal arms did not gain any conspicuous success in Jai Singh's invasion of Bijapur (first half of 1666), but these expeditions were of the nature of raids for extortion, and not deliberate schemes of conquest.

A more formidable but distant trouble was the revolt of the Yusufzai clan and their allies on the Afghan frontier, (begun in 1667). The war against these sturdy hillmen dragged on for many years; successive Mughal generals tried their hands and buried their military reputation there, and at last peace was purchased only by paying a large annual subsidy from the Indian revenue to these "keepers of Khyber gate."

A state of war also continued against the Bijapur King and Shivaji for many years: but the Mughal generals were bribed by the former to carry on the contest languidly, and the latter was more than able to hold his own. These operations present us with nothing worthy of note. The Muhammadan kings of the Deccan, in fear of the Mughals, courted the alliance of Shivaji, who rapidly grew in wealth, territory, armed strength, and prestige, and had made himself the foremost power in the Deccan when death cut his activity short at the age of 52, (5th April, 1680).

Meantime Aurangzib had begun to give free play to his RELIGIOUS BIGOTRY. In April, 1669 he ordered the provincial governors to "DESTROY the TEMPLES and schools of the Brahmans...and to utterly put down the teachings and religious practices of the infidels." The wandering Hindu saint Uddhav Bairagi was confined in the police lock-up. The Vishwanath temple at Benares was pulled down in August, 1669. The grandest shrine of Mathura, Kesav Rai's temple, built at a cost of 33 lakhs of rupees by the Bundela Rajah Birsingh Dev, was razed to the ground in January, 1670, and a mosque built on its site. "The idols were brought to Agra and buried under the steps of Jahanara's mosque that they might be constantly trodden on" by the Muslims going in to pray. About this time the (new?) temple of Somnath on the south coast of the Kathiawar peninsula was demolished, and the offering of worship there ordered to be stopped. The smaller religious buildings that suffered havoc were beyond count. The Rajput War of 1679-80 was accompanied by the destruction of 240 temples in Mewar alone, including the famous one of Someshwar and three grand ones at Udaipur. On 2nd April, 1679, the JAZIYA or poll-tax on non-Muslims was REVIVED. The poor people who appealed to the Emperor and blocked a road abjectly crying for its remission, were trampled down by elephants at his order and dispersed. By another ordinance (March, 1695), "all Hindus except Rajputs were forbidden to carry arms or ride elephants, *palkis*, or Arab and Persian horses." "With one stroke of his pen he dismissed all the Hindu clerks from office." Custom duties were abolished on the Muslims and doubled on the Hindus.

The discontent provoked by such measures was an ominous sign of what their ultimate political consequence would be, though Aurangzib was too blind and obstinate to think of the future. A rebellion broke out among the peasantry in the Mathura and Agra districts, especially under Gokla Jat (1669), and the Satnamis or Mundias rose near Narnol (March and April, 1672), and it taxed the imperial power seriously to exterminate these 5,000 stubborn peasants fighting for church and home. The Sikh Guru Tegh Bahadur was tortured in prison till he courted death as a release (1675), but his followers thereafter gave no rest to the Panjab officers.

At last Aurangzib threw off all disguise and openly ATTACKED THE RAJPUTS. Maharajah Jaswant Singh of Jodhpur died in the Emperor's service at Peshawar (10th December, 1678). Immediately Aurangzib sent out officers to take possession of his kingdom and himself marched to Ajmir to overawe opposition. Two wives of the Maharajah delivered two sons after reaching Lahore in the following February. Aurangzib sold the Jodhpur throne for 36 lakhs of rupees to a worthless nephew of Jaswant and ordered the late Maharajah's widows and new-born babes to be seized and detained in his Court till the latter should come of age. But thanks to the devotion of their Rathor guards, all of whom died like heroes, and the sagacity and loyalty of Durgadas, (one of the noblest characters in Rajput history), Ajit Singh, the surviving infant of Jaswant and the future hope of Marwar, was safely conveyed to Jodhpur (23rd July, 1679). But Aurangzib was up to any trick: he proclaimed Ajit Singh to be a counterfeit prince, and for many years cherished a beggar boy in his Court under the significant name of Muhammadi Raj, as the true son of Jaswant! All Rajputana (except ever-loyal Jaipur) burst into flame at this outrage to the head of the Rathor clan. The Maharana, Raj Singh, chivalrously took up the defence of the orphan's rights. The war dragged on with varying fortune; the country was devastated wherever the Mughals could penetrate; the Maharana took refuge in his mountain fastnesses. At last PRINCE AKBAR, the fourth son of Aurangzib, REBELLED (January, 1681,) joined the Rajputs, and assumed the royal title. For a few days Aurangzib was in a most critical position, but his wonderful cunning saved him: by a false letter he sowed distrust of Akbar in the minds of the Rajputs, the prince's army melted away, and he fled, leaving all his family and property behind and reaching the Maratha Court after a perilous journey under the guidance of the faithful Durgadas (May, 1681). The Emperor patched up a peace with the Maharana (June, 1681), both sides making concessions. But henceforth the Rajputs ceased to be supporters of the Mughal throne; we no longer read of large Rajput contingents fighting under the imperial banner; he had to depend more on the Bundelas. The Rathors continued the war till the close of Aurangzib's life. Here ends the first and stable half of Aurangzib's reign—the period passed in Northern India.

IV.

AURANGZIB'S REIGN IN THE DECCAN.

We next enter on a scene of unceasing but fruitless exertion for 26 years,—the war with the "slim" Marathas, which ruined the Emperor's health, the *morale* of his army, and the finances of the State,—a war of which all saw the futility and all were heartily tired, all save Aurangzib, who pursued one policy with increasing obstinacy, till at last the old man of 90 sank into the grave amidst despair, darkness, and chaos ready to overwhelm his family and empire.

Shivaji's eldest son Shambhu was a more daring raider than his father and deterred by no fear of consequences. With Akbar as his pensioner, what might he not do against the Mughal crown? Moreover, all of Aurangzib's generals and even his sons sent against the kingdoms of the Deccan had failed of conquest, and were rightly suspected of corruption. So there was nothing left for Aurangzib but to conduct the war in person. With this object he left Ajmir for the Deccan (8th September, 1681, never again to return to Northern India alive or dead. The capital Aurangabad was reached on 22nd March, 1682. Thence, on 13th November, 1683, he arrived at Ahmadnagar, a town to which he was destined to return 23 years afterwards only to die. Two of his sons and some nobles were despatched against the Bijapuris and the Marathas, but they effected nothing decisive, though a large number of Shambhu's forts were captured. A large force which penetrated into

Ram-derah in the Konkan under Prince Muazzam, returned with failure and heavy loss (September, 1683,—May, 1684).

Fierce as was Aurangzib's hatred of the Hindus (the vast majority of his subjects), it was equalled by his AVERSION FOR THE SHIAHS,—who supplied him with some of his best generals and all his ablest civil officers. To him the Shiah was a heretic (*ráfizi*); in one of his letters he quotes with admiration the story of a Sunni who escaped to Turkey after murdering a Shiah at Isfahan, and draws from it the moral, "Whoever acts for truth and speaks up for truth, is befriended by the True God!" In another letter he tells us how he liked the naming of a dagger as the 'Shiah-slayer' (*Ráfizi-kush*), and ordered some more of the same name to be made for him. In his correspondence he never mentions the Shiahs without an abusive epithet: 'corpse-eating demons' (*ghul-i-bayábáni*), 'misbelievers' (*bátil mazhabán*), are among his favourite phrases. Indeed, even the highest Shiah officers had such a bad time of it in his Court that they often played the hypocrite to please him! Aurangzib threw the cloak of Sunni orthodoxy over his aggressive conquest of Bijapur and Golkonda, of which the rulers were Shiahs. The Shaikh-ul-Islam (son of the Chief Qazi Abdul Wahhab and one of the purest characters of the age,) tried to dissuade the Emperor from these "wars between Muslims" as opposed to Islam. But Aurangzib got displeased at the opposition; the honest and manly Shaikh resigned his post, left the

Court, and for the rest of his life rejected the Emperor's repeated solicitations to resume his high office.

On 1st April, 1685 the SEIGE OF BIJAPUR was begun by Ruhullah Khan and Khan-i-Jahan Bahadur. The Emperor advanced to Sholapur (24th May) to be near the seat of war. A terrible famine desolated the besiegers; but reinforcements soon arrived with provisions, though scarcity of a kind continued in a chronic state in the Mughal camp. The relieving armies of Beydurs and Marathas were beaten back and the siege pressed on. The garrison fought with the heroism of despair. Aurangzib himself arrived in the environs of the city to superintend the siege operations (3rd July, 1686). At last, on 12th September, Sikandar, the last of the Adil-Shahi kings, surrendered, and his kingdom was annexed.

Meantime another force had been sent under Prince Muazzam or Shah Alam (28th June, 1685) against Golkonda to prevent aid from coming from that quarter to Bijapur. It captured the rich city of Haidarabad, making an immense loot (October). The king, Abul Hassan, a worthless voluptuary and the exact counterpart of Wajid Ali of Oudh, helplessly SHUT himself UP in the FORT OF GOLKONDA. But his chiefs were seduced by the Mughals; there was discontent among his Muhammadan officers at the power of his Brahman minister Madanna Pant. The besiegers, too, had a hard time of it before that impregnable fort: a terrible famine raged in Haidarabad, but the rains and swollen rivers rendered the transport of grain impossible, and the most ghastly scenes were acted by the sufferers. At an immense cost the Mughals filled the moat and also erected a huge barrier wall of wood and clay completely surrounding the fort and preventing ingress and egress. Aurangzib himself arrived near Golkonda on 28th January, 1687, and pressed on the siege. But mining and assault failed, and it was only the treachery of a Golkonda officer that opened the gate of the fort to the Mughals at midnight (21st September, 1687). The king was dragged out and sent to share the captivity of his brother of Bijapur. His kingdom was annexed. Two years later, SHAMBHUJI, the brave but dissolute Maratha king, was surprised by an energetic Deccani officer (Muqarrab Khan), ignominiously paraded through the imperial camp like a wild beast, and EXECUTED with prolonged and inhuman tortures (11th March, 1689). His capital Raigarh was captured (19th October) and his entire family, "mothers, wives, daughters, and sons" made prisoner by the Mughals. His eldest son, Sahu, was brought up in the imperial Court in gilded fetters.

All seemed to have been gained by Aurangzib now, but in reality all was lost. It was THE BEGINNING OF HIS END. The saddest and most hopeless chapter of his life now opened. The Mughal empire had become too large to be ruled by one man or from one centre. Aurangzib, like the boa constrictor, had swallowed more than he could digest. It was impossible for him to take possession of all the provinces of the newly annexed kingdoms and at the same time to suppress the Marathas. His enemies rose on all sides, he could defeat but not crush them for ever. As soon as his army marched away from a place, the enemy who had been hovering round occupied it again, and Aurangzib's work was undone! Lawlessness reigned in many places of Northern and Central India. The old Emperor in the far-off Deccan lost control over his officers in Hindusthan, and the ADMINISTRATION grew SLACK and corrupt; chiefs and zamindars defied the local authorities and asserted themselves, filling the country with tumult. In the province of Agra in particular, there was chronic disorder. Art and learning decayed at the withdrawal of imperial patronage,—not a single grand edifice, finely written manuscript, or exquisite picture commemorates Aurangzib's reign. The endless war in the Deccan exhausted his treasury; the Government turned bankrupt; the soldiers, starving from arrears of pay, mutinied; and during the closing years of his reign the revenue of Bengal, regularly sent by the faithful and able diwan Murshid Quli Khan, was the sole support of the Emperor's household and army, and its arrival was eagerly looked forward to. Napoleon I. used to say, "It was the Spanish ulcer which ruined me." The Deccan ulcer ruined Aurangzib.

To resume the narrative, imperial officers were despatched to all sides to take over the forts and provinces of the two newly annexed kingdoms from their local officers, many of whom had set up for themselves. The Beydurs, a wild hill tribe, whom Col. Meadows Taylor has described in his fascinating *Story of My Life*, were the first to be attacked. Their country, situated between Bijapur and Golkonda, was overrun, their capital Sakhkhar captured (28th Nov., 1687), and their chief Pid Naik, a strongly built uncouth black savage, brought to the Court. But the brave and hardy clansmen rose under other leaders and the Mughals had to send two more expeditions against them.

A desolating epidemic of BUBONIC PLAGUE broke out in Bijapur (early in November, 1668), sparing neither prince nor peasant. The imperial household paid toll to Death in the persons of Aurangabadi Mahal (a wife of the Emperor), Fazil Khan the *Sadr*, and the bogus son of Jaswant Singh. Of humbler victims the number is said to have reached a *lakh*.

After Shambhu's capture, his younger brother Rajah Ram made a hairbreadth escape to the fort of Jinji, (Gingee in the S. Arcot district of Madras), which was besieged by the Mughal general Zulfiqar Khan Nusrat Jang and Prince Kam Bakhsh (December, 1691), and fell on 7th February, 1698. Soon afterwards Rajah Ram, the last king of the Marathas, died. But the MARATHA captains, each acting on his own account incessantly raided the Mughal territory and did the greatest possible injury by their GUERILLA WARFARE. The two ablest, most successful, and most dreaded leaders of this class were Dhanna Jadon and Santa Ghorpure (and latterly Nima Sindhia), who dealt heavy blows at some important Mughal detachments. They seemed to be ubiquitous and elusive like the wind. The movable columns frequently sent from the imperial headquarters to "chastise the robbers," only marched and counter-marched, without being able to crush the enemy. When the Mughal force had gone back the scattered Marathas, like water parted by the oar, closed again and resumed their attack, as if nothing had happened to them.

V.

THE LAST PHASE.

After moving about almost every year between Bijapur in the south and the Manjira river in the north, Aurangzib (21st May, 1695) finally made Brahmapuri on the Bhima river, east of Pandharpur, his Base Camp, and named it Islampuri. Here a city sprang up from his encampment, and it was walled round in time. Here his family was lodged when he was out on campaign.

On 19th October, 1699, after a four years' stay at Islampuri, Aurangzib, now aged 81 years, set out to besiege the Maratha forts in person. The rest of his life is a repetition of the same sickening tale: a hill fort captured by him after a great loss of time men and money, recovered by the Marathas from the weak Mughal garrison after a few months, and the seige begun again after a year or two! The soldiors and camp-followers suffered unspeakable hardships in marching over flooded rivers and rain-soaked roads, porters disappeared, transport beasts died of hunger and overwork, scarcity of grain was chronic in the camp. The officers all wearied of this labour of Sisyphus; but Aurangzib would burst into wrath at any suggestion of retreat to Hindusthan and taunt the unlucky counsellor with cowardice and love of ease! The mutual jealousies of his generals, Nusrat Jang and Firuz Jang, Shujaet Khan and Muhammad Murad Khan, Tarbiyat Khan and Fathullah Khan, spoiled his affairs as thoroughly as the French cause in the Peninsular War was damaged by the jealousies of Napoleon's marshals. Therefore, the Emperor must conduct every operation in person, or nothing would be done!

A bare RECORD OF HIS SIEGES will suffice here:

BASANTGARH (surrenders 25th November, 1699).

SATARA (siege, 8th December, 1699—21st April, 1700).

PARLIGARH near Satara (siege, 30th April—9th June).

Halt at Khawaspur for the rainy season of 1700— (from 30th August).

PANHALA (siege, 9th March—28th May, 1701), also Pawangarh captured.

Halt at Khatanun for the rainy season of 1701, (29th May—7th November).

Capture of Wardhangarh (6th June, 1701), Nandgir, Chandan and Wandan (6th October) by Fathullah Khan.

KHELNA (siege, 26th December, 1701—4th June, 1702).

Halt at Bahadurpur for the rainy season of 1702, after

a most painful march from 10th June to the third week of October!

KONDANA (siege, 27th December, 1702—8th April, 1703).

Halt at Puna for the rainy season of 1703, (1st May—10th November).

RAJGARH (siege, 2nd December, 1703—16th February, 1704).

TORNA (siege, 23rd February—10th March).

Halt at Khed for the rainy season of 1704 (17th April—22nd October).

WAKINKHERA (siege, 8th February—27th April, 1705).

Halt at Dewapur, 6 miles from Wakinkhera *for the rainy season* of 1705, (May—23rd October).

This was the last of his sieges, for here he got a warning of what was to come. At Dewapur a severe illness attacked him, which was aggravated by his insistence to transact business as usual. The whole camp was in despair and confusion: who would extricate them from that gloomy mountainous region if the Emperor died? At last Aurangzib yielded to their entreaty and probably also to the warning of approaching death, and RETREATED TO Bahadurpur (6th December, 1705), whence he reached AHMADNAGAR (20th January, 1706), to die a year later.

The last few years of his life were inexpressibly sad. On its public side there was the consciousness that his long reign of half a century had been a colossal failure. "After me will come the deluge!" this morose foreboding of Louis XV. was repeated by Aurangzib almost word for word (*Az ma-st hamah fasad-i-báqi.*) His domestic life, too, was loveless and dreary, and wanting in the benign peace and hopefulness which throw a halo round old age. One daughter, Zinat-un-nissa, already an old maid, looked after his household, and his youngest concubine, Udaipuri, bore him company. But he had, at one time or other, to imprison all his five sons except one! By his own conduct in the War of Succession he had raised a spectre which relentlessly pursued him: what if *his* sons should treat him in his weak old age as he had treated Shah Jahan? This fear of Nemesis ever haunted his mind, and he had no peace while his sons were with him! Lastly, there was the certainty of a deluge of blood when he would close his eyes, and his three surviving sons, each supported by a provincial army and treasury, would fight for the throne to the bitter end. In two most pathetic letters written to his sons when he felt the sure approach of death, the old Emperor speaks of the alarm and distraction of his soldiery, the passionate grief of Udaipuri, and his own bitter sense of the futility of his life, and then entreats them not to cause the slaughter of Musalmans by engaging in a civil war among themselves. A paper, said to have been found under his pillow after his death, contained a plan for the peaceful partition of the empire among his three sons. Meantime death was also busy at work within his family circle. When Gauharara, the last among

Aurangzib's brothers and sisters, died, (about March, 1706,) he felt that his own turn would come soon. Some of his nephews, daughters, and grandsons, too, were snatched away from him in the course of his last year. In the midst of the darkness closing around him, he used to hum the pathetic verses:—

> By the time you are 80 or 90 years of age,
> You will have felt many hard blows from Fate;
> And when you reach the stage of a 100 years,
> Life will be the image of death to you.

And also,—

> In a moment, in a minute, in a breath,
> The condition of the world may become different.

His last illness overtook him at Ahmadnagar, late in January, 1707; then he rallied for 5 or 6 days, sent away his two sons from his camp to their provincial governments, and went through business and daily prayers regularly. But that worn-out frame of 91 years had been taxed too much. A severe fever set in, and in the morning of Friday, 20th February, 1707, he gradually sank down exhausted into the arms of death, with the Muslim confession of faith on his lips and his fingers on his rosary.

The corpse was despatched to Khuldabad, six miles from Daulatabad, and there buried in the courtyard of the tomb of the saint Shaikh Zainuddin, in a plain low red sandstone sepulchre built by Aurangzib in his own lifetime. The tombstone, 9 feet by 7 feet, is a few inches in height, and has a cavity in the middle which is filled with earth for planting fragrant herbs in.

Aurangzib's wife DILRAS BANU BEGAM, the daughter of Shah Nawaz Khan Safawi, died on 8th October, 1657, after bearing him Zeb-un-nissa, Azam and Akbar. A secondary wife (*mahal*) NAWAB BAI, the mother of Sultan and Muazzam, does not seem to have been a favourite, as her husband seldom sought her society after his accession. Of his three concubines (*parastar*), Hira Bai or ZAINABADI, with whom he was infatuated almost to madness, died very young; AURANGABADI, the mother of Mihr-un-nissa, died of the plague in November, 1688; UDAIPURI, the favourite companion of Aurangzib's old age and the mother of his pet son Kam Bakhsh, entered his harem after his accession. She is said to have been a Circassian slave-girl of Dara, gained by Aurangzib among the spoils of victory. But another account which describes her as a Kashmiri woman, is more likely to be true, because the *Masir-i-Alamgiri* calls her *Bai*, a title which was applied to Hindu women only. Her descent from the royal house of Mewar is a fanciful conjecture of some modern writers. We also read of a woman named *Dilaram*, as having been his *parastar* in his early life; but she was probably a handmaid only.

Aurangzib's eldest son, SULTAN, chafing under the restraints of his father's officers, during the war in Bengal, fled to Shuja and married his daughter, but in a few months returned to his father. The foolish youth, then only 20 years old, was kept in prison for the rest of his life. (Died 3rd December, 1676.)

His second son, MUAZZAM, (also *Shah Alam*), who in 1707 succeeded his father on the throne as Bahadur Shah I., incensed Aurangzib by intriguing with the besieged kings of Bijapur and Golkonda, and was placed in confinement (20th February, 1687). After his spirit had been thoroughly tamed, his captivity was relaxed little by little (in a rather amusing fashion), and at last, on 9th May, 1695, he was sent to Agra as Governor, (afterwards getting the Panjab to govern).

The third prince, AZAM, stepped into the vacant place of the heir-apparent (*Shah-i-alijah*) during Muazzam's disgrace, and was made much of by his father. But he was extremely haughty, prone to anger, and incapable of self-restraint.

The fourth, AKBAR, rebelled against his father in 1681, and fled to Persia where he died an exile in November, 1704. His presence at Farah, on the Khurasan frontier, was long a menace to the peace of India.

The youngest, KAM BAKHSH, the spoilt child of his father's old age, was worthless, self-willed, and foolish. For his misconduct during the siege of Jinji he was put under restraint, and again confined for his fatuous attachment to his foster-brother, a wretch who had tried to assassinate an excellent officer. The third and fifth brothers fell fighting in the struggle for the throne which followed Aurangzib's death, (1707 and 1709).

AURANGZIB'S CHARACTER.

So lived and so died Aurangzib, surnamed Alamgir Shah, the last of the Great Mughals. For, in spite of his religious intolerance, narrowness of mind, and lack of generosity and statesmanship, he was great in the possession of some qualities which might have gained for him the highest place in any sphere of life except the supreme one of rule over men. He would have made a successful general, minister, theologian, or school-master, and an ideal departmental head. But the critical eminence of a throne on which he was placed by a freak of Fortune, led to the failure of his life and the blighting of his fame.

Pure in his domestic relations, simple and abstemious like a hermit, he had a passion for work and a hatred of ease and pleasure which remind one of George Grenville, though with Grenville's untiring industry he had also got Grenville's narrowness and obstinacy. European travellers observed with wonder the greyheaded Emperor holding open Court every day, reading every petition and writing orders across it with his own hand. Of the letters dictated by him, those that are known to exist in Europe and India, number about two thousand. (I have got copies of all of them as far as known to me). Many more must have perished.

In matters of official discipline and Court etiquette he was a martinet and enforced the strictest obedience to rules and established usages: "If I suffer a single regulation to be violated, all of them will be disregarded," was his frequent remark. But this punctilious observance of the form must have led to neglect of the spirit of institutions and laws.

His passion for doing everything himself and dictating the minutest particulars to far-off governors and generals, robbed them of all self-reliance and power of initiative, and left them hesitating and helpless in the face of any unexpected emergency. His suspicious policy crushed the latent ability of his sons, so that at his death they were no better than children though turned of sixty years of age. Alike in his passion for work, distrust of the man on the spot, preference for incompetent but servile agents, and religious bigotry, he resembled his contemporary in Europe, Louis XIV.

His coolness and courage were famous throughout India: no danger however great, no emergency however unlooked for, could shake his heart or cloud the serene light of his intellect. Indeed, he regarded danger as only the legitimate risk of greatness. No amount of exertion could fatigue that thin wiry frame. The privations of a campaign or forced ride had no terror for him. Of diplomacy he was a past master, and could not be beaten in any kind of intrigue or secret manipulation. He was as much a "master of the pen" as a "master of the sword."

From the strict path of a Muslim king's duty as laid down in the Quranic Law nothing could make him deviate the least. And he was also determined not to let *others* deviate too! No fear of material loss or influence of any favourite, no tears or supplication could induce him to act contrary to the *Shara* (Canon Law). Flatterers styled him "a living saint," (*Alamgir zinda pir*). Indeed, from a very early period of his life he had chosen "the strait gate and narrow way which leadeth unto life"; but the defects of his heart made the gate straiter and the way narrower.

He lacked that warm generosity of the heart, that chivalry to fallen foes, and that easy familiarity of address in private life, which made the great Akbar win the love and admiration of his contemporaries and of all posterity. Like the English Puritans, Aurangzib drew his inspiration from the old law of relentless punishment and vengeance and forgot that mercy is an attribute of the Supreme Judge of the Universe.

His cold intellectuality, his suspicious nature, and his fame for profound statecraft, chilled the love of all who came near him. Sons, daughters, generals, and ministers, all feared him with a secret but deep-rooted fear, which neither respect nor flattery could disguise.

Art, music, dance, and even poetry (other than "familiar quotations") were his aversion, and he spent his leisure hours in hunting for legal precedents in Arabic works on Jurisprudence.

Scrupulously following the rules of the *Quran* in his own private life, he considered it his duty to enforce them on everybody else; the least deviation from the strict and narrow path of Islamic orthodoxy in any part of his dominions, would (he feared) endanger his own soul. His spirit was therefore the narrow and selfish spirit of the lonely recluse, who seeks his individual salvation, oblivious of the outside world. A man possessed with such ideas may have made a good *faqir*, —though Aurangzib lacked the *faqir's* noblest quality, charity;—but he was the worst ruler imaginable of an empire composed of many creeds and races, of diverse interests and ways of life and thought.

"The nature of man is intricate; the objects of society are of the greatest possible complexity; and therefore no simple disposition or direction of power can be suitable either to man's nature, or to the quality of his affairs......Political reason is a computing principle; adding, subtracting, multiplying, and dividing true moral denominations......The true lawgiver ought to have an heart full of sensibility. He ought to love and respect his kind, and to fear himself. Political arrangement is to be only wrought by social means. There mind must conspire with mind." (*Burke*).

Aurangzib utterly lacked sympathy, imagination, breadth of vision, elasticity in the choice of means, and that warmth of the heart which atones for a hundred faults of the head. These limitations of his character completely undermined the Mughal empire, so that on his death it suddenly fell in a single downward plunge. Its inner life was gone, and the outward form could not deceive the world long. Time relentlessly sweeps away whatever is inefficient, unnecessary, or false to Nature.

AURANGZIB'S DAILY LIFE.

I have already described how the Emperor Shah Jahan spent his time. I shall now present to the reader an account of his successor Aurangzib's daily life at Delhi at the beginning of his reign, as supplied by the contemporary Persian history *Alamgirnamah*. Aurangzib was a strict Muhammadan, a veritable Puritan in the purple. Hence his life was marked by greater seriousness, religious devotion, and aversion to amusement than his father's. He scorned delights and lived laborious days.

AURANGZIB'S ROUTINE OF WORK.

A.M.

5 ...Wakes—Morning Prayer—Devotional reading.

7-30...Justice in Private Chamber.

8-30...*Darshan*—Review—Elephant fights.

9-15...Public Darbar.

11 ...Private Audience.

11-50...Harem—Siesta.

P.M.

2 ...*Zuhar* Prayer.

2-30...Private Chamber—Study—Business—*Asar* Prayer—State affairs.

5-30...Evening salute in the Private Audience Hall—Sunset Prayer.

6-40...*Soiree* in the *Diwan-i-khas*.

7-40...Court dismissed—*Isha* Prayer.

8 . In the Harem—Religious meditation and reading—Sleep.

MORNING PRAYER.

Rising from his bed some time before dawn, the Emperor performed his morning ablutions, went from the *harem* to the mosque attached to the Hall of Private Audience (*Diwan-i-khas*), and sat there facing the west, waiting for the time of the morning prayer as indicated by the *Hadis* (or Muhammad's Traditions). After performing this religious rite, he read the *Quran* and the Prophet's *Traditions* till the breakfast hour, (say 7-30 A.M.).

COURT OF JUSTICE IN CHAMBER.

Then he went to his private chamber (*khilwatgah*), to which only a few confidential officers and his personal attendants were admitted, and sat on the throne dispensing justice, the first duty of an eastern king. The superintendents of the law-courts presented to him all aggrieved persons, who had come either from the capital or from the provinces to seek justice at its fountain head. Their plaints were reported, and then the Emperor personally examined them to find out the truth.

On the basis of the facts so ascertained, all cases coming under Canon Law were decided according to the *Quranic* injunctions. Common-law cases were tried according to the customary procedure and regulations of the Empire, evidently at the Emperor's own discretion. Needy and miserable plaintiffs were helped with money from the public treasury.

DARSHAN.

Next, he entered the bed-chamber and showed his face at one of its windows, called 'the window of *darshan,'* which overlooked the broad sandy beach of the Jumna. A vast and varied crowd filled this plain at the foot of the fort, in expectation of the Emperor's appearance. Here the army was often reviewed, and here too were paraded the retainers of the nobles who accompanied the Emperor when he rode out in procession to perform the Friday prayer in the vast Jumma Masjid of Delhi. Elephant combats, the training of war-elephants to charge cavalry without fear, and the parade of newly captured untamed elephants, took place in this plain, as was also the case under Shah Jahan.

PUBLIC DARBAR.

After passing three quarters of an hour at the *darshan* window, the Emperor, at about 9-15 A.M., took his seat in the alcove overlooking the *Diwan-i-am,* and transacted public affairs of the same kind and in the very same way as Shah Jahan had done. This took nearly two hours.

PRIVATE AUDIENCE.

Some time before noon he withdrew to the *Diwan-i-khas,* and held a private or select audience, conducting confidential business and bestowing gifts till noon. Here were admitted a few nobles, clerks, servants, mace-bearers, the imperial retinue, his special watchmen (*Khas-chawki*), many slaves, the standard-bearers and such other necessary persons only. At this audience his business and pleasure were identical with those of Shah Jahan, as described in another essay. The despatches of the provincial viceroys and governors of towns were either read by the Emperor or reported in brief abstracts by the Grand *Wazir*. The Emperor's orders were taken, and their purport dictated by the Wazir to the secretaries (*munshis*), who drafted the replies. Many of these were looked over and revised by the Emperor; then they were copied out fair and placed before His Majesty for being signed and sealed. Sometimes he wrote in his own hand the beginnings of the letters to the high grandees, either to do them greater honour, or to make the orders more urgent, or to remove all doubt as to their genuineness.

HAREM.

It was now almost noon, and the Emperor retired to the *harem* to take his well-earned rest. After eating his meal, he slept for an hour to refresh his body and spirits.

PRAYER.

But shortly before the *Zuhar* prayer (about 2 P.M.) he was up again, washed himself, and waited in the palace mosque reciting God's names and telling his beads. This prayer was performed in company, as recommended by the Prophet. The congregation privileged to join the Emperor in his devotions, consisted of *ulema* (theologians), Syeds, Shaikhs, *faqirs*, and a few of His Majesty's close attendants and *khawases*.

IN THE PRIVATE CHAMBER.

Thereafter the Emperor went to his Private Chamber, situated between the *harem* and the Hall of Private

Audience (named the *Ghusal-khanah*), and engaged in works of piety, such as, reading the *Quran*, copying it, collating his transcript of it, hunting through Arabic jurisprudence for precedents in Canon Law, &c. Or His Majesty read the books and pamphlets of the Islamic pious men and saints of all ages. Then, urgent affairs of State forced themselves on his attention. The petitions of aggrieved parties rich enough to buy the mediation of the favourite courtiers, were now submitted. On some days, work being over, His Majesty visited the *harem* again for an hour, heard the petitions of poor women, widows, and orphans, and satisfied them with money, lands, or ornaments.

By this the time for the *Asar* prayer (4 P.M.) arrived. It was performed in company in the mosque close to the Hall of Private Audience; afterwards the Emperor returned to his Private Chamber and spent the remaining short period of the day in the work of administration.

EVENING SALUTE AND PRAYER.

About half an hour before sunset, His Majesty visited the Hall of Private Audience again and sat on the throne. A little work was done. The courtiers made their bows. The nobles and officers, who had sentry duty that night, presented themselves in full accoutrement, and were marshalled by the Mir Tuzuk and the sergeants according to their ranks on the two sides of the imperial standard of cows' tails and balls. The chief men formed a line in front; the rear ranks were made up by the subordinates. The Paymasters made them salute, according to the imperial regulations.

The sun was now setting. Piercing the evening air came the loud cry,—

God is most great! God is most great! I testify that there is no deity except God and that Muhammad is His Apostle! Come to prayer! Come to prayer! Come to salvation!

It was the *muazzin* or crier of the mosque, chanting from the church-spire the call to prayer. What the *angelus* is to the French peasantry, the *azan* is to the Muslim world. All work was at once suspended. The Emperor withdrew his mind from earthly affairs, and listened with great reverence to the call. At every pause in the crier's voice, he interjected, like a pious Musalman, these responses:—

Yes, God is most great! I testify that there is no deity except God and that Muhammad is the Apostle of God! I have no power or strength except from God! What He willeth shall be, and what He willeth not shall not take place.

Then he rose from the throne, went to the mosque in full congregation and performed the evening prayer and certain non-obligatory extra rites of devotion (*viz.*, the *sunnah* and the *nafl*). These acts of piety occupied more than half an hour.

SOIREE IN THE DIWAN-I-KHAS.

The *Diwan-i-khas* (or Hall of Private Audience) was lit up wih camphorated candles and torches, and golden lanterns, making it rival the vault of the sky dotted wih myriads of twinkling stars. The Emperor arrived here from the mosque and occupied the throne. The *Wazir* reported on all affairs of the revenue department, both general and particular, and got his orders. Other kinds of State business were also done. There was no music or dance, as Aurangzib had banished these mundane vanities from his Court in the 11th year of his reign (1668 A.D.) The assembly continued for more than an hour; and shortly before 8 P.M., the call to the *Isha* prayer was heard; the Court was dismissed.

The Emperor prayed in the adjoining mosque with only his close attendants and *khawases*, and then retired to the *harem*, but not to sleep. Several hours were here spent in prayer and religious meditation, before his tired frame sank into the necessary repose.

This routine was varied on three days of the week. On Friday, the Islamic Sabbath, no Court was held. WEDNESDAY was sacred to justice, and no public darbar was then held, but the Emperor went straight from the *darshan* to the Private Audience Hall, thronged with the law officers, *qazis*, *muftis*, scholars, theologians (*ulema*), judges, and the prefect of police for the City. None else was admitted unless his presence was needed. The Emperor went on personally judging cases till noon.

On THURSDAY he gave his Court a half-holiday, as we get on Saturday in British India. The usual routine was followed up to noon; but there was no afternoon Court, nor any assembly in the *Diwan-i-khas* at night. The whole evening was spent in prayer and sacred reading, and the world and its distractions were kept out.

If we may believe the Court historian, Auranzib slept only three hours out of twenty-four.* It was a very strenuous life that this Emperor led. All work and no play gave to his Court a cold, sombre and dreary aspect. He seems to have taken for his motto the following words of Louis XIV., whom he greatly resembled in his foreign policy, religious intolerance, love of centralised imperialism, and unbounded egotism and industry :—"One must work hard to reign, and it is ingratitude and presumption towards God, injustice and tyranny towards man, to wish to reign without hard work."

---

* The materials for this essay have been mainly taken from the *Alamgirnamah* 1096-1106.

THE EDUCATION OF A MUGHAL PRINCE.

Some letters of Aurangzib preserved in the Persian manuscript *Adab-i-Alamgiri*, give us interesting information about the way in which Mughal princes were educated and the ideas of etiquette and decorum held in the seventeenth century. In October, 1654, Aurangzib was Viceroy of the Deccan and his eldest son, Muhammad Sultan, then in his 15th year, was marching towards Ajmir to be presented to the Emperor Shah Jahan. The father was naturally anxious that his boy should make a good impression at the imperial court. Minute directions were sent to the prince regulating every act of his life and prescribing a strict routine for every hour of the day. This is how the prince was commanded to spend his time.

"Whether you are in residence or on a march, get up from bed 72 minutes before sunrise. After spending 48 minutes in bathing and getting ready, come out of your rooms for the morning prayer. After saying the prayer and reciting set passages, read one section of the *Quran*. Breakfast in the inner apartments will come next. If you are on a march, take horse 48 minutes after sunrise. Should you hunt on the way, take care to reach the halting place appointed for that day punctually. Arriving there, if you are so inclined or have the necessary time, read something in Arabic; otherwise take rest. About 24 minutes after noon, when the sun begins to decline, come out of your tent for the *zuhar* prayer which should be performed in full congregation. The principal meal and some repose—(evidently the siesta or afternoon nap so popular in the hot countries of Europe and Asia alike) will fill your time till two hours before sunset, when the *asar* prayer should be said. But if the meal alone suffices to refresh you spend the interval in improving your handwriting, composing letters, or reading Persian prose and poetry. After the *asar* prayer, read Arabic for a short time, and then, some 24 minutes before sunset, hold a 'select audience,' where you should sit till 48 minutes after nightfall. Then leave the chamber and read a section of the *Quran*, and retiring to the inner apartments, go to bed at 9 P.M.

"If you are on a journey, but it is a day of halt, do the other works mentioned above at the stated time, but (in the place of riding) spend 48 minutes of the morning in archery and musketry practice, and one hour and twenty-four minutes after sunrise hold a public court for about 48 minutes or more as the business requires. Then, if there is important work to be done, hold a private council for about an hour with your chief officers. Otherwise this period (four *gharis*) should be spent in reading Arabic.

"On a day of march read two sections and on a day of halt three of the *Quran*.—If the stage to be covered is a long one, take horse immediately after performing the morning prayer and eat your breakfast on the way, otherwise you should break your fast before starting. No march should be begun at such an unseasonable time as the morning twilight or after 9 A.M. If you want to hunt on the way, send your army to the halting-place by the shortest route in charge of the Paymaster of the Forces, and go to the hunting ground with a few attendants only."

The Mughal government of India was essentially of the nature of a military occupation and the stability of the throne depended on the efficiency of the army, and the military capacity of the princes. Aurangzib, therefore, advises his son, "Gradually make yourself perfect in the habit of wearing arms. Let your sweat dry before you take off your coat and lie down, lest you should fall ill." Strict discipline was to be maintained in the army, and every one taught to keep his station. The prince is thus instructed on the subject:

"Don't allow any of my officers except Muhammad Tahir (the prince's guardian), or any servant of the Emperor below a commander of 2,000 horse, to ride in front of your army, (where the prince marched.)" Certain specified officers were to be posted right and left of him and therefore in the van of the army, but they were to be accompanied by not more than two valets. The prince is commanded to see to this rule strictly, "as the crowding of the vulgar in front of the army destroys its order and discipline."

The commander should not make himself too affable, lest familiarity should breed contempt. "At all times, —whether marching or holding court,—speak just as many words as are necessary. As for those who are not high enough to be personally spoken to by you, contrive to evade them politely. This sort of behaviour keeps fear and reverence alive (in their hearts.) A sketch plan is sent herewith to show how you should marshal the officers at the public and private *darbars* that you hold."

This prince seems to have been too fond of hunting and rather averse to study. His father complains, "I regret very much that I took him out with myself to hunt at too early an age, for after once tasting the delights of sport, he has got a dislike for reading, writing and similar accomplishments and given up cultivating them." To the study of the Turkish language,—so necessary for the Mughal emperors who entertained large numbers of Turkish soldiers and generals,—Muhammad Sultan had a rooted aversion. The Prince is censured for leaving his Turki tutor behind him when setting out for Northern India. He pleads in excuse that the tutor was too old and weak to bear the fatigue of a march! Aurangzib angrily retorts that the prince had ignored the tutor even when in residence at Aurangabad. "He has been engaged for a year's time and drawn a lot of money as his salary, but you never tried to study with him." The prince is now ordered to call the tutor to himself and converse with him in Turki to learn the language. The father remarks indignantly, "You refuse to learn the accomplishments of (gentle) men and kings. What does it matter to *me*? You are now old enough to know good from evil."

As might be expected in a noble Muhammadan

family, the highest importance is attached to etiquette. The prince is told whom to admit to his 'select audience' and whom to keep out, how to arrange the *mansabdars* at court, and whom to address and whom not. He must be particular about his dress. "Your father has been shocked to hear that you sometimes go to prayer in undress, wearing a waist-coat and trousers only. This is a matter of surprise, as you have long lived with him and watched his (decorous) habits and manners."

Special attention is directed to style. "Read the *Akbarnamah* at leisure, so that the style of your conversation and writing may become pure and elegant. Before you have thoroughly mastered the meanings of words and the proper connection in which they may be used, do not employ them in your speeches or letters. Ponder carefully on what you speak or write."

This advice had a most comic effect. The *Akbarnamah* is the despair of readers and the rage of critics, by reason of its extravagant, involved and pedantic style. It is the worst possible literary model for a slow-witted lad of fourteen to imitate. Muhammad Sultan's next letter to his father made him open his eyes wide in astonishment. The poor child had written to his father an exact copy of one of the letters of Akbar to his subjects as drafted by Abul Fazl! It began with Akbar's favourite motto *Allahu akbar! Jall-i-jalaluhu!* in the place of the orthodox *Bismillah*, and the writer had applied to himself the imperial phrases and epithets of Akbar's letter though addressing his own father!

In deep vexation Aurangzib wrote back, "I had advised you to study the *Akbarnamah* of Abul Fazl, to make you follow its style and not to make you adopt the author's creed, who had changed the orthodox Sunni practices by his hertical innovations. You designate your letter as 'my imperial letter' (*nishan-i-wala*) and your seal as 'His Majesty's seal' (*muhar-i-khas*). In what terms will you then describe the Emperor's letter and seal?"

However, in spite of this poor success in improving Sultan's style and literary knowledge, he was very graciously received by his grandfather at Hindun (in December next), and loaded with gifts and other marks of favour.

The reader may be interested in the later history of this unpromising scholar. Three years after this, when the war for the throne of Delhi broke out, he accompanied his father's army to the North and often acted as his lieutenant, as we should expect of an eldest son. At the great battles of Dharmat, Samugarh, and Khajwah he commanded his father's vanguard. Indeed, his firm stand is said to have snatched victory out of the jaws of defeat at Khajwah. When Shah Jahan helplessly surrendered, Muhammad Sultan was sent to see him in Agra Fort and arrange about his confinement. Thereafter he was sent under the guardianship of Mir Jumla to chase Shuja back to Bengal. Here, during the operations round Rajmahal he resented the control of his guardian and his father's treatment, and listened eagerly to Shuja's emissaries who offered him marriage with Shuja's daughter Gulrukh Banu Begam, to whom he is said to have been betrothed in childhood. The infatuated young man deserted his army and fled to his uncle's camp one dark night (8 June, 1659,) and was married to his beloved. Eight months later, Shuja was hopelessly defeated, and Sultan left him to return to Mir Jumla. Stern was the punishment meted out by Aurangzib to the deserter. He was taken to Delhi under strong guard and confined in the Gwalior State prison for the rest of his life. While there his portrait was occasionally taken and sent to the Emperor for inspection. Thus only did the father know of his erring son's health! Death put an end to his miseries on 3rd December, 1676, when he was about to complete his 37th year. Only four years before his death was he brought closer to his father, by being removed to the fortress of Salimgarh (Delhi), restored to favour in a small degree—being thrice married in this short period.

ZEB-UN-NISSA.

Zeb-un-nissa, or the Ornament of Womankind, was the eldest child of Aurangzib and his Persian wife Dilras Banu Begam. Born at Daulatabad in the Deccan on 15th February, 1638, she was educated by a learned lady named Hafiza Mariam (the wife of Mirza Shukrullah of Kashmir whose family originally came from Naishabur in Khurasan.)

She inherited her father's keenness of intellect and literary tastes, and completely mastered the Arabic and Persian languages. For her success in committing the whole *Quran* to memory she received from her delighted father a purse of 30,000 gold pieces. She could write the different kinds of Persian hand,—*nastaliq*, *naskh*, and *shikasta* with neatness and grace. Her library surpassed all other private collections of books, and she employed many scholars on liberal salaries to produce new works or copy old manuscripts for her. Aurangzib disliked poets as lying flatterers and their poetry as vain babblings; but his daughter's liberality compensated for the lack of Court patronage of literature in that reign, and most of the poets of the time were maintained by her. Supported by her bounty, Mulla Safiuddin Ardbeli lived in comfort in Kashmir and translated the gigantic Arabic *Tafsir-i-Kabir* (Great Commentary) into Persian and named it after his patroness, *Zeb-ut-tafasir*. Other theological tracts and books, written by her pensioners, bore her name. Zeb-un-nissa is said to have written Persian poetry under the pseudonym of *Makhfi* or the Concealed One. But the extant *Diwan-i-Makhfi* cannot be her work.* The title of *Makhfi* was borne by several other poets, notably a wife of Akbar and Nur Jahan. (*M. A.* 538.)

Zeb-un-nissa, is the heroine of some love-tales current in modern Indian literary circles. She was a gifted poetess and is alleged to have claimed an artist's independence of morality. Similar discreditable legends about Kalidas's life have long circulated among our old school of Sanskritists, but are discredited by sober historians (*Ind. Antiq.*, 1878, 115.) We shall to-day try to ascertain whether the traditions about the Princess Royal of Delhi had a stronger basis in fact than those about the laureate poet of the court of Ujjayini.

No mention of Zeb-un-nissa's love-intrigue with Aqil Khan, or indeed with any person whatever, is made in any work of her father's reign or even for half a century after his death. We can easily explain the silence of the court historians and other official writers, who would naturally suppress every scandal about royalty. But perfect freedom of speech was enjoyed by the private historians of the reign (especially the two Hindu authors, Bhimsen and Ishwardas), by Khafi Khan who wrote a quarter of a century after Aurangzib's death, and by the author of the biographical dictionary of the Mughal Peers (*Masir-ul-umara*), who lived a generation later still.

* The subject has been fully discussed by Khan Sahib A. Muqtadir in the O. P. L. *Persian Catalogue*, Vol. III, pp. 250-1.

The European travellers, Bernier and Manucci, wrote for the eyes of foreigners, and had nothing to fear from the wrath of Aurangzib or his posterity. Manucci, in particular, revelled in court scandals, so much so that his history of the Mughals (*Storia do Mogor*) has been well called a *chronique scandaleuse.* Would he have passed over Zeb-un-nissa's failings, if he had heard of any, as such a topic would have made excellent "copy" for his book? The gossipy and outspoken Khafi Khan does not assail Zeb-un-nissa's character, though he openly proclaims the shames of Jahangir and Nur Jahan. The story of our heroine's love-intrigues is modern,—a growth of the 19th century and the creation of Urdu romancists, probably of Lucknow. The pretended Urdu Life of Zeb-un-nissa that holds the field at present is the *Durr-i-Maktum* of Munshi Ahmaduddin, B.A., of Lahor, who quotes from an earlier work, *Haiyat-i-Zeb-un-nissa* by Munshi Muhammad-ud-din Khaliq.

This story, in its most developed form is conveniently summarised in English (evidently from Ahmaduddin's Urdu work) in Mrs. Westbrook's introduction to her *Diwan of Zeb-un-nissa* in the "Wisdom of the East Series" (1913). She writes:

"In the beginning of 1662 Aurangzib was taken ill, and, his physicians prescribing change of air, he took his family and court with him to Lahor. At that time Aqil Khan, the son of his *wazir*, was governor of that city. He was famous for his beauty and bravery, and was also a poet. He had heard of Zeb-un-nissa, and knew her verses, and was anxious to see her. On pretence of guarding the city, he used to ride round the walls of the palace, hoping to catch a glimpse of her. One day he was fortunate, he caught sight of her on the housetop at dawn, dressed in a robe of *gul-anar*, the colour of the flower of the pomegranate. He said, *A vision in red appears on the roof of the palace.* She heard and answered, completing the couplet, *Supplications nor force nor gold can win her.*

She liked Lahor as a residence, and was laying out a garden there : one day Aqil Khan heard that she had gone with her companions to see a marble pavilion which was being built in it. He disguised himself as a mason, and, carrying a hod, managed to pass the guards and enter. She was playing *chausar* with some of her girl friends, and he, passing near, said, *In my longing for thee I have become as the dust wandering round the earth.* She understood and answered immediately : *Even if thou hadst become as the wind, thou shouldst not touch a tress of my hair.* They met again and again, but some rumour reached the ears of Aurangzib, who was at Delhi, and he hastened back. He wished to hush up the matter by hurrying her into marriage at once. Zeb-un-nissa demanded freedom of choice, and asked that portraits of her suitors should be sent to her ; and chose naturally that of Aqil Khan. Aurangzib sent for him ; but a disappointed rival wrote to him : 'It is no child's play to be the lover of a daughter of a king. Aurangzib knows your doings ; as soon as you come to Delhi, you will reap the fruit of your love.' Aqil Khan thought the Emperor planned revenge. So, alas for poor Zeb-un-nissa ! at the critical moment her lover proved a coward ; he declined the marriage, and wrote to the king resigning his service. Zeb-un-nissa was scornful and disappointed, and wrote : '*I hear that Aqil Khan has left off paying homage to me*'—or the words might also mean, '*has resigned service*'—'*on account of some foolishness.*' He answered also in verse, '*Why should a wise man do that which he knows he will regret ?*' (Aqil also means, a wise man.)

But he came secretly to Delhi to see her again, perhaps regretting his fears. Again they met in her garden ; the Emperor was told and came unexpectedly, and Zeb-un-nissa, taken unawares, could think of no hiding-place for her lover but a *deg*, or large cooking-vessel. The Emperor asked, 'What is in the *deg* ?' and was answered, 'Only water to be heated.' 'Put it on the fire, then,' he ordered ; and it was done. Zeb-un-nissa at that moment thought more of her reputation than of her lover, and came near the *deg* and whispered, 'Keep silence if you are my true lover, for the sake of my honour.' One of her verses says, '*What is the fate of a lover ? It is to be crucified for the world's pleasure.*' One wonders if she thought of Aqil Khan's sacrifice of his life.* After this she was imprisoned in the fortress of Salimgarh." (Pp. 14-17.)

Now, examining the above account in the light of known history we at once find that the story of the smuggled lover being done to death in a *deg* in the harem has been transferred to Zeb from her aunt Jahanara, of whom it is told by Manucci (*Storia*, i. 218) and Bernier (p. 13). The recorded facts of the life of Aqil Khan also contradict the story in every particular.

Mir Askari, afterwards surnamed Aqil Khan, was a native of Khwaf (in Persia)—and not the son of a Delhi *wazir*. He entered the service of Aurangzib in Shah Jahan's reign and attended the Prince during his second viceroyalty of the Deccan (1652-1657) as his equerry (*jilaudar*). He had already made his mark as a poet and adopted the pen-name of *Razi* from the saint Burhanuddin

* This conjecture is incorrect. According to the conventions of Persian poetry the type of the perfect lover is the moth which consumes itself in the flame of a lamp without uttering a groan. Cf. Carlyle's 'Consume your own smoke'.

Raz-ullah whom he venerated. When Aurangzib started from the Deccan to contest the throne, he left his family behind in the fort of Daulatabad (6th February —December, 1658), and Aqil Khan acted as the governor of the city from 6th February and of the fort from August 1658 till near the end of 1659. Arriving at Delhi on 8th February 1660, he was, two months later, made *faujdar* of the land between the Ganges and the Jumna (Mian Duab), but replaced by another officer in July, 1661. In the following November he temporarily retired from service on the ground of ill-health and was permitted to reside at Lahor on a pension of Rs. 750 a month. When in November 1663 Aurangzib was passing through Lahor with his family, on his return from Kashmir, Aqil Khan waited on him (2nd November) and was taken into the Emperor's train and appointed Superintendent of the Hall of Private Audience, a position of very close contact with the Emperor, (January, 1664). Evidently he continued to enjoy high favour, being promoted in October 1666 and given a royal present in May next. Later on he was made Postmaster-General (Darogha of Dak Chauki), but resigned in April 1669 and seems to have lived under a cloud for the next seven years, as we find no mention of him till October, 1676 when he was granted an allowance of Rs. 1,000 a month. In January, 1679 he was taken back into service as Second Paymaster. Being appointed *Subahdar* of Delhi in October 1680, he held that office till his death in 1696.

Thus we find that the story of young Aqil Khan

having been roasted to death in a cauldron by order of Aurangzib, is utterly false. No man below thirty could have been put in charge of a fort containing Aurangzib's wives and children on the eve of the war of succession, and, therefore, Aqil Khan must have been an old man at the time of his death in 1696.

So far was Aqil Khan from being cut off in the prime of youth through the vindictiveness of his mistress's father that he married, raised a family and died at the age of more than seventy surrounded by his grand-children. The *Letters of Mirza Bedil* (a favourite of Aqil Khan, when governor of Delhi towards the end of the 17th century,) mentions Qayyum Khan as this noble's son, and Shukrullah Khan and Shakir Khan as his sons-in-law.

And yet the Urdu biographer of Lahor has the audacity to say that Dr. Bernier witnessed the boiling of young Aqil Khan in a cauldron in the harem! Bernier's story refers to Jahanara's lover, and he took all his facts from Manucci.

From the life-sketch of Aqil Khan we find that he was at the same place with Zeb-un-nissa first at Daulatabad in 1658 (some ten months), then at Lahor in 1663 for a week only, thenceforth with the imperial Court at Delhi and Agra till his resignation in April 1669, again with the Court during the Rajput wars of 1679 and 1680, and finally at Delhi from January 1681 to 1696. It was only during the first and last of these periods that he could have been tempted to court the Princess by the absence of her august father.

The Khan's temporary retirement from service and residence at Lahor away from the court (November, 1661 --October, 1663) could not have been due to imperial displeasure as he was given a large pension all the time. But his long removal from the capital and Emperor's entourage for ten years (1669—1679) during the first seven of which he was denied any imperial bounty shows that he had for some reason, unknown to us, fallen under the Emperor's wrath.

Was it a punishment for making love to Zeb-un-nissa? A letter to her from her brother Prince Akbar, written in 1680, contains the statement, "As the Emperor has now ordered that no packet (*nalwo*) bearing the seal of Aqil should be admitted to the ladies' apartments of the palace, it is certain that papers will have to be now sent [by me?] after careful consideration."

Was this Aqil her alleged lover Aqil Khan Razi the poet? I think, not. There was at this time in Akbar's camp a Mulla named Muhammad Aqil, who afterwards signed a manifesto pronouncing canonical sentence of deposition on Aurangzib in favour of Akbar, for which the luckless theologian was imprisoned and severely bastinadoed when his patron's rebellion failed. Zeb being herself a Quranic scholar and a patron of new commentaries on the Muslim scripture, correspondence between her and a noted theologian like Mulla Muhammad Aqil would naturally pass unsuspected. The writer of the letter implies that his own confidential letters to his sister used to be sent under cover of Aqil's envelopes, which could reach her unchallenged, while packets bearing his own seal on the cover might have been intercepted by his enemies. This is quite clear from the concluding part of the letter: "The delay that has taken place in my writing to you is solely due to the fear lest my letters should fall into the hands of other people [lit., strangers, *i.e.*, enemies.]"

The theory that the Emperor stopped the poet and noble Aqil Khan's correspondence with his daughter on detecting an intrigue between them, is discredited by the fact that only a few months afterwards he was appointed to the highly responsible post of viceroy of Delhi, the very place where she was sent as a State-Prisoner early next year.

Zeb-un-nissa was imprisoned by her father in January 1681, and the official history establishes beyond dispute the fact that it was in punishment of her complicity with Prince Akbar who had rebelled against the Emperor.

The letter from which we have quoted contains several passages showing how deeply engaged she was in her brother's interests. He says, "What belongs to you is as good as mine, and whatever I own is at your disposal," and, again, "The dismissal or appointment of the sons-in-law of Daulat and Sagar Mal is at your discretion. I have dismissed them at your bidding. I consider your orders in all affairs as sacred like the *Quran* and *Traditions* of the Prophet, and obedience to them as proper."

When Akbar's rebellion frizzled out and his abandoned camp near Ajmir was seized by the imperialists (16th January, 1681), "Zeb-un-nissa's correspondence with him was discovered, she was deprived of her pension of four lakhs of Rupees a year, her property was confiscated, and she was lodged in the fort Salimgarh at Delhi." (*Masir-i-Alamgiri*, 204.) Here she lived till her death on 26th May, 1702. It would be sweet to imagine that during this captivity our

High born maiden
In her palace-tower
Soothed her love-laden
Soul in secret hour
With music sweet as love, which overflowed her power.

and that she wrote at this time the pathetic laments which Mrs. Westbrook has translated on page 17:—

So long these fetters cling to my feet!
My friends have become enemies, my relations are strangers to me.
What more have I to do with being anxious to keep my name undishonoured,
When friends seek to disgrace me?
Seek not relief from the prison of grief, O Makhfi; thy release is not politic.
O Makhfi, no hope of release hast thou until the Day of Judgment come.

But history is silent on the point. On the other hand our ardour to weave a romance out of her captive life is chilled by the reflection that she was now an old maid of 43 and Aqil Khan was at least twelve years older and a grandfather.

Another legend makes her fall in love with Shivaji the Maratha hero at first sight on the occasion of his being presented to the Emperor at Agra on 12th May, 1666. Fifty years ago a novel was written by Bhudev Mukherji in Bengali describing how the lovers exchanged rings and parted. But it is a fiction and nothing more. Not to speak of the Persian histories of the time, no Marathi life of Shivaji mentions that a Mughal princess interested herself in the fate of the captive chieftain in her father's capital. None of them gives the smallest hint of the champion of Hindu revival having coquetted with a Muslim sweet-heart in the enemy's den. Zeb-un-nissa's æsthetic sense, too, would have saved her from throwing her heart away to a rugged and illiterate Deccani. The whole story is not only unhistoric, but improbable.

Her captivity at Delhi does not seem to have been relaxed during her life. The official history records her death thus:—"The Emperor learnt from the news-letter of Delhi that the Princess Zeb-un-nissa had drawn on her face the veil of God's Mercy and taken up her abode in the palace of inexhaustible Forgiveness, [26th May, 1702]. At the parting of his child, dear as his life, his heart was filled with grief and his eyes with tears. He could not control the weakness that overpowered him. [At last] he recovered self-possession [somehow], and ordered Syed Amjad Khan, Shaikh Ataullah, and Hafiz

Khan to give away alms [at her funeral] and build a place of repose for her, as had been decided beforehand, in the Garden of Thirty Thousand [outside Delhi] which was a bequest from Jahanara." (*M.A.*, 462.)

A short letter from Aurangzib to Zeb-un-nissa has been preserved in *Faiyyaz-ul-qawanin*, (p. 369); half of it is in Arabic and it tells us nothing about her life. Similarly, some letters written to her by her brother Akbar in 1679-80 and given in *Adab-i-Alamgiri* throw no light on her biography. An Aligarh College manuscript contains some letters written by her Secretary Mirza Khalil, thanking [? her] for presents of fruit, game, ice, and a pair of spectacles! In the 32nd year of Aurangzib's reign (1688-1689) Inayet-ullah, the son of her lady-tutor, was appointed steward (*Khan-i-saman*) of her household. (*M. U.*, ii. 828.)

She was buried in the "Garden of Thirty Thousand Trees" outside the Kabuli gate of Delhi; but her tomb was demolished in making the Rajputana railway line.

THE NEMESIS OF AURANGZIB.

"...............But in these cases
We still have judgment here ; that we but teach
Bloody instructions, which being taught return
To plague th' inventor : this even-handed justice
Commends th' ingredients of our poison'd chalice
To our own lips."—*Macbeth*.

We all know that the Emperor Aurangzib gained the throne by deposing his father and murdering his brothers. But it is not so well-known that an exactly similar fate threatened him in 1681, when his fourth son, Muhammad Akbar, made an attempt to seize the throne.

This prince was born at Aurangabad on 11th September, 1657. As his mother, Dilras Banu Begam, died within a month of his birth, the young orphan was treated by his father with special tenderness. "God be my witness that I have loved you more than my other sons," as Aurangzib says in a letter to Akbar. The prince served the usual apprenticeship in government by acting as viceroy in some provinces.

On 10th December, 1678, Maharajah Jaswant Singh of Jodhpur died in the imperial service at Jamrud in Afghanistan. The Emperor immediately seized Jodhpur and sent an army into Marwar to bring it under his direct rule. The deceased Maharajah's property in the fort of Siwana was ordered to be confiscated. His widowed queens delivered two sons on reaching Lahor in February, 1679, and then proceeded to Delhi intending to return to Jodhpur. But meantime Aurangzib had sold the kingdom of Marwar to Jaswant's nephew Indra Singh, destroyed the temples of Jodhpur, and ordered the cart-loads of idols brought from the city to be flung down in the cavalry square of the imperial court and under the steps of the Juma Masjid to be trodden on by the Muslims. From 2nd April the *jaziya* or poll-tax was reimposed on the non-Muslims in order, as the official history of the reign asserts, "to spread the law of Islam and to overthrow the practices of the infidels." (*Masir-i-Alamgiri*, 171--177.)

At Delhi the leading Rathor adherents of Jaswant,—Durgadas, Ranchhordas, and Raghunath Bhatti,—continued to urge the Emperor to allow Jaswant's surviving infant, Ajit Singh,—the other having died in the meantime,—to go home and declare him as the heir of Marwar. But Aurangzib (15th July) ordered the baby prince to be seized and confined in the prison of Nurgarh. The Rathor escort offered a most heroic resistance to the arrest, and their leaders, by successively sacrificing themselves and their devoted followers in rearguard actions, carried Ajit Singh away in safety to Jodhpur (23rd July), after maintaining a running fight with the Mughal army for some days. One of the Ranis was killed to save her from capture.

The Rathor ministers immediately got possession of Jodhpur. The Mughal *faujdar* of Jodhpur and the *faineant* Rajah Indra Singh were dismissed by the Emperor for incompetence. Mughal armies now marched into Rajputana to wrest Jodhpur from the Rathors. The Emperor himself went to Ajmir (25th September) to be near the seat of war. Prince Akbar accompanied him, and moved in advance with the vanguard. Maharana Raj Singh of Udaipur having taken up the cause of the orphan heir of Jodhpur, the imperial army started from Ajmir (30th November) to punish him. Prince Akbar entered Udaipur (in January, 1680), after its evacuation by the Maharana. Mewar was ravaged by the Mughals and 176 temples were destroyed at Udaipur and its environs, besides 63 others in Chitor (*Masir-i-Alamgiri*, 183-188.) The war dragged on for some time. In this war, Prince Akbar commanded the Mughal vanguard, and gained some victories through his able lieutenants Tahawwur Khan, and Syed Hassan Ali Khan. But when posted in the Chitor district, he suffered some heavy losses by surprise attacks on the part of Maharana Raj Singh. The Emperor in anger transferred him to Jodhpur (June, 1680), where he fought languidly against the Rajputs for some time longer, but in the end formed a treasonable plot with the Rajputs to depose his father and crown himself!

The Emperor had been staying at Ajmir, the bulk of his army being detached under Akbar. On 7th January, 1681, he received the startling news that Prince Akbar had rebelled "at the instigation of the Rathors and some traitors among the imperial servants," proclaimed himself Emperor, and was planning to attack Aurangzib, who was slenderly guarded. But loyal officers made forced marches to join the Emperor, who boldly issued from Ajmir and reached Dorahah (10 miles southwards) on the 15th. Akbar too arrived within three miles of the place and encamped for the night. The battle was fixed for the next morning. But at night Tahawwur Khan (surnamed Padishah Quli Khan), the chief adviser of Akbar, came to the Emperor's court at the invitation of his father-in-law, a loyal officer. As he declined to take off his arms before entering the Emperor's tent, there was an altercation with the courtiers; then he turned to go back, but was beaten to death by the imperial guards. Aurangzib also sent a false letter to Akbar and contrived that it should fall into the hands of the Rajputs. In it he praised the prince for his success in pretending to rise in rebellion in order to deceive the Rajputs and bring them easily within the clutches of the imperial army!

The Rajput leaders on intercepting this letter went to Akbar for an explanation, but could not see him as he was then sleeping. The journey of Padishah Quli Khan to the imperial camp doubled their suspicion of a trap having been laid against them; the vast Rajput army melted away during the night and Aurangzib was saved! Next morning (16th January) Akbar woke to find himself utterly deserted, and he fled from his camp, leaving his family and children behind. Durgadas returned to him when the truth became known.

After passing some months in Marwar and Mewar, incessantly hunted by the imperial forces, Akbar at last fled to the Deccan under the escort of the faithful

Durgadas, crossing the Narmada on 9th May 1681, and passing by way of Burhanpur, Talnair and Baglana into Shambhuji's territory. A very amusing correspondence was now carried on between father and son, Aurangzib professing the greatest love and forgiveness for Akbar and that prince taunting the Emperor in scathing terms and doggrel verses for his administrative failure and claiming that in rebelling against his father he was only following a course sanctified by the example of Aurangzib himself!

Accounts vary as to the treatment of Akbar by Shambhuji. Khafi Khan says that he was at first well received and lodged in a palace six miles from Raigarh, but that afterwards he was treated with scant courtesy and allowed too small a pension for the support of his followers. Bhimsen, on the other hand, says that Shambhu gave the refugee a royal welcome and a liberal allowance. But the fact is clear from the following letters that Akbar tried to play the Padishah in his exile, while Shambhu stood on his own dignity and could never forget that the self-styled Emperor of Delhi was really a beggar living on his bounty. Besides, Akbar was ever haunted by the fear that the Maratha Court would make terms with the Imperial Government by delivering him up to his father's vengeance. At last, in search of a securer haven, Akbar left Shambhu, went to the European possessions on the Bombay coast and there took ship for Persia at the end of January, 1683. (*Masir-i-Alamgiri*, 224.)

At the Persian court he demanded armed aid for the conquest of Hindusthan; the Shah replied that he could not abet his attempt against his father's throne, but would gladly help him with men and money in a war of succession with his brothers. Nothing was now left for Akbar but to wear his heart out in patient waiting at Farah on the Persian frontier and to wickedly pray for his father's speedy death. Aurangzib on hearing of his unnatural son's aims, smiled grimly and repeated the following Persian quatrain:

> "My heart cannot forget the speech of the potter
> Who addressed a fragile cup that he had made,—
> 'I know not whether the stone from the sky of Fate
> Will break you or me first.'"

In fact Akbar died in 1704, three years earlier than the author of his being. The following letters have been translated from Persian Ms. No. 71 of the Royal Asiatic Society's Library, (London.) The first two of them also occur, with many variants of reading, in the Bengal Asiatic Society's Ms. F. 56, the lithographed *Zahir-ul-insha*, and a Persian Ms. belonging to me.

I.—AURANGZIB TO HIS SON MUHAMMAD AKBAR.

Muhammad Akbar, my son! close to my heart, a piece of my liver [as it were], dear as my life—be assured of and exalted with my sincere kindness, and know:—

God be my witness, that I held you dearer and more beloved than all my other sons. But you, through your own ill-luck, were tempted by the deception and stratagem of the Rajputs, those Satans in a human shape, to lose your portion of the wealth of Paradise and to become a wanderer in the hill and wilderness of Misfortune. What remedy can I contrive and what help can I give? My heart became plunged in extreme sorrow and grief when I heard of your present miserable condition of anxiety, perplexity, ruin and wretchedness. Nay more, life itself tasted bitter to me; what need I say of other things? Alas! a thousand times alas! leaving out of your sight your [legitimate] pride of rank and majesty as a prince and Emperor's son, you in your simplicity took no pity on your own [extrême] youth; you showed no regard for your wives and children, but in the most wretched condition threw [them] into the captivity of those beast-looking beast-hearted wicked Rajputs! And you are roaming in all directions like a polo ball, now rising, now falling, now fleeing!

As the Universal Father has planted in all fathers' bosoms affection for their sons, I do not, in spite of the heavy sins you have committed against me, wish that you should meet with the due punishment of your deeds:—(*Verses*)

Even though the son may be a heap of ashes
His father and mother regard him as collyrium for their eyes!

Let what is past, be past! Now if you are so guided by Fortune as to repent of your improper deeds, you may wait on me at any place that you like; the pen of forgiveness will be drawn across the pages of your book of errors and offences; and such favours and grace will be shown to you as you have not conceived in your mind;

and all your troubles and hardships will be compensated for. Although the granting of my favours does not depend upon your presenting yourself before me, yet, as the cup of your disgrace has fallen from above, it is proper that you should come to my presence even once to remove the shame of evil repute from yourself. Jaswant, the chief of Rajputs, assisted and joined Dara Shukoh, [but that prince] met with nothing save humiliation and reverses in consequence. Know for certain [that the same will be your fate, too.] Providence befriend you! God make it your lot to follow the right path.

II. Muhammad Akbar to the Emperor Aurangzib.

The petition of the humblest of sons, Muhammad Akbar, who performs all the necessary ceremonies of adoration and devotion, submission and obedience, and like an atom lays the following before your Majesty,—the centre of adoration and the holiest shrine of this world and the next:—

The royal letter which, in a spirit of graciousness to slaves, had been addressed to this the humblest of sons, arrived at the happiest of times and the best of places. I laid that auspicious celestial disc on the crown of my head, and rubbed its white portion into my eyes like light and its black portion like collyrium, and illuminated my heart and eyes by reading its gracious contents. I submit a short commentary on all matters which have flowed from your pen, so full of advice and graciousness,—which [commentary], as Truth is the essence of a matter, will not be far [from appropriate] in proportion as it approaches Justice.

Your Majesty has written with your gem-scattering pen, "I have loved this son *above* all my other sons, but he through his own ill-luck has lost his share of [my] great wealth and thrown himself into the tempest of thoughtlessness." Hail, Lord of the inner and outer worlds! Just as it is the duty of a son to seek the satisfaction of his father and devote himself to his father's service, so, too, it is an obligation and duty on the part of the father to bring up *all* his sons and attend to their interests, material and moral, and their rights. God be praised, that I have not hitherto failed in any way in rendering all the devotion of a son. How can I narrate in detail all the favours and graces of your Majesty, of which I cannot write of even one in a thousand or of a few out of many? The care and protection of the younger son is everywhere and always the paramount aim of [all] great fathers. But your Majesty, contrary to the practice of the world, has shown small regard for all your younger sons and honoured your eldest son with the title of Shah [Alam], and appointed him as your heir. In what [code] of justice and equity can we enter this act? All sons have equal claims to the property of their father. Under what rule of the Holy Law and Faith can one [son] be exalted and the others thrown down? Although the True Emperor is another being, in whose administration "when" and "why" have no jurisdiction, and the raising or overthrowing [of kings] belongs to Him of luminous splendour,—yet, [how does such partiality consist with] your Majesty's devotion to the Canon Law, love of the righteous path, spiritual insight, and regard for truth, which are known and manifest to the world and its inmates, [as is proved by Shah Jahan's verses on your Majesty in youth] (*Verse*)

Whom will he wish for as a friend,
and to whom will his heart incline ?

Verily, the guide and teacher of this path [of rebellion against a reigning father] is your Majesty; others are merely following your footsteps. How can the path which your Majesty himself chose to follow be called "the path of ill-luck ?" (*Verses*)

My father bartered away the garden of Eden for
two grains of wheat ;
I shall be an unworthy son if I do not sell it for a
grain of barley

Hail, centre of the worlds, spiritual and temporal! Men draw hardship and labour on themselves. Former emperors like Akbar, Jahangir and Shah Jahan [deliberately] raised troubles, and in the end attained to their hearts' desires. The volumes of history prove that so long as a king [like Alexander the Great] does not penetrate to the wilderness of gloom (*zulmat*) he cannot taste the water of eternal life. No rose without a thorn, and no buried treasure without [its guardian] snake. (*Verses*)

That man alone can tightly clasp the bride of Fortune in his arms,
Who can plant kisses on the lip of the keen-edged sword.

Since ease has been ordained as the result of every fatigue, I firmly hope that, through the grace of the Doer of All Works,—the Cherisher of His slaves,—my heart's desire will soon manifest itself in the happiest manner, and all my anxieties and exertions will be converted into rejoicing.

Your Majesty has written, "Jaswant was the chief of the Rajputs; what sort of assistance and support he rendered to Dara Shukoh is known to the world. Hence the words of this false race do not deserve trust." Your Majesty has spoken very well indeed, but has not reached the marrow of the matter. In fact Dara Shukoh bore hatred and antipathy to this race, and what he suffered was the consequence of it. If he had agreed with them from the outset, his affairs would not have come to such a pass. Former emperors like Akbar had contracted alliance and kinship with this race and conquered the realm of Hindusthan with *their* help. This is the race with whose aid and support Mahabat Khan made the Emperor Jahangir his captive and meted out due punishment to the tricksters and deceivers. This is the race who, when your Majesty was adorning the throne at Delhi, and the Rajputs [there] did not number more than three hundred men, performed heroic deeds, whose narrative is manifest to the age; such heroism and victory [were theirs] as the commanders of the age have not heard of. Jaswant it was who in the midst of the battle with Shuja displayed unpardonable insolence and violence to your Majesty; and yet your Majesty knowingly and deliberately overlooked his act. The same Jaswant it was whom your Majesty won over with many charms and soft speeches and detached from the side of Dara Shukoh, so that victory fell to your side. Blessings be on this race's fidelity to salt, who, without hesitation in giving up their lives for their master's sons, have done such deeds of heroism that for three years the Emperor of India, his mighty sons, famous ministers and high grandees have been moving in distraction [against them], though this is only the beginning of the contest.

And why should it not be so, seeing that in your Majesty's reign the ministers have no power, the nobles enjoy no trust, the soldiers are wretchedly poor, the writers are without employment, the traders are without means, the peasantry are down-trodden? So, too, the kingdom of the Deccan—which is a spacious country and a paradise on earth,—has become desolate and ruined like a hill or desert; and the city of Burhanpur,—a mole of beauty on the cheek of the earth,—has become ruined and plundered; the city of Aurangabad, glorified by connection with your Majesty's name, is perturbed like quicksilver at the shock and injury given by the enemy's armies. On the Hindu tribes two calamities have descended, (first) the exaction of the *jaziya* in the towns and (second) the oppression of the enemy in the country. When such sufferings have come down upon the heads of the people from all sides, why should they not fail to pray for or thank their ruler? Men of high extraction and pure breed belonging to ancient families, have disappeared, and the offices and departments of your Majesty's government and the function of counselling on the affairs of the State, are in the hands of mechanics, low people and rascals,—like weavers, soap-venders and tailors. These men, carrying the broad cloaks of fraud under their arms, and the snare of fraud and trickery, (to wit, the rosary) in their hands, roll on their tongues certain traditions and religious maxims. Your Majesty trusts these confidants, counsellers and companions as if they were Gabriel and Michael, and places yourself helplessly under their control. And these men, showing wheat [as samples] but selling barley,—by such pretexts make grass appear as a hill and a hill as grass [to you.] (*Verses*)

In the reign of King Alamgir, the Holy Warrior,
Soap-venders have become Sadar and Qazi!
Weavers and Jolahas are boasting
That at this banquet the king is their confidant!
Low people have gained so much power,
That cultured persons have to seek shelter at their doors!
Such rank has been acquired by fools
As even scholars can never attain to!
God protect us from this calamitous age,
In which the ass kicks at the Arab steed!
The supreme magistrate is [vainly] treading on the wind,
While justice has become [as rare] as the phœnix itself!

The clerks and officers of State have taken to the

practice of traders, and are buying posts with gold and selling them for shameful considerations. Every one who eats salt destroys the salt-cellar. The day seemed near when the palace of the State would be cracked.

When I beheld this to be the state of affairs [in the realm] and saw no possibility of your Majesty's character being reformed, kingly spirit urged me to cleanse the realm of Hindusthan of the brambles and weeds (*viz*, oppressors and lawless men), to promote men of learning and culture, and to destroy the foundations of tyranny and meanness,—so that mankind might, in easy circumstances and peaceful minds, engage in their respective professions, and good name,—which is synonymous with 'next life' and 'eternal existence'—might remain [for me] in the pages of [the history of] the age. How happy would it be if Providence so befriends [your Majesty] that leaving this work in the hands of the humblest of your sons, your Majesty seeks the blessedness of going on a pilgrimage to the Holy Cities [Mecca and Medina], and thereby induces the whole world to utter praises and prayers for you!

Hitherto your Majesty has spent all your life in the quest of the things of this world—which are even more false than dreams, and even less constant than shadows. Now is the proper time for you to lay in provisions for the next life, in order to atone for your former deeds, done out of greed for this transitory world against your august father and noble brothers in the days of your youth. (*Verses*)

O! thou art past eighty years and art still asleep!
Thou will not get more than these few days.

As for the lecture your Majesty has read to me in your letter, I am ashamed of your presumption [in writing in that strain.] (*Verses*)

What good did you do to your father,
That you expect all these [services] from your son?
O thou that art teaching wisdom to mankind,
Administer to thy ownself what thou art preaching to others!
Thou art not curing thyself,
Then, for once, give up counselling others!

Concerning what your Majesty has written to me to go to your presence, although it is the highest blessing to enter your presence, yet by reason of my youth and my apprehension of your Majesty's vengeance—who have behaved so notoriously towards your father and brothers—my heart is naturally full of suspicion of such undeserved punishment. If, however, your Majesty goes to Ajmir with a small body of attendants, all these fears will be removed from my heart; it will gain confidence, and I shall secure the honour of waiting on you. Thereafter, with perfect composure of mind I shall carry out all your commands. To write more would be impolite.

[NOTES. *My father bartered away, etc.*—In Muslim theology Adam is said to have been expelled from Paradise for breaking God's command by eating two grains of wheat (*i.e.*, the fruit of the forbidden tree) at the instigation of Satan.

Wilderness of gloom.—There is a Muslim tradition that Alexander the Great penetrated through the Egyptian desert to a terrible dark region where the *elixir vitae* was preserved. He tasted it as the reward of his daring and hardiness. The poet Sadi uses the story in his *Gulistan.*

Your Majesty at Delhi.—The allusion is to the desperate battles by which Durgadas and other Rathors carried off Jaswant's infant son Ajit Singh from Delhi where Aurangzib tried to imprison him. See my *History of Aurangzib*, iii. 377.

The battle with Shuja—The battle of Khajwa, 5th January, 1659, on the eve of which Jaswant treacherously plundered Aurangzib's camp and then fled to Jodhpur. See my *History of Aurangzib*, ii. 146.

For three years the Emperor of Hindusthan, etc.—The allusion is to the war which broke out in Rajputana early in 1679, when Aurangzib tried to annex Marwar on the death of Jaswant Singh. Mewar was speedily involved in it, and though the new Maharana Jai Singh made peace on 14th June, 1681, the quarrel was soon afterwards renewed. With the Rathor followers of Ajit Singh the war continued without cessation for 30 years, and ended only with his formal recognition by Aurangzib's successor in August, 1709.

The spirited defence of the Rajput character for fidelity and of Jaswant's memory against Aurangzib's aspersions, shows that this letter was inspired by Durgadas. The stinging satire on Aurangzib contained in the second half of the letter could never have been forgiven by that Emperor.]

III. Aurangzib to Prince Akbar.

Alas for this son's lack of wisdom and sense, who has stepped aside from the path of obedience and devotion,—which befits the relation of a son to a father,—displayed crookedness of action and evil disposition, and, with the aim of gaining the crown and the throne, has uplifted the sword in his hand against his own father! In the race of the Emperors of India which son ever fought against his father? You have advanced most presumptuously. If your heart's desire is to play your sword and conquer kingdoms, what can be better? With faithful nobles and devoted followers go to Persia, whose king Shah Abbas [the Second] has fought battles with thy father and broken his coin of Qandahar. You ought to destroy *his* cities, for such is the duty of true sons. Why engage in battle with your own father in the hope of sitting on the throne? The key to the locks of endless victories lies in the hands of the Divine Treasurer, and kingship is His holy gift. What better than this? You, my son, ought to turn the rein of your enterprise from that side with all the circumstances of humility and defeat, and put the ring of servitude and obedience in the ear of your life, and come like a point to the centre of [my] celestial power, and rub the forehead of gratitude on the dust of my imperial threshhold. Then, probably, will my grace be your lot. Know that my wish is urgent in this matter; delay not in acting up to my command.

[Notes. *Qandahar.*—After Shah Abbas II. had

captured the fort of Qandahar from its Mughal garrison, Aurangzib besieged it twice without success.

Ring in the ear.—Slaves in Islamic countries (as also among the ancient Teutons) were distinguished by putting rings in their ears.]

IV. Muhammad Akbar to Shambhuji.

Shambhuji, the chief of great Rajahs, etc.! hope for my boundless favours and know that,—

From the beginning of his reign it was the intention of Alamgir to utterly ruin all the Hindus alike. On the death of Maharajah Jaswant Singh this intention became revealed to all. His war with the Rana [Raj Singh, of Udaipur] was also the outcome of this design.

As all men are the creation of God, and He is the protector of them all, it is not proper for us as Emperors of India to try to uproot the race of landowners, for whom is India. Emperor Alamgir had carried matters beyond their limit, and I became convinced that if these men were overthrown then Hindusthan would not continue to be in the hands of our family. Therefore, with a view to saving my heritage and also taking pity on this race [Rajput Rajahs] who have been loyal to us from olden times,—I decided, at the request of Rana Raj Singh and Durgadas Rathor, to ride to Ajmir and fight a battle for the throne, so that the intention of God might become known. In this state of things, as the Rana happened to die, the business was delayed. One month afterwards, Rana Jai Singh submitted the same prayer of his father [to me,] through Padishah Quli Khan,—who had gone to Jilwar in order to plunder his dominions,—saying, "If you wish that the honour of Hindusthan should remain [inviolate], then we all, laying our hands on the skirt of your robes, hope for our deliverance and benefit from your Majesty."

At the request of these two great clans, I set about to take possession of my heritage. I arrived within two miles of the encampment of Alamgir, it was three hours after sunset,—the battle having been fixed for the next morning,—when Death dragged the coward Padishah Quli Khan bound [with ropes, as it were,] to the court of Alamgir, who slew him immediately on his arrival. Although the going away of any one was not really subversive of my undertaking, yet, as Padishah Quli Khan had been the intermediary in bringing over to my side the Sisodias and Rathors, both these clans were seized with a groundless suspicion that the whole affair was a stratagem [of Alamgir]. So they decamped towards their homes, without informing me. At their departure my soldiers lost heart and fled, so that the battle was not fought.

At this I took a small portion of my family retainers with me and went towards Marwar. The night of the next day Durgadas Rathor saw me with all his troops, and decided to accompany me. I made two or three trips and circuits in the kingdom of Marwar. As Muazzam,—who had been appointed to pursue me,—could not overtake [me] in these rambles, he divided his troops and stationed them in different parts of the kingdom of Marwar as outposts. Therefore, I passed [into the dominion of] Rana Jai Singh, and he, after offering to me horses and other presents, begged me to remain in his kingdom. But as his country was close to the seat of the Emperor, I did not consider it prudent to stay there. Therefore, bearing in mind your bravery and high spirit, I decided to march [to your country.] So, helped by the favour of the gracious Accomplisher of Tasks, on the 1st Jamadi-ul-awwal, year 1092 A. H. (=9th May, 1681), I safely forded the river Narmada at Bhaiswarah. Durgadas Rathor is with me. Keep your mind composed about me and cherish the hope that, God willing, when I have gained the throne, the name will be mine and the State will be yours. Fully realising Alamgir's enmity to yourself and to me, set your heart on this that we should act so as to promote our business. (*Verses*)

As the world does not stay in the same condition
It is better to have a good name, which endures as a memorial.

This is what we expect from a man and a hero. What more need I say than that 'A hint is enough for the wise?' Written on 3rd Jamadi-ul-awwal, year 1092, (=11th May, 1681).

[NOTES.—Maharana *Jai Singh* was the son and successor of Raj Singh. *Jilwar* probably stands for the Jilwarra pass leading into Mewar. Akbar forded the Narmada "at one of the crossing places appertaining to the ferry of Akbarpur, at a distance of 16 miles, close to the frontier of Rajah Mohan Singh," according to Khafi Khan (ii. 276). Akbarpur is south of Mandu. The word written as *Bhaiswarah* in the MS. may be a copyist's error for Maheshwar, a noted place 8 miles east of Akbarpur. The year is wrongly given in the MS. as 1098.]

A MUSLIM HEROINE.

A WARDEN OF THE MARCHES.

A noble Persian family of Yezd took refuge in India early in the seventeenth century and rose to high distinction in the service of the Mughal Emperors. One grandson of the first immigrant was Paymaster under Shah Jahan, and another, named Khalilullah Khan, was a provincial governor and married a niece of the Empress Mumtaz Mahal. Their son Amir Khan was a noble of the first rank in the reign of Aurangzib and governed Afghanistan for 22 years with remarkable success and reputation.

He acquired his knowledge of mountaineers and hill-fighting by acting as the military commander of the Jammu hills and afterwards leading a punitive expedition against the Yusufzai Afghans of Shahbazgarhi (near Langarkot), whose villages he destroyed and whose cattle he drove away with great ability and firmness. Even when posted in Bihar as Governor, he was not rid of the Afghans; there was a colony of these turbulent men in Shahjahanpur and Kant-golah, who rebelled and were defeated and captured by Amir Khan.

After these preparatory experiences came the great opportunity of his life; in March, 1677, he was appointed *subahdar* (viceroy) of Afghanistan, and filled the post with undimmed brilliancy till the day of his death, 28th April, 1698.

His first meeting with his new subjects was not a happy one. An Afghan named Aimal Khan had set up as king of the hillmen and struck coins in his own name. The first expedition against the rebels near the Lamghanat ended in the rout of the imperial forces. The sword having failed, the new governor took to policy. He engaged himself in winning the hearts of the Afghans with such success that the chiefs of the clans "left their shy and unsocial manners and began to visit him without any suspicion."

His statesmanship bore such good fruit that "during his government of 22 years no disaster befell him, and no administrative failure or disorder took place. Robbery and oppression were kept down by his firmness and activity. Whatever he planned succeeded; all his desires were fulfilled."

The tribal chiefs became thoroughly obedient to him: every one of them looked up to him for advice in conducting his own affairs. Under his astute guidance they ceased to trouble the Imperial Government and spent their energies in internecine quarrels! His cleverness made him triumph over every difficulty.

Once there was a great gathering of the Afghans under Aimal. There was hardly any tribe that did not join him. Every male fighter in the hills took provisions for a few days and attended the muster. The *subahdar's* army was too small to encounter a nation in arms. Amir Khan was alarmed, took counsel with a very clever subordinate, Abdullah Khan Kheshgi, and made him write feigned letters to the head of every tribe in the rebel camp, saying, "We had long been waiting for such a happy event as that the government of the country would pass to the Afghans. Thank God, our long deferred hope is at last being fulfilled. But we do not know the character of your new king. If he is worthy to rule, write, and we shall join you, as service under the Mughals is not to our liking."

The Afghan chieftains highly praised Aimal Khan in their replies. Then Abdullah Khan wrote again, "All this praise is good no doubt; but is your leader so eminently just as to treat his kinsmen and strangers with impartial equality? Try him by asking him to parcel out among the clans the land already conquered. Then you will find out whether he has any greed or reluctance to be impartial to all."

At this the tribesmen made the proposal to him. Aimal declined, saying, "How can a small territory be divided among so many men?"

All was now dissension in the Afghan camp. Many of the hillmen immediately returned home in anger. Aimal Khan had at last to make a division of land; but as he naturally showed greater consideration to his own clan and kinsmen, the quarrel broke out afresh. All the other chiefs left him in disgust, and wrote to dissuade Abdullah Khan from joining such a bad king! Surely the policy of *divide et impera* has never triumphed so well in Afghanistan.

A WOMAN WHO RULED THE AFGHANS.

Amir Khan's wife, SAHIBJI (=Her Ladyship), was a daughter of Ali Mardan Khan, a highly gifted Persian, who rose to be the Premier Noble of the Court of Shah Jahan. She was a wonderfully clever and expert woman. In conducting the administration she was her husband's partner. His success in many a difficulty was due to her wise suggestions and business capacity. *She* was the real Governor of Kabul.

One night the Emperor Aurangzib learnt from the report of Kabul the news of Amir Khan's death. Immediately summoning Arshad Khan (who had formerly acted as *Diwan* of Afghanistan), he said in concern, "A great difficulty has cropped up. Amir Khan is dead. That province, which is ever ripe for a thousand disturbances and troubles, has now none to govern it. A disaster may happen before the arrival of his successor."

Arshad Khan boldly replied, "Amir Khan lives. Who calls him dead ?"

The Emperor handed him the report from Kabul. The Khan read it and added, "Yes; but then it is Sahibji who governed and controlled the province. So long as *she* lives your Majesty need not fear any disorder."

The Emperor at once wrote to the lady to guard the province till the arrival of her husband's successor in office, which, however, happened two years afterwards. During this interval she was the sole Governor of Afghanistan, as she had been in all but the name in her husband's lifetime.

Death overtook Amir Khan when he was out among the valleys. If the fact had got wind, the Afghans would have taken heart and massacred his leaderless escort in their narrow defiles. Sahibji with great presence of mind suppressed her grief, concealed his death, dressed a man like Amir Khan, made him sit in a *palki* with glass doors, and thus marched long distances. Every day she inspected the troops and received their salute. It was only after issuing safely from the hills that she went into mourning.

After her husband's death, all the Afghan chieftains sent their relatives to condole with her. She treated them with great respect and sent word to the headmen, "Take your customary dues. Do not rebel or rob, but remain obedient as before. Otherwise I defy you to a fight.* If I defeat you, my name will remain famous to the end of time."

The headmen out of regard for fair play gave her new promises and assurances of their loyalty and did not break out in lawlessness.

Her courage and presence of mind had been as conspicuous in her youth. Years ago at Delhi she was passing by a lane in a *chaudol* (sedan chair). The Emperor's own elephant—the chief of its species—appeared in an infuriated (*mast*) condition before her. Her attendants wanted to turn it back. But the *mahouts* as a class are vicious, and this one was further proud of being the Emperor's own driver. So he urged the

* Lit., "Here is the ball and here the polo field," *i.e.*, a challenge to a contest.

elephant rashly onward. Her escort pulled out their arrows from the quivers; but the brute flung its trunk on the *chaudol* to seize and trample it down. The porters dropped it and fled. Quick as thought Sahibji jumped out, ran into a money-changer's shop hard by, and shut the door. This was no common feat of agility, as a Muslim noblewoman travelling on the public road must have been securely wrapped up like a parcel sent by post in the rainy season.

She had saved her life, but alas! she had broken *pardah*,—an unpardonable offence against Indian etiquette. Amir Khan was angry at her audacity, and for a few days lived in separation from her. Then the Emperor Shah Jahan told him frankly, "She has played a man's part; she has saved her own and your honour at the same time. If the elephant had seized her and exposed her (bare body) to the public, what privacy would have been left?"

So she was taken back by her husband. Amir Khan might have cried out to his heroic wife,

> "Bring forth men children only!
> For thy undaunted mettle should compose
> Nothing but males."

But unfortunately she was childless like Lady Macbeth. Her husband, in fear of her, durst not take another wife, but kept a secret harem and had children by them. At last Sahibji discovered it, but adopted and lovingly brought up her step-sons.

On being relieved of the government of Kabul, she made a pilgrimage to Mecca and Medina, where she spent large sums in charity and was highly honoured by the Sheriff and other people.†

† The materials of this sketch have been taken from the Persian *Masir-ul-umara* i. 277—286.

THE FERINGI PIRATES OF CHATGAON, 1665 A.D.

[*From the contemporary Persian account of Shihabuddin Talish, in the Bodleian Ms. 589.*]

ARRACAN DESCRIBED.

The fort of Châtgâon is an appurtenance of the kingdom of Arracan, which is a large country and great port of the east. One side of it is enclosed by high hills which join the mountains of Kashmir, China, Cathay, and Mahachin. Another side is bordered by the ocean. Deep rivers and wide oceans enclose the western side, which adjoins Bengal. The land and water routes alike for entering the country are very difficult. Its conquest is an extremely hard task. The people of the country are called Maghs,—which is an abbreviation of *Muhamil-i-sag* (=despicable dog), according to [the proverb] "The name descends from heaven." They do not admit into their country any other tribe than the Christians, who visit it by the sea-route for purposes of trade. Good elephants abound; horses are totally wanting. This writer has heard from the Khân Khânân [Mir Jumla] that the elephants of Arracan surpass all other elephants in beauty of appearance and character. Some mines of metals are said to exist in the country. The inhabitants have no definite faith or religion, but incline [a little] to the Hindu creed. Their learned men are called *Rawlis;* they do not transgress the guidance of the latter in their earthly affairs. The *Rawlis* have the ways of the *Sewrahs* [=Shwetambar

Jains]. The Rajahs of this country hold pre-eminence over other lower rulers, by reason of their large forces, spacious country, and great splendour. The Governors of the ports and islands of the east always show respect and meekness to them. These Rajahs are so proud and foolish that as long as the sun does not decline from the zenith they do not put their heads out of the doors of their palace; they say, "The sun is our younger brother. How can we hold Court while he is over our heads and we below him?" In their decrees and letters they give themselves the titles of "Elder brother of the Sun, Lord of the Golden House and White Elephant." Of their offspring that base-born son is considered the proper heir to the throne whom they have begotten on the person of their own sister. After the conquest of Chatgaon [by Shaista Khan] it was found from the records of the place that the year was written as 1127.* On being asked to account for the date, the people said that the beginning of the era was the beginning of their royal dynasty, and that the aforesaid years had passed since the establishment of the rule of these Rajahs. This fact makes it clear that in this long period [of 1127 years] no foreigner had succeeded in conquering the country, and no outsider had got into it. Their cannon are beyond numbering, their flotilla (*nawwara*) exceeds the waves of the sea [in number]. Most of their ships are *ghurabs* and *jalbas; khalus* and *dhums*

* This should be 1027. In the Burmese vulgar era, used also in Arracan, 1027 corresponds to 1665 A.D. *(Bengal and Agra Gazetteer.)*

are larger than *ghurabs;* these are so strongly made of timber with a hard core (*az chob-i-qalbdar*) that the balls of *zamburaks* and small cannon cannot pierce them. [Latterly] the Rajah appointed the Feringi pirates to plunder Bengal, and hence he did not send the Arracan fleet for the purpose.

OLD CHATGAON DESCRIBED.

Chatgaon is a tract adjacent to Bengal and Arracan alike. From Jagdia, where there was a [Mughal] outpost, to Chatgaon lay a wilderness. On the skirt of the hill was a dense jungle, without any vestige of habitation or living being. The river Feni, rising in the hills of Tipperah, passes by Jagdia* and falls into the ocean. Ninety-nine *nullahs*, which contain water even in seasons other than the monsoons, intervene between Feni and Chatgaon. After the capture of Chatgaon, bridges (*pul*) were built by Shaista Khan's order over all these *nullahs*. From Dacca to Chatgaon six creeks (*bahar*) have to be crossed in boats; one of them is the river of Sripur, which is so broad that a boat can perform only one trip across it and back in the whole day.

On the bank of the Karnafuli river are some hills, high and low, situated close to each other. The lower hills have been heaped over with earth and raised to the level of the higher ones; all these hills have been scarped cylindrically, fortified, and named the fort [of Chatgaon]. In strength it rivals the rampart of Alexander, and its

* In Rennell's *Atlas*, Sheet 1, Jagdia is on the Little Feni River.

towers (*burj*) are as high as the *falak-ul-baruj*. Fancy cannot sound the depth of its moat, imagination cannot reach its niched parapet.

In the fort has been dug a deep ditch, about eight yards in breadth; on the eastern side, close to the edge of the ditch, flows the river Karnafuli, which descends from the Tipperah hills to the sea. On the north side is a large wide and deep tank close to the ditch. Behind the tank, along the entire north side and a part of the western side, are hills. The hills are so high and the jungle so dense, that it is impossible to traverse them even in imagination. Within the fort two springs flow, the water of which runs into the Karnafuli river in the monsoons, when the channel of the springs becomes so broad that a *jalba* boat can easily pass through it. As the people of the fort use all the water [that issues] in seasons other than the rainy, they dam the springs and block the outlet to the Karnafuli river. On a height within the fort is a tomb, known as the *âstanâ* of Pir Badar; the attendants of the shrine perform prayer and fast. The Magh infidels..... have settled some villages in *waqf* on this tomb; they make pilgrimage to the holy dead and offer presents. It is said that if one could perform the impossible feat of dragging a large gun to the top of the hill at the western angle [of the fort]—which adjoins Tipperah—its balls would fall within the fort. On the other side of the Karnafuli there is a lofty and strong fort, opposite the fort of Chatgaon; it is full of defence-materials.

Every year the Rajah of Arracan sends to Chatgaon a hundred ships full of soldiers and artillery munitions, with a new *Karamkari* (commandant, superintendent), when the former *Karamkari*, with the ships of last year, returns to Arracan. There is always some trustworthy relative or faithful clansman of the Rajah in charge of the government of Chatgaon. He issues gold coins stamped with his own name at this place and its dependencies.

In bygone times, one of the Sultans of Bengal named Fakhruddin fully conquered Chatgaon, and built an embankment (*al*) from Chandpur, opposite the outpost of Sripur across the river, to Chatgaon. The mosques and tombs which are situated in Chatgaon were built in Fakhruddin's time. The [existing] ruins prove it.

CHATGAON IN MAGH HANDS.

When Bengal was annexed to the Mughal empire, and included in the records of the *qanungo* department, Chatgaon was entered in the papers of Bengal as one of the defaulting unsettled [districts]. When the *mutasaddis* of Bengal did not really wish to pay any man whose salary was due, they gave him an assignment on the revenue of Chatgaon! Towards the end of the rule of the Bengal kings and the early years of the conquest of Bengal by the Mughals, when great confusion prevailed in the country, Chatgaon again fell into the hands of the Maghs, who did not leave a bird in the air or a beast on the land [from Chatgaon] to Jagdia, the frontier of Bengal, increased the desolation, thickened the jungles, destroyed the *al*, and closed the road so well that even the snake and the wind could not pass through. They built a strong fort, and left a large fleet to guard it. Gaining composure of mind from the strength of the place, they turned to Bengal, and began to plunder it. None of the Viceroys of Bengal [before Shaista Khan] undertook to put down this trouble and punish them. Only Ibrahim Khan Fatih Jang, in the Emperor Jahangir's reign, resolved to conquer Chatgaon and destroy the wicked Maghs. [This expedition failed.]

DOINGS OF THE PIRATES OF CHATGAON.

From the reign of the Emperor Akbar, when Bengal was annexed to the Mughal empire, to the time of the conquest of Chatgaon during the viceroyalty of Shaista Khan, Arracan pirates, both Magh and Feringi, used constantly to [come] by the water-route and plunder Bengal. They carried off the Hindus and Muslims, male and female, great and small, few and many, that they could seize, pierced the palms of their hands, passed thin canes through the holes, and threw them one above another under the deck of their ships. In the same manner as grain is flung to fowl, every morn and evening they threw down from above uncooked rice to the captives as food. On their return to their homes, they employed the few hard-lived captives that survived [this treatment] in tillage and other hard tasks, according to their power, with great disgrace and insult. Others were sold to the Dutch, English, and French merchants at the ports of the Deccan.

Sometimes they brought the captives for sale at a high price to Tamluk, and the port of Baleshwar, which is a part of the imperial dominions and a dependency of the province of Orissa. The manner of the sale was this:—The wretches used to bring the prisoners in their ships, anchor at a short distance from the shore off Tamluk or Baleshwar, and send a man ashore with the news. The local officers, fearing lest the pirates should commit any depredation or kidnapping there, stood on the shore with a number of followers, and sent a man with a sum of money to the pirates. If the terms were satisfactory, the pirates took the money and sent the prisoners with the man. Only the Feringi pirates sold their prisoners. But the Maghs employed all their captives in agriculture and other kinds of service. Many high-born persons and Sayyads, many pure and Sayyad-born women, were compelled to undergo the disgrace of the slavery, service or concubinage (*farash wa suhabat*) of these wicked men. Muslims underwent such oppression in this region of war (*dar-ul-harb*) as they had not to suffer in Europe. It was less in some Governors' time and more in others'.

As they for a long time continually practised piracy, their country prospered, and their number increased, while Bengal daily became more and more desolate, less and less able to resist and fight them. Not a householder was left on both sides of the rivers on their track from

Dacca to Chatgaon. The district of Bagla,* a part of Bengal, lying in their usual path, was [formerly] full of cultivation and houses, and yielded every year a large amount to the Imperial Government as duty on its betel-nuts. They swept it with the broom of plunder and abduction, leaving none to inhabit a house or kindle a fire in all the tract. Matters came to such a pass that the Governor of Dacca confined his energies to the defence of that city only, and the prevention of the coming of the pirate fleet to Dacca, and stretched some iron chains across the *nullah* of Dacca and set up some bridges of bamboo (*nai*, reed) on the stream (*nahar*) of the city.

DEMORALISED BENGAL NAVY.

The sailors of the Bengal flotilla were in such a fright, that I may say without exaggeration that whenever 100 war-ships of Bengal sighted four ships of the enemy, if the distance separating them was great the Bengal crew showed fight by flight, considered it a great victory that they had carried off their lives in safety, and became famous in Bengal for their valour and heroism! If the interval was small and the enemy overpowered them, the men of the Bengal ships—rowers, sepoys, and armed men alike—threw themselves without delay into the water, preferring drowning to captivity.

Once Ashur Beg, an officer of Prince Shujâ was cruising with about 200 boats, when a few of the enemy's

* *Bagla* included Backerganj and part of Dacca (*J. A. S. B.*, Pt. I., 1873, p. 209).

fleet, in number not even one-tenth of the imperial flotilla, came in sight. Ashur Beg was mortally frightened; in great agitation he cried to the *mânjhi* or captain of his ship, "*Ai bâi âsh bedeh!*"* The *manjhi* in perplexity asked, "*Mir-jiu!* whence can I get broth at such a time? Just now these pirates will cook a nice broth for you!" Ashur Beg in agitation and bewilderment kept up crying, "You confounded fellow, give *âsh*," and the *mânjhi* went on replying, "I have not got it with me. Whence can I bring it?" [The fact is] sailors use the term *wars* to mean, 'backing the boat'; Ashur Beg in his terror had forgotten the word and used *âsh* instead! In no other part of the Mughal empire has any neighbouring infidel [king] the power to oppress and domineer over Muslims; but rather do [infidel kings] show all kinds of submission and humility in order to save their homes and lands, and the [Mughal] officers of those places engage in making new acquisitions by conquest. In Bengal alone the opposite is the case; here the mere preservation of the imperial dominion is considered a great boon. Those Governors in whose times these piracies were less frequent, congratulated themselves and exulted at it. None of them tried to stop the path of oppression and domination of this wicked tribe through their fear of the necessary expenditure and exertion, weakness of faith and trust, and the [false] notion of their lack of power.

* "Ho, brother, give [me] broth." *Bai* is the Dacca pronunciation of *Bhai*.

ROUTES OF THE PIRATES.

In Jahangir's reign, the Magh pirates used to come to Dacca for plunder and abduction, by the *nullah* which leaves the Brahmaputra, passes by Khizirpur, and joins the *nullah* of Dacca. Khizirpur is situated on the bank of the Brahmaputra, on a narrow embankment (*âl*). In the monsoons all the land except the sites of the houses is covered with water. The Governors of Dacca, therefore, at the end of the monsoons and during the winter, which was the season of the coming of the pirates, used to go to Khizirpur with an army and encamp there. After some years, the *nullah* dried up, and many places in the track of the pirates in the Brahmaputra river also became fordable. Thus their [water] route to Dacca was closed on this side, and restricted to the side of Jattrapur* and Bikrampur. Recently as the pirates could more easily carry out their chief design of kidnapping men in the villages of Dacca and other *parganahs*, they did not exert themselves to reach Dacca town.

When the pirates came from Chatgaon to molest Bengal, they passed by Bhalua, a part of the imperial dominions, on the right, and the island of Sondip, belonging to the zamindar Dilawwar, on the left, and reached the village of Sangramgarh. [From this point] if they wished to plunder Jessore, Hughli, and Bhushna, they moved up the Ganges; if they wanted to raid Bikrampur, Sunargaon, and Dacca, they proceeded up the

* In Rennell, Sheet 1, Jattrapur is given 30 miles west of Dacca.

Brahmaputra. Sangramgarh* is the land at the extremity of the island (*i.e.*, delta) which contains Dacca and other towns and villages. In front of it the Ganges and the Brahmaputra unite. The mingled stream, after passing by Bhalua and Sondip, falls into the sea. In ancient times, a man named Sangram had built a fort here to repel the Magh raids into Bengal. In Hindi a fort is called a *garh*. By the combination of these two words the name of the place has been formed. If a fort were built here and stored with weapons, munitions, and materials of defence, and a large force and well-equipped flotilla kept here, the oppression of the pirates and the raids of the Maghs into Bengal could most probably be prevented.

FERINGI PIRATES.

Many Feringis lived happily at Chatgaon† and used to come to the imperial dominion for plunder and abduction. Half their booty they gave to the Rajah of Arracan, and the other half they kept. This tribe was called *Harmad*.‡ They had 100 swift *jalba* boats full of war-materials. The Governors of Bengal were disturbed by their robbery and were too weak to prevent it. As the Harmads [=Feringi pirates] were not in

* No trace of Sangramgarh is found in Rennell. The *Alamgirnamah*, p. 943, says that its name was changed to Alamgirnagar, and that it was 21 *kos* from Sripur (p. 944). It must have been near Rennell's *Mendigunge*. Khafi Khan calls it Sangramnagar, ii. 188.

† Their settlement was called *Feringi-bandar* or *Bandar*, on the south bank of the Karnafuli, very close to its mouth.

‡ This word is evidently *armad*, a corruption of *armada*. *Armad* is used in the sense of fleet in the *Kalimat-i-tayyibat*.

need of the help of the Arracan fleet, the king of Arracan did not send his ships to practise piracy in Mughal territory (Bengal). He considered the Feringi pirates in the light of his servants, and took the booty they brought [as his share].

[In December, 1665, the Feringis of Chatgaon, partly in fear of Arracanese treachery and partly won over by Shaista Khan's tempting overtures] came with all their families in 42 *jalbas* and took refuge with Farhad Khan, the Mughal *thanahdar* of Noakhali. The Khan sent their chief, Captain Moor, with a few of their great men to Shaista Khan at Dacca, while he kept all the others with their ships at Noakhali, showing them great attention and kindness. The Captain and other leaders of the Feringis had audience of the Nawwab at night, and received splendid robes of honour and other unexpected favours. The Nawwab asked them, "What did the zamindar of the Maghs fix as your salary?" The Feringis replied, "Our salary was the imperial dominion! We considered the whole of Bengal as our *jagir*. All the twelve months of the year we made our collection [*i.e.*, booty] without trouble. We had not to bother ourselves about *amlas* and *amins;* nor had we to render accounts and balances to anybody. Passage over water was our [land-] survey. We never slackened the enhancement of *our* rent, *viz.*, booty. For years we have left no arrears of [this] revenue. We have with us papers of the division of the booty village by village for the last 40 years." One can infer from this answer the condition of things and the weakness of the Governors of Bengal. The coming over of the Feringis gave composure to the hearts of the people of Bengal. Two thousand rupees were presented from the Nawwab's own purse as reward to Captain Moor and the other Feringis who had come from Chatgaon, and from the Imperial Treasury a monthly stipend of Rs. 500 was settled on the Captain, and other comfortable salaries on others of the tribe.

THE CONQUEST OF CHATGAON, 1666 A.D.

(From Shihabuddin Talish's account as preserved in the Bodleian Ms. 589, supplemented by the Alamgirnamah.)

DECAY OF THE BENGAL FLOTILLA.

During the viceroyalty of Prince Shuja, when great confusion was caused by his negligence, the extortion and violence of the clerks (*mutasaddis*) ruined the *parganahs* assigned for maintaining the *nawwara* (=flotilla). Many [naval] officers and workmen holding *jagir* or stipend were overpowered by poverty and starvation. Day by day their distress and ruin increased. When Mir Jumla came to Bengal as Viceroy, he wished to make a new arrangement of the expenditure and *tankhah* of the flotilla, which amounted to 14 lakhs of rupees. After abolishing the old system, and just before beginning the re-organisation, he was overcome by the spells of Assam [*i.e.*, died of the Assam queen's witchcraft]. Many naval officers and men too perished in the expedition; so that at Mir Jumla's death the flotilla was utterly ruined.

[Early in 1664] the pirates came to Bagadia, a dependency of Dacca, and defeated Munawwar Khan, zamindar, who was stationed there with the relics of the *nawwara*—a few broken and rotten boats—and who bore the high title of cruising admiral (*sardar-i-sairab*). Munawwar fled in confusion. Ismail Khan Tarin and other Nawwabi officers, whom [Shaista Khan's son and

Deputy Governor at Dacca] Aqidat Khan had sent with a small force to Munawwar, prevented the crew of their own boats from retreating by turning them round. The crew, on seeing their passengers averse to flight, jumped into the sea and swam ashore to safety. Ismail Khan and his comrades boldly made a firm stand and repelled with their bows and guns the enemy who had advanced to seize them. A musket-shot grazed the leg of Ismail Khan. The current drove their sailorless boats lo the bank, and they escaped destruction. The few boats that still belonged to the *nawwara* were thus lost, and its name alone remained in Bengal.

SHAISTA KHAN'S RESOLVE TO SUPPRESS PIRACY.

On 8th March, 1664, the new Viceroy, Shaista Khan, entered Rajmahal [the western capital of Bengal]. When he learnt that the cause of the ravages of the pirates was the power and equipment of their fleet and the dilapidation of the Bengal fleet, he gave urgent orders to Muhammad Beg [Abakash, the *darogha* of the *nawwara*] to restore the flotilla, wrote to Aqidat Khan also [on the subject], accepted the suggestions of Muhammad Beg, appointed at his request Qazi Samu as *musharraf* of the *nawwara*, and sent them back to Dacca with robes of honour and presents. As timber and ship-wrights were required for repairing and fitting out the ships, to every *mauza* of the province that had timber and carpenters, bailiffs (*muhasal*) were sent with warrants (*parwanah*) to take them to Dacca. It was ordered that at the ports of Hughli, Baleshwar, Murang, Chilmari, Jessore, and Karibari, as many boats should be built as possible and sent [to Dacca]. The Nawwab spoke to the Captain of the Dutch, who was present at the audience, "You make vast amounts every year by your trade in the imperial dominions, for which you have to pay no duty or tithe. For this reason, the path of the profit of Muslim and Hindu *beparis* and merchants in the imperial dominions, especially in Bengal, has been closed. In gratitude for such favour and bounty you should call for ships from your country, and co-operate with the imperial forces in the expedition against Arracan for extirpating the Maghs, which I have in view. Abolish the factories (*kothi*) that you have in Arracan. Otherwise, know for certain that trade and traffic with you will be forbidden all over the empire, and your gains stopped." The Captain replied, "I cannot agree to this great and serious proposal without first writing to our head, the General [Governor-General of the Dutch Indies], and getting his consent." The Nawwab, accepting the Captain's entreaty, said, "Write and call for a reply," and entrusted to the Captain a *parwanah* on the above subject, one suit of *khilat* and one jewelled saddle-cover, for the General. Through God's grace, their help was at last found unnecessary.

As the Feringis engaged in piracy, kidnapping and plundering the inhabitants of Bengal, and lived at Chatgaon under the protection of the zamindar of Arracan, giving half their booty from Bengal to him, the

Nawwab sent Shaikh Ziauddin Yusuf, one of his own officers, as *darogha* of the port of Ladhikol,* which is near Dacca and where Feringi merchants, engaged in the salt trade, live; he ordered the Shaikh to manage that these Feringis should write to their brethren, the pirates of Chatgaon, offering assurances and hopes of imperial favours and rewards, and thus make them come and enter the Mughal service. Ziauddin, too, was to send conciliatory letters [of his own] to them.

SHAISTA KHAN CREATES A NEW FLOTILLA.

On 13th December, 1664, Shaista Khan first entered Dacca. He devoted all his energy to the rebuilding of the flotilla: not for a moment did he forget to mature plans for assembling the crew, providing their rations and needments, and collecting the materials for ship-building and shipwrights. Hakim Muhammad Husain, mansabdar, an old, able, learned, trustworthy and virtuous servant of the Nawwab, was appointed head of the ship-building department. The *musharrafi* of the flotilla was given, *vice* Qazi Samu, to Muhammad Muqim, an expert, clever, and hardworking officer serving in Bengal, whom Mir Jumla had left at Dacca in supervision of the *nawwara* at the time of the Assam expedition. Kishor Das, an imperial officer, a well-informed and experienced clerk, was appointed to have charge of the *parganahs* of the *nawwara*, and the stipend of the jagirs assigned to the [naval] officers and

* In Rennell, Sheet 1, *Luricool*, 13 miles west of Chandpour.

men. To all posts of this department expert officers were appointed. Through the ceaseless exertions of the Nawwab, in a short time nearly 300 ships were built and equipped with [the necessary] materials. Those who had seen the [sorry] plight of the *nawwara* after the death of Mir Jumla, can understand the great change effected by Shaista Khan in a short time.

SECURING BASES FOR THE WAR.

Sangramgarh is situated at the point of land where the Ganges and the Brahmaputra unite. The Nawwab ordered Muhammad Sharif, the late *faujdar* of Hughli, to go to Sangramgarh as *thanahdar*, with many men, officers, and guns, and build a fort there. Abul Hassan was posted there with 200 ships to patrol and check the pirates. Muhammad Beg Abakash, with a hundred ships, was stationed at Dhapa, with orders to go and reinforce Abul Hassan whenever he heard of the coming of the pirates.

A wide high road (*al*) was built from Dhapa* to Sangramgarh, so that even in the monsoons horse and foot could proceed on land from Sangramgarh to Dacca, a distance of 18 *kos*.

[Sondip was a halfway house between Sangramgarh and Chatgaon, and formed an excellent base. Hence the Nawwab decided to wrest it from its zamindar Dilawwar before sending the expedition to Chatgaon. On 12th November, 1665, Sondip was conquered and a Mughal *thanah* established there.]

* The site of Dhapa is given in Rennell (sheet 12) as *Dhape ki Kila*, 6 m. s. e. of Dacca.

THE FERINGIS DESERT TO THE MUGHAL SIDE.

Ever since his coming to Bengal the Nawwab had been planning how to put down the root of disturbance, the Feringi pirates, either by winning them over or by slaying them. As already narrated, Shaikh Ziauddin Yusuf told the Feringis of Ladhikol what the Nawwab had said, and they wrote to their piratical brethren of Chatgaon reassuring them and asking them to visit the Nawwab. When the Nawwab was making his progress [from Rajmahal] to Dacca, the [Portuguese?] Captain of the port of Hughli interviewed him on the way. The Nawwab, after gracing him with favours, asked him to write to the Feringi pirates of Chatgaon tempting them to come over to the Nawwab's service. When he reached Dacca, the Captain of Tamluk also was ordered to write letters of invitation to them. When these successive letters arrived at Chatgaon, and the news of the conquest of Sondip and the establishment of a Mughal *thanah* there spread abroad, spies reported these matters to the king of Arracan. The news threw him into terror, and he wrote to his uncle's son, the Governor of Chatgaon, to look carefully to the defence of the country and fort, conciliate the Feringi pirates, and send to Arracan their families and children, and informed him that a large fleet equipped for battle was being shortly sent to Chatgaon for reinforcement. As he had from the above causes come to entertain suspicion [of the fidelity] of the Feringis, he really wished to lure their families to Arracan and massacre the Feringis themselves at Chatgaon at an opportune time. The hearts of the Feringis were distracted and shaken by the arrival of the tempting letters and the news of the Mughal establishment at Sondip. On learning of the wishes of the Magh chief, they fled with their families in 42 *jalbas* to Farhad Khan at Noakhali for protection.* [They were taken into imperial service and liberally rewarded by the Nawwab.]

INVASION IMMEDIATELY DECIDED ON.

Captain Moor, the Feringi leader, reported to the Nawwab "Owing to their pride and folly, the king and counsellors of Arracan have neglected the defence and munitions of the fort, and mostly depended on us [for this purpose]. But now that they have heard of the conquest of Sondip, they have ordered a large army and fleet to reinforce [the defence of Chatgaon]. If the Mughal force attacks the fort before the arrival of this reinforcement, its capture will probably be very easy." The Nawwab, who had been day and night thinking how to realise this object, regarded the coming over of the Feringis as the commencement of the victory, and decided not to let this opportunity slip away.

From Jagdia, the frontier of Mughal Bengal, to Chatgaon, a distance of 30 *kos*, is an utterly desolate

* The *Alamgirnamah*, p. 947, says: "The Feringis, learning [of the intended Arracanese treachery,] resisted and fought the Arracanese, burnt some of the ships of the latter, and started for service in Bengal with all their goods and ships. On 19th December, 1665, fifty *jalbas* of the Feringis, full of guns, muskets, and munitions, and all the Feringi families, reached Noakhali."

wilderness. The expeditionary force would have to be supplied with provisions [from Bengal] till after Chatgaon was reached, besieged, and captured. As the Bengal crew were mortally afraid of the Magh flotilla, provisions could not be sent by water, though the means of transport in this province are confined to boats. Hence, when in Jahangir's reign, Ibrahim Khan Fatih Jang decided to attack Chatgaon, for two years before setting out he collected provisions at Bhalua and Jagdia.

COMPOSITION OF THE EXPEDITION.

It was decided that the Nawwab's son, Buzurg Ummed Khan, with 4,000 troopers should conduct the campaign, while the Nawwab would look after the work of keeping the army supplied with provisions. If the siege were protracted he would quickly go and join his son. On 24th December,* 1665, at a moment auspicious for making a beginning, Buzurg Ummed Khan started from Dacca. Under him were appointed Ikhtisas Khan, a commander of 2,500 (1,000 extra troopers), Sarandaz Khan, a commander of 1,500 (800 troopers), Farhad Khan, a commander of 1,000 (150 troopers), Qarawwal Khan, a commander of 1,000 (800 troopers), Rajah Subal Singh Sisodia, a commander of 1,500 (700 troopers), Ibn Husain, *darogha* of the *nawwara*, a commander of 800 (200 troopers), Mir Murtaza, *darogha* of the artillery, a commander of 800 (150 troopers), other imperial officers with their

* The *Alamgirnamah*, p. 948, gives 25th December as the date, and says that the expeditionary force was composed of "Buzurg Ummed Khan with *two* thousand troopers of the Nawwab's own *tabinan* (followers), Syed Ikhtisas Khan Barha, Subal Singh Sisodia, Miana Khan, Karn Khaji and some others."

followings, all the *naqdis* and *ahadis* except a few who were engaged in special works, and 2,500 troopers in the Nawwab's pay. All the *amirs*, *mansabdars*, *sardars*, and *jamadars* were presented with robes of honour, horses, swords, and shields, according to their ranks. Mir Abul Fath was appointed *diwan* and Muhammad Khalil paymaster and newswriter of the force. From Dacca Mir Murtaza, and from Sondip Ibn Husain, Muhammad Beg Abakash, Munawwar Khan zamindar and other zamindars of the *nawwara*, and Haiat Khan *jamadar* with the Nawwab's soldiers, who had accompanied him to the conquest of Sondip, were ordered to go to Noakhali, join Farhad Khan and Captain Moor and other Feringi pirates who had come from Chatgaon and entered the imperial service, and then proceed on land and sea as van of Buzurg Ummed Khan's army.

Askar Khan, who had been posted to Ghoraghat, returned opportunely and was stationed at Dacca.*

The imperial fleet under Ibn Husain consisted of 288 ships, as described below:—

Ghurab	... 21	*Jalba*	...	96
Salb	... 3	*Bachari*	...	2
Kusa	... 157	*Parenda*	...	6
		[Not specified]		3
				288

* The *Alamgirnamah*, p. 948, adds: "Kamal, a former Arracanese king's son, who in Shah Jahan's reign had fled to Dacca from the oppression of the present king, was ordered to accompany Mir Murtaza with a band of the Maghs who lived at Dacca, on the assurance that he would be made chief of his tribe. A letter (*parwanah*), inviting submission to the Mughals and offering conciliatory favours from the Imperial Government, was written to the Governor of Chatgaon and sent to him with one of the Maghs."

NAWWAB'S VIGOROUS EXERTIONS.

Before this Mir Murtaza had collected many axes at Dacca. From the *parganahs*, too, axes had been brought by issuing *parwanahs*, so that several thousands of them had been collected. These were sent with the expedition for clearing the jungle. Every day the Nawwab wrote to the officers of the expedition letters full of plans and advice, and inquiries addressed to the Khan about the condition of the enemy and the state of the road. On the first day [when the expedition left Dacca] the Nawwab stayed outside [the harem] till noon, and again from the time of the *asar* prayer to one *prahar* of the night, and supervised this business. Even when he was in the harem, if any good plan struck him, he at once sent word to the officers to carry it out. Muhammad Khalil was ordered to keep him daily informed of the occurrences. Shaikh Mubarak, an experienced and trusted servant, appointed to command the Nawwab's retainers accompanying Buzurg Ummed Khan, was ordered to report all the daily events, great and small, to the Nawwab, and give the Khan every advice that he considered fit.

FEEDING THE ARMY.

The officers of the *golahs* (granaries) were ordered that one-half of all the grain that *beparis* brought into Dacca should be sent to the army. To the *faujdars* of all parts of Bengal urgent *parwanahs* were issued directing that every kind of provision that they could secure should be despatched to the expeditionary force. *Yasawwals* were appointed by the Nawwab to see to it. So excellent were the Nawwab's arrangements that from the beginning till now the price of grain in the army has been to the price in Dacca as ten to nine.

MUGHAL ADVANCE BY LAND AND SEA.

Buzurg Ummed Khan moved quickly on, carried his entire army over the deep river in a few days, crossed the river of Feni,* entered the Magh territory, and advanced cutting the jungle and making a road. According to the Nawwab's command a *thanah* was established on the river of Feni, under Sultan Beg, *mansabdar*, with a contingent of horse and foot. As the river of Feni joins the sea, it was feared that the enemy's ships would pass up the river and harass the imperial army's passage. It was, therefore, decided that out of the commanders at Noakhali, Ibn Husain should advance with the *nawwara* by the sea and Farhad Khan, Mir Murtaza, and Haiat Khan by land, in aid of the *nawwara*.

* The *Alamgirnamah*, p. 949, describes the movements of the expedition thus: Farhad Khan, appointed a force of pioneers, wood-cutters, and some infantry armed with bows and muskets for making a road and clearing the jungle. On 12th January, 1666, marching from Noakhali with Mir Murtaza and other comrades, he reached the outpost of Jagdia. Ibn Husain and his comrades on board weighed anchor. On the 14th, Farhad Khan and his party crossed the Feni river and advanced cautiously. On the 20th, he reached a tank, from which Chatgaon was one day's journey, and waited for Buzurg Ummed Khan's arrival. That general, after crossing the Feni on the 17th......... arrived on the 21st at a place 8 *kos* behind the position of Farhad Khan and Mir Murtaza, which [latter] was ten *kos* from Chatgaon fort, and where the jungle was very thick and the road very bad,—and halted there. Farhad Khan daily advanced a little, cutting the jungle and levelling the road. The flotilla waited for the army at Dumria, a dependency of Chatgaon, which was about 20 *kos* from the halting-place of Buzurg Ummed Khan.

If they could, they should enter the Karnafuli river and occupy its mouth, and also attack Chatgaon. Otherwise they should stay in the neighbourhood and wait for Buzurg Ummed Khan's arrival. The jungle was thereafter to be cut along the sea stage by stage, the flotilla to advance by sea and the Khan by its coast; in march and halt the land and sea forces were never to be separated.

These officers started from Noakhali. Ibn Husain with the flotilla soon arrived at the creek of Khamaria, two stages from Chatgaon, and began to cut the jungle *before* towards Chatgaon and *behind* towards the advancing army. Farhad Khan, Mir Murtaza and other commanders of the land force too advanced cutting the jungle, and joined hands with Ibn Husain on 21st January, 1666. Buzurg Ummed Khan who was hastening clearing the jungle, arrived with the [main] army within three *kos* of Khamaria.

FIRST NAVAL BATTLE, *23rd January.*

On the evening of 22nd January,* the scouts (*qarawwals*) of Ibn Husain brought news that the enemy's flotilla having come from Chatgaon was staying in the creek of Kathalia, six hours' journey from their place. Ibn Husain, after informing the imperial and Nawwabi servants who were on board most of the ships, got ready for action. At night he sent a few ships to

* Text gives the 24th, which is wrong. *Alamgirnamah*, p. 950, mentions the 23rd as the day of the *battle*.

the mouth of the creek, telling the passengers to keep a good look out. Next morn, the scouts reported that the enemy's flotilla had started from Kathalia to fight the imperial *nawwara* and might come immediately. Ibn Husain, after sending a man to inform Buzurg Ummed Khan of the matter, set out to meet the enemy, though the wind had freshened, and the sea was raging in billows threatening to sink the imperial ships. Abul Qasim, who was in the ship of Muhammad Beg Abakash, narrates that when in this tempest he unmoored his ship to join Ibn Husain, one of the Türkish soldiers standing on the bank cried to M. Beg Abakash in Turki, "Are you mad, that you put your boat out during tempest in such a deep and terrible sea?" He replied, "Brother, if I were not mad, I should not have become a soldier!" Farhad Khan, Mir Murtaza, and Haiat Khan advanced by land to co-operate with the navy, following the road cleared by the men of the ships. Beyond the clearing they could not go on account of the density of the jungle.

Ten *ghurabs* and 45 *jalbas* of the enemy hove in sight and began to discharge their guns. Captain Moor and the other Feringis, who led the van, boldly steered their ships up to the enemy, Ibn Husain coming behind them. The enemy could not resist the onset; the men of their *ghurabs* jumped overboard, and the *jalbas* took to flight. Ibn Husain, seizing the *ghurabs*, wanted to pursue. But the Bengal sailors, who had never even seen in their minds the vision of a victory over the Magh fleet, objected, saying that that day's victory—the like of which even centenarians had not seen—ought to content them. Ibn Husain had to yield; but advancing a little from the spot where the *ghurabs* had been captured, he decided to stay there till evening and to return to the creek of Khamaria at night.

Suddenly two or three ships with flags (*bairaq*) were seen afar off. The Maghs, when they left the Kathalia creek that morning for fight and reached the creek of Hurla close to Khamaria, in their pride left their large ships—called *khalu* and *dhum*,—and [some] other ships here, and sent on only ten *ghurabs* and 45 *jalbas* as sufficient for [defeating and] capturing the imperial flotilla. The two or three ships with flags now seen were among those *khalus* left in the creek.

Ibn Husain encouraged his crew, saying, "Now that the fugitive *jalbas* have joined their larger fleet, the enemy have surely been seized with terror. It behoves [us] as brave men not to give the enemy time, nor let the opportunity slip out of our grasp, but attack them in full reliance on God." These words had effect on the Bengal crew; they agreed and started for Hurla. The enemy learning of it issued from the creek and stood at sea in line of battle. Ibn Husain arriving there found their line stronger than Alexander's rampart. He felt that to run his smaller ships against the [enemy's] larger ones,—whose many guns would, at every discharge, command [his ships],—was to court needless ruin, but that he ought to stop in front of the enemy, engage in firing, and wait for the arrival of his larger ships (*salbs*,) when he would put the latter in front and attack the enemy. He therefore began firing his guns and sent a man to hurry up the *salbs*. These arrived at the time of the evening prayer. From that time to dawn, there was cannonade between the two sides.*

SECOND NAVAL ENCOUNTER, *24th January*.

Next morning, the Muslims flying their victorious banners, beating their drums, and sounding their bugles and trumpets, advanced towards the enemy firing guns and in this order: First the *salbs*, then the *ghurabs*, and last the *jalbas* and *kosas* side by side. . The enemy lost all courage and firmness, and thought only of flying. They turned the heads of their larger ships away from the Imperialists, attached their *jalbas* to them, and began to tow back these big ships, fighting during their flight.

Ibn Husain without throwing away caution or making rash haste advanced in his previous formation. At

* The *Alamgirnamah*, p. 950, says :—"[After the first naval battle] the enemy fled; Ibn Husain with his light and swift ships gave chase and captured 10 *ghurabs* and three *halias* [=*jalbas*] from them. Soon afterwards, the larger ships (*nawwara-e-buzurg*) of the enemy came in sight, for a second time fought a long and severe fight, and at sunset fled from the scene of action. Ibn Husain pursued them, [p. 951] but as the enemy's ships entered the Karnafuli, and his own larger ships had not come up with him, he thought it inadvisable to advance, but withdrew his fleet to a suitable place, and passed the night in keeping watch.

When Buzurg Ummed Khan heard of it, he wrote strongly urging Farhad Khan and Mir Murtaza not to wait for clearing the jungle and making a road, but to hurry up and join hands with the *nawwara*. He himself gave up road-making and advanced quickly. Next day [24th January,] Farhad Khan arrived at the bank of the river [Karnafuli]. The enemy lost heart at the sight of the Islamic army."

last at about 3 P.M., the enemy entered the mouth of the Karnafuli, reached the island in mid stream in front of Chatgaon fort, and drew up their ships off the bank on which Chatgaon stood. The imperial fleet too came to the Karnafuli and seized its mouth. On the [further] side of the Karnafuli, near the mouth and close to the village called Feringi-bandar, where the Feringi pirates had their houses, the enemy had built three bamboo stockades on the brink of the water, and filled them with artillery, many Telingas (as the fighting men of Arracan are called) and two elephants, in preparation for fight. When the imperial flotilla entered the mouth of the Karnafuli, these forts opened fire on them with muskets and guns. Ibn Husain sent most of his ships up the river and many of the soldiers by the bank, and attacked them. After making some vain efforts the garrison of the stockades took to flight. The Mughals burned the forts and returned.

ARRACAN NAVY ANNIHILATED.

Now with a strong heart and good hope, Ibn Husain dashed upon the enemy's ships. Captain Moor and other Feringi pirates, the Nawwab's officers [such as] Muhammad Beg Abakash and Munawwar Khan zamindar, came swiftly from different sides. A great fight was fought. Fire was opened [on the Mughals] from the fort of Chatgaon also. At last the breeze of victory blew on the banners of the Muslims. The enemy were vanquished; some of their sailors and soldiers jumped overboard;

some remaining in their ships surrendered as prisoners. Most of the former carried off their lives, only some being drowned. Many were slain by the swords, arrows, and spears of the victors. A few, reaching the bank, carried the news to the fort. Many of the enemy's ships were sunk by the fire or ramming of the Mughal fleet; the rest, 135 ships, were captured by the Imperialists* and consisted of :—

Khalu	... 2	*Kosa*	... 12		
Ghurab	... 9	*Jalba*	... 67	[Should be 68]	
Jangi	... 22	*Balam*	... 22		

Meantime, Buzurg Ummed Khan, hearing of the naval battle, hastened to the neighbourhood of Chatgaon. The *chawkidars* of the fort informed the garrison of the near approach of the Mughal army. This news and the spectacle of the victory of the imperial fleet struck such terror into the hearts of the garrison and soldiers of the country, that in spite of their large number they fled.

NIGHT AFTER BATTLE.

That night† Ibn Husain, sending to the fort two

* The operations in the Karnafuli are thus described in the *Alamgirnamah*, p. 952 :—"[On 24th January,] Ibn Husain with the Imperial fleet entered the Karnafuli river and attacked the enemy's fleet that had fled there. A second terrible battle was fought for two *prahars* of the day. At last the Imperialists gained the victory, and the enemy fled, many of them being killed, many others taken prisoner, many drowned after jumping overboard."

† The *Alamgirnamah*, p. 951, says :—"After the victory the Imperial fleet halted in the Karnafuli below the fort of Chatgaon. Some of the Feringis of Chatgaon who had remained there, and many [p. 952] other Feringis who at this time had come from Arracan to aid them, interviewed Ibn Husain. Captain Moor, who accompanied the Imperial forces in this expedition, did excellent service. Next day [25th January,] Buzurg Ummed Khan arrived at the foot of the fort of Chatgaon with the rest of the

trustworthy men out of those taken prisoner in the ships, wrote to the *qiladar* who represented the Rajah of Arracan, "Why should you needlessly destroy yourself and your family? Before you are forcibly seized and sacrificed to our swords, give up your fort, and save your life and property." The *qiladar*, feeling himself helpless and in need of protection, sent back the reply that he should be granted respite for the night and that next morning he would admit them.

CHATGAON FORT SURRENDERS.

In the morning of 26th January, 1666, which was the sunset of [the glory of] the Maghs, the commandant opened the fort gate and informed Ibn Husain, who started for the fort. But Munawwar Khan zamindar had entered it before him, and his companions had set fire to it. Ibn Husain entered soon afterwards, and tried his best to put out the fire, but in vain. The fire was so violent that he could not stay there, but came out bringing the *qiladar* away with himself.

When the fire went out, he again proceeded to the

army. The Imperial forces by land and sea encircled the fort. The garrison, after making great exertions, found that they could not resist the Mughal army, and at last sought safety. The second day of the siege, 26th January, 1666, the Imperial army gained possession of the fort, the whole province of Chatgaon, and the entire artillery and navy of the place......[p. 953]. The Governor of Chatgaon, who was the son of the Arracan king's uncle, was taken prisoner with one son and some other relatives, and nearly 350 men of the tribe, 132 ships of war, 1,026 guns made of bronze and iron, many matchlocks and *zamburaks* (camel pieces), much shot and powder, other artillery materials, and three elephants, were captured. Large numbers of the peasants of Bengal who had been carried off and kept prisoner here, were now released from the Magh oppression and returned to their homes."

fort and attached the property. He sent the *qiladar* with the news of victory to the Nawwab at Dacca, and also informed Buzurg Ummed Khan of the happy event.

The Maghs who were in the fort on the other side of the river, fled, and that fort, too, fell into Mughal hands. The peasantry on the further side of the river, who were mostly Muslims kidnapped from Bengal, attacked the Maghs that fled yesterday and to-day, slew one of their leaders, captured two of their elephants, and brought them to Ibn Husain. Of the four elephants in the fort of Chatgaon, two were burned in the fire and two were secured by the Mughals.

REWARDS TO THE VICTORS.

On 29th January the news of the conquest reached Dacca. The Nawwab after thanking God, began to give to all the army liberal rewards consisting of robes, horses, and elephants, distributed alms to the poor, and ordered the music of joy to play. Wealth beyond measure was given to the Feringi pirates and one month's pay as bounty to his own officers and the crew of the *nawwara*.

That very day the Nawwab sent a despatch on the victory to the Emperor. When it arrived at Court,* the Emperor ordered joyous music to be played. Rewards were given to all concerned in the conquest: the Nawwab was presented with a costly jewelled sword of the Emperor, two elephants, two horses with gold trappings,

* "At the end of Sh'aban [February 1666]" according to the *Alamgirnamah*, p. 956. "The Emperor ordered Chatgaon to be renamed Islamabad."

a special *khilat*, and an imperial *farman* of praise. Buzurg Ummed Khan, Farhad Khan, Mir Murtaza, Ibn Husain, and Muhammad Beg Abakash were promoted. Ibn Husain got the title of Mansur† Khan, and Mir Murtaza that of Mujahid Khan.

NEW GOVERNMENT OF CHATGAON.

On 27th January,‡ 1666, Buzurg Ummed Khan entered the fort of Chatgaon, reassured the people that their lives were safe, and firmly forbade his soldiers to oppress the people, in order to cause the place to be well-populated and prosperous.

[Here the Bodleian Ms. ends abruptly. I give the concluding portion of the campaign from the *Alamgir-namah*, pp. 953-956.]

Buzurg Ummed Khan stayed at Chatgaon for some time to settle its affairs. Miana Khan was sent to the north of Chatgaon to reassure the peasantry and to establish a *thanah*. Taj Miana, with his followers and 100 musketeers, was appointed as *thanahdar* and guard of the roads from Chatgaon to the bank of the Feni river.

RAMBU TAKEN AND ABANDONED.

The port of Rambu* is four days' journey from Chatgaon, and midway between Chatgaon and Arracan. A large body of the enemy defended its fort. Mir Murtaza was ordered to that direction, to win over the

† *Muzaffar* according to the *Alamgirnamah*.

‡ The date is left blank in the Bodleian Ms. I have supplied it from the *Alamgirnamah*.

* *Ramoo* in Rennell, Sheet I.

peasantry, learn all about the paths and ferries of that region, and, if he found it possible, to go to the place and besiege it. The Mir, after traversing difficult roads, dense jungles, and terrible rivers, at the end of 12 days arrived within one *kos* of Rambu. Next day, at morn he stormed the fort. The Arracan king's brother named Rawli, who held the government of the place, tried his best to oppose, but being worsted, he fled with the garrison to a jungle close to a hill near the fort. Mir Murtaza giving chase slew many of them and captured many others. Some of the enemy, who had taken refuge in the hill, came out to surrender, and were made prisoner. Many Muslim ryots of Bengal, who had been kept as captives here, were liberated and returned home.

Buzurg Ummed Khan hearing of the victory and learning that the king of Arracan was sending a force by land against Rambu, despatched Miana Khan, Jamal Khan Dilzaq, and many others to reinforce Mir Murtaza. The Mir, after his victory, had posted a company of musketeers on the bank of the river one and a half *kos* from Rambu, to keep watch for the enemy's arrival. One day a large force of the enemy with seven elephants suddenly issued from the jungle, fell upon the musketeers, and dispersed some of them. Mir Murtaza hearing of it, rode with a force to the bank of the river, and in spite of its water being deep and the enemy having begun to make entrenchments on the [other] bank, boldly plunged in with his comrades and crossed over in safety. The enemy, after a hard fight, fled. The victors pursued, slew and captured many of them, and seized 80 guns, many muskets, and other war material.

As the space between Chatgaon and Rambu is very hard to cross, full of hills and jungles, and intersected by one or two streams which cannot be crossed without boats, and as in the rainy season the whole path is flooded, and this year there was only a small store of provisions and the rainy season was near,—therefore the sending of the Mughal army into Arracan was put off. Buzurg Ummed Khan, in view of the roads being closed and reinforcements and provisions being cut off by the rains, very wisely ordered Mir Murtaza to evacuate Rambu and fall back with the chiefs, zamindars, prisoners, and peasants of Rambu, on Dakhin-kol,* which is close to Chatgaon. He did so.

---

* *i. e.*, 'The southern bank of the river.'

SHAISTA KHAN IN BENGAL (1664-'66).

THE MANUSCRIPT.

When Mir Jumla invaded Kuch Bihar and Assam, he had in his train an officer named Shihabuddin Talish, who has left a detailed history of the expedition, named by the author the *Fathiyyah-i-ibriyyah*. A long abstract of it was given by Mr. Blochmann in the Bengal Asiatic Society's Journal for 1872, Part I, No. 1 pp. 64-96. This Society has a fine old Ms. of this work (D. 72), and the Khuda Bakhsh Library three others. All these end with the death of Mir Jumla, 31st March, 1663.

But the Bodleian Library possesses a Ms. of the work (No. Bod. 589, Sachau and Ethe's *Catalogue*, Part I, No. 240), supposed to be the author's autograph, which contains a continuation (folios 106*a*-176*b*), relating the events immediately following and bringing the history down to Buzurg Ummed Khan's victorious entry into Chatgaon (Chittagong), 27th January, 1666. This portion is absolutely unique and of the greatest importance for the history of Bengal.

The internal evidence is overwhelming in favour of the *Continuation* being regarded as Shihabuddin Talish's work. The style is marked by the same brilliancy of rhetoric; many favourite phrases and turns of expression are common to both; and one peculiar sentence, which I have found in no other Persian history, occurs in both (*Conquest of Assam*, p. 58 of Ms. D. 72, and *Continuation*, folio 124*a*). We have here (*f.* 156*b*) one instance of the author's imitation of Amir Khusrau's vicious rhetorical trick of running the variations of a single simile through a whole page of which there are three examples in the *Conquest*. The writer is the same hero-worshipper, only Shaista Khan here takes the place of Mir Jumla.

The author evidently died shortly after writing the *Continuation*, for it ends abruptly, without carrying on the campaign in the Chatgaon District to its conclusion. He had no time to give it the finishing touches: the material is loosely arranged; there is no regular division into chapters as in the *Conquest*, only three headings (*surkhi*) being (*ff.* 150*b*, 153*a*, and 161*b*). Moreover, the author has left blanks for dates in two places (*ff.* 149*b* and 175*b*), which he evidently meant to fill up after consulting other sources. Wrong dates are given in 106*a* and 167*a* and some obscurity has been introduced into the narrative by his passing over the first day of the siege of Chatgaon (25th January, 1666) in absolute silence.

The *Continuation* supplies us with useful and original information on the following four subjects:—

(1) Shaista Khan's administration of Bengal up to January, 1666. (2) The system of piracy followed by the Feringis of Chatgaon, and a record of the various Magh incursions into Bengal and Bengal attacks on the Maghs. (3) A description of Sondip and the history of its conquest. (4) A description of Chatgaon and the history of its conquest.

I shall here deal with the first.

Shaista Khan's Civil Administration.

(*Translation*)

[117*a*] The mansabdars had their jagirs situated in different parganahs, and the multiplicity of co-partners led to the ryots being oppressed and the parganahs desolated. Large sums were wasted [in the cost of collection] as many *shiqdars* and *'amlas* had to be sent out by [every] jagirdar. Therefore, the Nawwab ordered the *diwan-i-tan* to give every jagirdar *tankha* in one place only; and, if in any parganah any revenue remained over and above the tankha of a jagirdar [117*b*], it was to be made over to the jagirdar for collection and payment into the public treasury. Thus the department of Crown-lands would make a saving by not having to appoint collectors [of its own in the parganahs of jagirdars]; and, secondly, it was not good for one place to have two rulers [*viz.*, the jagirdars and Government collectors]. The *diwan-i-tan* set himself to carry out this work.

Next, Shaista Khan learnt the truth about the appointments and promotions made after Mir Jumla's death by the acting Subahdars. Most of these men were now dismissed; a few, who were really necessary for the administration, were retained in service. I have noted this difference between Shaista Khan and other servants of the Crown, in the matter of saving Government money, that they desired solely to gain credit with the Emperor, while his aim is pure devotion and loyal service. He considers the parading of this fact as akin to hypocrisy and remote from true devotion and fidelity.

At this time the *aimadars* and stipend-holders of the province of Bengal began to flock to the Nawwab to make complaints [118*a*]. The facts of their case were:—After the reign of Shah Jahan, the late Khan-i-khanan [Mir Jumla] confirmed in his own jagirs many of these men who were celebrated for devotion to virtue and love of the Prophet's followers, and some who had got *farmans* of the Emperor. All other men who had been enjoying *madad-i-m'aâsh* and pensions in the Crown-lands and fiefs of jagirdars, were violently attacked by Qazi Rizwi, the Sadr; their *sanads* were rejected and their stipends and subsistence cancelled. It was ordered that the *aimadars* should take to the business of cultivators, till all the lands they held in *madad-i-m'aash*, and pay revenue for them to the department of Crown-lands or to the jagirdars. And, as in carrying out this hard order these poor creatures could not get any respite, many who had the capability sold their property, pledged their children [as serfs], and thus paid the revenue for the current year [118*b*], preserving their lives as their only stock for the next year. Some, who had no property, brought on themselves torture and punishment, gave up their lives, and thus escaped from all anxiety about the next year.

(*Verse*)

Like fire they ate sticks [*i.e.*, received beating] and
gave up gold [or sparks],
And then, through loss of strength, they fell down
dead in misery.

And now even by the resumption of the cultivated lands sufficient gain in the form of produce cannot be collected, because the *aimadars* abstain from tilling the lands that have been escheated to the State; and even the chastisement and pressure of the *'amlas* cannot make them engage in cultivation. And so the land remains waste and the *aimadars* poor and aggrieved. Owing to the great distance and the fear of calamities, these poor perplexed sufferers could not go to Delhi to report their condition fully to the Emperor and get the wicked and oppressive officials punished [119*a*]. Hence their sighs and lamentations reached the sky.

One Friday, the Nawwab, as was his custom, went [to the mosque] to offer his Friday prayer. After it was over he learnt that an old *aimadar* had suspended his head upside down, one yard above the ground, from a tree near the mosque, and that he was on the brink of death and was saying: (*Verse*)

Shall my life return [to my body] or shall it go out,—
what is thy command?

The Nawwab ordered the author to go and ask the reason. I went to the old man and inquired. He replied, "My son, who held thirty *bighas* of land in *madad-i-m'aash*, has died. The *amlas* now demand from me one year's revenue of the land. As I have no wealth, I shall give up my life and thus free myself [from the oppression]." I reported the matter to the Nawwab, who gave him a large sum, and then confirmed his son's rent-free land on him. (*Verse*)

God favours that man,
Whose life gives repose to the people. [119b.]

The wise know that the resumption of the lands of *aimadars* and the cutting off of the subsistence of stipend-holders bring on great misfortunes and terrible consequences [on the wrong-doer]. I have seen some among the rulers of this country who engaged in this wicked work and could not live through the year. (*Verse*)

The dark sigh of sufferers, in the heart of dark nights,
Snatches away by [God's] command the mole of prosperity
from the cheek of the oppressor.

It is a lasting act of virtue and an undying deed of charity to bestow *imlak* on the needy and *idrar* on the poor. The hindering of such liberality and the stoppage of such charity does not bring any gain in this world and involves one in the Creator's wrath in the next.........

[120*a*] One day there was a talk on this subject in the Nawwab's court. As "the words of kings are kings among words," he remarked, "If a man has not grace enough to increase the gifts made to these [poor] people, he should at least not deprive them of what others gave them [120*b*], because.........these people, too, should be counted among the needy. And one should not through his own meanness of spirit and vileness of heart resume the charitable gifts of others."

In short, the Nawwab's natural kindness having been excited, he ordered that Mir Sayyid Sadiq, the Sadr, should fully recognise the *madad-i-m'aash* and *wazifa* which these men had been enjoying in the Crown-lands according to the reliable *sanads* of former rulers. As for what was held [rent-free] in the fiefs of jagirdars, if it amounted to one-fortieth of the total revenue of the jagirdar, he should consider it as the *zakat* (tithe) on his property and spare it. But if the rent-free land exceeded one-fortieth [of the total jagir], the jagirdar was at liberty to respect or resume [the excess]. Whosoever held whatever rent-free land in the parganahs of the jagir of the Nawwab, on the strength of the *sanad* of whomsoever, was to be confirmed in it without any diminution, and was on no account to be troubled [by demand of revenue]. As for those who had no means of subsistence and now, for the first time, begged daily allowances and lands in the jagir of the Nawwab, the *diwani* officers were ordered to further their desires without any delay.

The Sadr carried out the above order in the case of the Crown-lands and the jagirs of [other] jagirdars [121*a*]. In the jagir of the Nawwab his *diwan-i-bayutat*, Khawajah Murlidhar,—who had been brought up and trained in the Nawwab's household, was marked by honesty and politeness, possessed his master's confidence and trust, and, in spite of his still being in the flower of youth, had the wisdom and patience of old men,—displayed in this work of benevolence such zeal and exertion as, I pray, God may favour all Musalmans with. Every day two to three hundred *aimadars* presented their *sanads* to him and then departed. Next day, in the presence of the Nawwab, he passed them through the Record office and sealed them, and then gave them back to the *aimadars*. In short, he exhibited such great labour and praiseworthy diligence in this business, that every one of this class of men got what he desired. And the aforesaid Khawajah gained good name and respect for himself, temporal and spiritual welfare for his master, and prayers for the perpetuaton of the empire for the Solomon-like Emperor. (*Verse*) [121*b*].

That man's influence with the king is a blessed thing,
Who forwards the suits of the distressed.

SHAISTA KHAN'S GOOD DEEDS.

(*Translation.*)

[127*a*] I. His exertions for conquering the province and fort of Chatgaon; the suppression of the pirates, and the consequent relief of the people of Bengal.

II. Every day he held open *darbar* for administering justice, and quickly redressed wrongs. He regarded this as his most important duty.

III. He ordered that in the parganahs of his own jagir everything collected by the revenue officers above the fixed revenue should be refunded to the ryots. [127*b*].

IV. The former governors of Bengal used to make monopolies (*ijara*) of all articles of food and clothing and [many] other things, and then sell them at fanciful rates which the helpless people had to pay. Shaista Khan restored absolute freedom of buying and selling.

V. Whenever ships brought elephants and other [animals] to the ports of the province, the men of the Subahdar used to attach (*qurq*) them and take whatever they selected at prices of their own liking. Shaista Khan forbade it.

VI. His abolition of the collection of *zakat* (*i.e.*, one-fortieth of the income) from merchants and travellers, and of custom (*hasil*) from artificers, tradesmen and new-comers,* Hindus and Musalmans alike. The history of it is as follows:—

From the first occupation of India and its ports by the Muhammadans to the end [128*a*] of Shah Jahan's reign, it was a rule and practice to exact *hasil* from every trader,—from the rose-vendor down to the clay-vendor, from the weaver of fine linen to that of coarse cloth,—to collect house-tax from new-comers and hucksters, to take *zakat* from travellers, merchants and stable-keepers (*mukari*). As Sadi has said, "At first oppression's basis was small; but every successive generation increased it," [so it happened], till at last in all provinces, especially in Bengal, it reached such a stage that tradesmen and merchants gave up their business, householders took to exile, saying—(*Verse*)

"We shall flee from the oppression of the Age,
To such a place that Time cannot track us there."

The rulers, out of greed for *hasil*, gave them no relief.

* *Khush-nashin*, which may also mean 'well-to-do men.'

On the roads and ferries matters came to such a pass that no rider was allowed to go on unless he paid a *dinar*, and no pedestrian unless he paid a *diram*. On the river-highways if the wind brought it to the ears of the toll-collectors (*rah-dars*) that the stream was carrying away a broken boat without paying *hasil*, they would chain the river [128*b*]. If the toll-officers heard that the wave had taken away a broken plank [without] paying *zakat*, they would beat it on the back of its head in the form of the wind. They considered it an act of unparalleled leniency if no higher *zakat* was taken from rotten clothes actually worn [on the body] than from mended rags, and a deed of extreme graciousness if cooked food was charged with a lower duty than uncooked grains. None of the Delhi sovereigns, in spite of their efforts to strengthen the Faith and follow the rules of the Prophet, put down these wicked and [canonically] illegal practices, but connived at them. Only, we read in histories, Firuz Shah forbade these unjust exactions. But after him they were restored, nay increased. But when, by the grace of God [129*a*] Aurangzib ascended the throne, he sent orders to the governors of the provinces and the clerks of the administration not to do such things in future. He thus gave relief to the inhabitants of villages and travellers by [129*b*] land and sea from these harassments and illegal demands. The learned know that no other king of the past showed such graciousness, made such strong exertions, and remitted to the people such a large sum—which equalled the total revenue of Turan.

(Verse)

O God! Keep long over the heads of the people,
This King, the friend of holy men,
Whose shadow gives repose to the people.
Through the guidance of [Thy] service, keep his heart alive.

I strongly hope that, just as the peasants and merchants have been released from oppression and innovations [in taxation], so someone would fully and freely report to the Emperor the distress among the soldiery and the fact of their being harassed and crushed by the oppression of the thievish clerks, and thereby release the soldiers from the tyranny of these godless men [130*a*]. The army is treated by the Hindu clerks, and drowsy writers as more degraded than a fire-worshipping slave and more unclean than the dog of a Jew. Whenever that forked-tongued cobra, their pen, brings its head out of the hole of the ink-pot, it does not write on the account-book (*tumar*) of their dark hearts any letter except to pounce upon and snatch away the subsistence of the soldiers. Indeed, when their tongue begins to move in the hole of their mouth, it does not spit out anything except curtailing the stipends of the soldiery. At times they would senselessly split a hair, and do not abstain from numerous unjust fines.

Again, if after life-long exertion and the showering of bribes, they are induced to sign the *fard-i-chehra* of any soldier, then, at the time of branding (*dagh*), they designate a charger worthy of Rustam as a mere pack-horse, and on the day of verification (*tashiha*) they describe [in the records] a horse that stands erect as fit for the yoke, a horse that bends its leg as lame, a horse that shies as doubtful, a horse that lacks a particle of hair as Taghlibi. They call a Daudi coat of mail the film of a wasp and a steel helmet itself a small linen cap. They regard a Rustam as a Zal, and a Zal as a mere child. May God the Giver [130*b*] reward with the long life of Noah, the patience of Job, and the treasures of Corah that valiant man, brave like Asfandiar, who after traversing these hill-tops (=hindrances) gets his *tasdiq yad-dasht qabz* and *barat* passed through the Haft-khan of the accounts department, so that his business may be done. In the shambles of the *kachari* of Crown-lands stipend-holders have to flay themselves [before getting their dues], and at the sacrificial altar of the office of the *diwan-i-tan tankha-dars* find it necessary to root out their own lives. O ye faithful! Did man ever hear of such tyranny as that each letter of the identification-marks of the record office should be written by a [different] clerk? O ye Muslims! Did man ever see such oppression as that one word has to be written by ten men? In [making out] the assignment-paper (*barat*) they decrease the *tankha* due and magnify the deduction to be made. If, through a mistake, the balance is entered in the receipts (*qabuz*), they treat it as a true record and appropriate the amount to themselves. And they think that they have conferred a great obligation if they consent to [issue such a paper as] this:—"In the parganah of Wiranpur (city of Desolation) in the *sarkar* of

Adamabad (Depopulation), tracts are assigned on the revenue in jagir [to the duped soldier?] and [he should] demand from the jagirdar *Khana-kharab* (Ruined) the arrears of many years at this place." A day's difference in the verification (*tashiha*) is seized upon as a ground for making a year's deduction [from the trooper's pay.] If a man has entered service on the 1st Farwardi, they assign *tankha* to him from the end of the coming Asfandar. For the single grain of wheat (=fruit of the tree of knowledge, in Muslim mythology) which Father Adam, in his jagir of the *sarkar* of Jannatabad (Paradise), ate without [131*a*] authorisation, they demand from his progeny refund amounting to an ass's load. If a man's pay is due for 3 years, they designate it as one for many years and then write [only] one-half of it (?). The faces of the clerks of the *taujih* (description-roll) are disagreeable. The answer of the author of this journal is, "The state of not being in need is better, without the need of taking oaths [to it]." No harm has been done to me by these men (the clerks), and no confusion has been introduced into my affairs by them; but [I write] from seeing and hearing what they have done to the helpless and the weak in the court [of the Nawwab] and in the provinces far and near. (*Verse.*)

My heart is oppressed, and the pain is so great,
That so much blood gushes out of it.

In short, the Emperor's orders for abolishing *zakat* and *hasil*, sent to Bengal, were for abolishing them in the parganahs of the Crownland. The Nawwab had a free choice in his jagir with regard to all exactions except the *rahdari* and the prohibited cesses (*abwabs*). But this just, God-fearing, benevolent governor, out of his sense of justice and devotion to God, abolished the *hasil* amounting to 15 lakhs of rupees which used to be collected [131*b*] in his own jagir, and he thus chose to please God, relieve the people, and follow his religious master (Aurangzib).

VII. In many parganahs the despicable practice had long existed that when any man, ryot or newcomer (*khush-nashin*), died without leaving any son, all his property including even his wife and daughter was taken possession of by the department of the Crownlands or the jagirdar or zamindar who had such power; and this custom was called *ankura* [=hooking]. The Nawwab put down this wicked thing.

VIII. In the *kotwali chabutras* of this country it was the custom that whenever a man proved a loan or claim against another, or a man's stolen property [was recovered], the clerks of the *chabutra*, in paying to the claimant his due, used to seize for the state one-fourth of it under the name of "fee for exertion." The Nawwab abolished it.

IX. When the plaintiff and defendant presented themselves at the magistracy (*muhakuma*) both of them were kept in prison until the decision of their case, lest it should be wilfully delayed (?). And their liberators (*itlaq-goian*) took daily fees from the prisoners and paid them into the State. This custom, too, was now abolished.

X. The courtiers [132*a*] used daily to present to the Nawwab many needy persons, and he made them happy with gifts of money. When he set out on a ride or dismounted at a stage or took a walk, and also on the day of '*Id* and other holy days, in addition to [supporting] the established almshouses, he used to invite the populace and feed vast numbers to satiety at the tables he spread. His profuse charity so thoroughly removed poverty and need from Bengal that few hired labourers or workmen could be had [for money] to do any work...... Every year he used to send to all the provinces vast sums for the benefit of the faqirs, orphans, and motherless children, and thus laid in *viaticum* for his last journey.

THE REVENUE REGULATIONS OF AURANGZIB.

INTRODUCTION.

A Persian manuscript of the Berlin Royal Library (Pertsch's Catalogue, entry No. 15 (9) *ff.* 112*b*-125*a* and 15 (23) *ff.* 267*a*-272*a*) gives, among other things, two very beautifully written *farmans* of the Emperor Aurangzib. The text of the first *farman* is accompanied by a highly useful commentary in Persian, written on smaller leaves placed between but paged consecutively. The *farman* to Rasik-das is also to be found in Bibliotheque Nationale (Paris) Ms. Sup. 476 (*f.* 13*a*), in the India Office Library, and in a Ms. presented to me by Maulvi M. Abdul Aziz of Sayyidpur-Bhitari (Ghazipur.) The *farman* to Muhammad Hashim has been printed in the *Mirat-i-Ahmadi* (p. 283) and the Persian Reader, Vol. II. (Calcutta School Book Society, 1836); English translations of it are to be found in the last mentioned work and Noel Paton's *Principles of Asiatick Monarchies.* But the commentary occurs in the Berlin Ms. alone.

For the meanings of Indian revenue terms I have consulted (1) *British India Analyzed* (ascribed to C. Greville), London, 1795, Part I.; (2) Wilson's Glossary; and (3) Elliot and Beames's Supplementary Glossary, 2 vols.

TRANSLATION.

Farman of the Emperor Aurangzib-'Alamgir, in the year 1079 A.H., on the collection of revenue.*

[112 *b*.] Thrifty Muhammad Hashim, [diwan of Gujrat], hope for imperial favours and know—

That, as, owing to the blessed grace and favour of the Lord of Earth and Heaven, (great are His blessings and universal are His gifts!) the reins of the Emperor's intention are always turned to the purport of the verse, "Verily God commands with justice and benevolence," and the Emperor's aim is directed to the promotion of business and the regulation of affairs according to the Law [113, *a*] of the Best of Men, (salutation and peace be on him and his descendants, and on his most virtuous companions!)—and as the truth of [the verse] "Heaven and earth were established with justice" is always acceptable in the eyes [of the Emperor] as one of the ways of worshipping and honouring the Omnipotent Commander, and friendliness and benevolence to high and low is the aim of the illuminated heart [of the Emperor],—

Therefore, at this auspicious time, a *farman* of the high and just Emperor is issued,—

That officers of the present and future and *'amils* of the Empire of Hindusthan from end to end, should collect the revenue and other [dues] from the *mahals* in the proportion and manner fixed in the luminous Law

* June 1668—May 1669; the 11th year of the reign.

Second.—At the beginning of the year inform yourself, as far as possible, about the condition of every ryot, as to whether they are engaged in cultivation or are abstaining from it. If they can cultivate, ply them with inducements and assurances of kindness; and if they desire favour in any matter show them that favour. But if after inquiry it is found that, in spite of their being able to till and having had rainfall, they are abstaining from cultivation, you should urge and threaten them and employ force and beating. Where the revenue is fixed (*Kharaj-i-muazzaf*) proclaim to the peasants that [115, *a*] it will be realised from them whether they cultivate the land or not. If you find that the peasants are unable to procure the implements of tillage, advance to them money from the State in the form of *taqavi* after taking security.

[*Commentary*, 114 *a*:—The second clause proves that the only business of peasants is to cultivate and so pay the revenue of the State and take their own share of the crop. If they lack the materials of cultivation, they should get *taqavi* from the Government, because, as the king is the owner [of the land], it is mercy that when the cultivators are helpless they should be supplied with the materials of agriculture. The emperor's desire is the first. And threatening, beating and chastisement are [ordered] with this view that, as the king is the owner, [and] always likes mercy and justice,—therefore it is necessary that the ryots too should, according to their own custom, make great exertions to increase the cultivation, so that the signs of agriculture may daily increase.

and shining orthodox Faith, and [according to] whatever has been meant and sanctioned in this gracious mandate in pursuance of the correct and trustworthy Traditions,—

And they should not demand new orders every year, and consider delay and transgression as the cause of their disgrace [113*b*] in this world and the next.

[*Commentary*, 113 *b* margin:—The purport of the introduction is only the transaction of affairs and threatening with [the anger of] God for the performance of the royal order and for the sake of [according] justice to the officers, and benevolence mercy and convenience to the peasants in the collection of revenue, etc., agreeably to the Holy Law.]

First.—They should practise benevolence to the cultivators, inquire into their condition, and exert themselves judiciously and tactfully, so that [the cultivators] may joyfully and heartily try to increase the cultivation, and every arable tract may be brought under tillage.

[*Commentary*, 113 *b* margin:—Concerning what has been written in the first clause the wish of the just Emperor is, "Display friendliness and good management which are the causes of the increase of cultivation. And that [friendliness] consists in this that under no name or custom should you take a *dam* or *diram* above the fixed amount and rate. By no person should the ryots be oppressed or molested in any way. The manager of affairs at the place should be a portector [of rights] and just [in carrying out] these orders."]

This thing is the cause of the gain of the State and the benefit of the ryots.]

Third—About fixed revenue: If the peasant is too poor to get together agricultural implements and runs away leaving the land idle, give the land to another on ease or for [direct] cultivation [as a tenant at will ?], and take the amount of the revenue from the lessee in case of lease, or from the share of the owner in case of cultivation, taking the amount of the revenue from the lessee [in case of lease] and from the owner's share in case of [direct] cultivation, and paying one-half to the *malik*, *i.e.*, to the cultivator,—the word *malik* (owner) does not mean 'proprietor of the soil' but 'owner of the crop in the field'; because, if the word 'owner' meant 'proprietor lease it out before the next year.

[*Commentary*, 114 *b*:—In what has been written about giving lease, entrusting to cultivators for [direct] cultivation, taking the amount of the revenue from the lessee [in case of lease] and from the owner's share in case of [direct] cultivation, and paying one-half to the *malik*, *i.e.*, to the cultivator,—the word *malik* (owner) does not mean 'proprietor of the soil' but 'owner of the crop in the field'; because, if the word 'owner' meant 'proprietor of the soil,' then the owner would not run away through poverty and want of agricultural materials, but would rather sell his land and seek relief in either of these two ways: (i) throwing the payment

of Government revenue upon the purchaser, (ii) devoting the sale-proceeds of his owner's right to the removal of his own needs. As for the words "substitute another man for the [former] owner," the rightful substitute for a proprietor can be none but his heir, and this is the distinctive mark of ownership. Therefore, the word 'substitute' as used here means 'a substitute for the owner of the crop.' But in the case in which a man, after spending his own money and with the permission of Government, cultivates a waste land which had paid no revenue before, and having agreed to its assessment for revenue pays the revenue to the State,—such a man has [true] tenant's right to the land he cultivates, because he is the agent of reclaiming the land. The real owner is he who can create a substitute for the owner, *i.e.*, the king. It is a well-known maxim, "Whosoever wields the sword, the coins are stamped in his name." As for the expression "pay half [the produce] to the owner, and do not lease out the field to anyone else for a year afterwards,"—the intention is that, as the fixed
had paid no revenue before, and having agreed to its assessment for revenue pays the revenue to the State,
cultivator has to pay the revenue in cash. As the Emperor likes leniency and justice, [he here orders] that the officers should kindly wait for one year [for the return of a fugitive ryot] and, in the case of [direct] cultivation or lease, they should pay to him any surplus left above the Government revenue.]

Fourth.—Inform yourself about the tracts of fallow

(*uftada*) land which have not returned to cultivation. If they be among the roads and highways, enter them among the area (? *bana*) of towns and villages, in order that none may till them. And if you find any land other than these, which contains the remnant of a crop that stands in the way of its tillage, then do not hinder [the cultivation] for the sake of its revenue. But if it be capable of cultivation, or really a piece of land fallen into ruin (*bâir*), then in both these cases, in the event of the land having an owner and that owner being present and able to cultivate it, urge the owner to till it. But if the land has no owner, or if the owner is unknown, give it to a man who can reclaim it to reclaim. Thereafter, if the lessee be a Muhammadan and the land [117, *a*] adjoins a tract paying tithes, assess tithes on it; if it adjoins a rent-paying tract, or if the reclaimer of the land be an infidel, do not make abatement [of the full revenue on it.] In case the [standard] revenue has to be abated, then, as prudence may dictate, either assess the land at something per bigha by way of unalterable rent,—what is called *Kharaj-i-muqat'at**—or lay on it the prescribed revenue of half the crop,—which is called *Kharaj-i-muqasema*. If the owner be known, but is quite unable to cultivate it, then if the land had been previously subject to *Kharaj-i-muqasema*, act according to the order issued [for this class of revenue]. But if it be not subject to *Kharaj-i-muqasema* or is not bearing any crop, then do not trouble

* Bilmokta—'land held at a low unalterable rent.'—(*Brit. Ind*, p. 151.)

[the owner] for tithes or revenue. But if he be poor, engage him in cultivation by advancing *taqavi*.

[*Commentary*, 116*a*:—Fourth clause: "When the land forms part of highways or is really waste or owned by a person unknown, or when the owner is quite unable to till it," and other expressions. In all these cases the word owner is used in the former sense. And there is a possibility of ownership being used in the latter sense too, as described before. There are many proofs, more manifest than the Sun and more evident than yesterday, in support of 'owner' being used for the king. For the sake of brevity they have not been mentioned here.]

Fifth.—As for a desert tract (*badia*), if the owner be known, leave it with him; do not give possession of it to others, [117, *b*]. If the owner be not known, and there is no chance of '*audat* in the land, then, as policy may dictate, give the land to whomsoever you consider fit to take care of it. Whosoever makes it arable must be recognised as the owner of the tract and the land should not be wrested from him. If the land contains articles of '*audat* (?), do not issue any order that may hinder the '*audat* in the land; and as for the gain from the land, forbid sowing, etc.; and do not let anyone take possession of it, and recognise none as its owner.

If an entire (*darbast*, undivided) tract of waste land has been transferred for any reason, and a contrary state of things is brought about by a different cause, then regard the land as belonging to the man up to the time till when it was in his possession, and do not give possession of it to anybody else.

[*Commentary*, 116, *b*:—In the fifth clause it has been written: "If the owner of a desert tract be present, entrust it to him; otherwise, give it, as advisable, to a fit person who may reclaim it to cultivation; recognise him as its owner, do not wrest it from him,—if there is no probability of '*audat* in it," and other things. Here the word '*audat* has two meanings: (i) that the land is likely to contain mines, and (ii) that the [original] owner may return to it. The second alternative which has been stated before, is clearly evident here, "Whosoever makes a land fit for cultivation should be recognised as its owner." It means that, as with the permission of the ruler he cultivates a waste unproductive land and benefits the State, therefore he has a claim to the land based on his services. Hence the imperial order runs: "Whosoever makes a land fit for cultivation should be recognised as its owner, and the land should not be wrested from him." Then it is evident that none else can have any right to the land. "As for the gain from the land, etc."—*i.e.*, if hereafter someone else sets up a claim to ownership, he should not be given possession of the profit from this land, such as the price of crops or [the gain from] gardens, tanks, and such things. The reason is that this land had been paying no rent before, and therefore the man who has reclaimed it and none else has a right to it.

"And if a tract of waste land, etc."—*i.e.*, if a tract

of waste land is in its entirety transferred to another person, either on account of its having had no owner, or by reason of the man having reclaimed the land by his own exertions from unproductiveness and incapacity to pay revenue, then the man who first owned it and from whom it was transferred to the former, has a right to the price of the produce of the transferred land up to the time when it ceased to produce anything. This produce had no connection with the man to whom the land has been transferred, because the land belongs to him only from the time of the transfer.]

Sixth.—In places where no tithe or revenue has been laid on a cultivated land, fix whatever ought to be fixed according to the Holy Law. If it be revenue, fix such an amount that [119*a*] the ryots may not be ruined; and for no reason exceed half [the crop], even though the land may be capable of paying more. Where the amount is fixed, accept it, provided that if it be *Kharaj*, the Government share should not exceed one-half, lest the ryots be ruined by the exaction. Otherwise reduce the former *Kharaj* and fix whatever the ryots can easily pay. If the land is capable of paying more than the fixed [amount] take (?) more.

[*Commentary*, 118, *a*:—In the sixth clause: The wish of the be ruined whenever is that the belongs should be so fixed that the peasantry may not be ruined to depends of it. The land belongs to the king, but its cultivation depends on the ryots; whenever the ryots desert their places and are ruined, *i.e.*, when they are crushed by the excessive exactions and oppression of the officers, one can easily imagine what the condition of the cultivation would be. Hence urgent orders are issued in this clause. And the statement in the last portion, "If the land is capable of paying more than the fixed amount, take more," is contrary to the order in the first portion of the same clause. Probably it is an error of the scribe. He must have imagined that as this passage is insistent, it ought to be read as 'take.' The reason is that in the first portion there is a total prohibition of taking more revenue, "although it can pay more, do not take more than one-half," and again here the Emperor orders "do not take more order the changingd amount," such an order strengthens the fixe fixed nay more, the repetition of the order is for the changing of revenue insistence.

Seventh.—You may change fixed revenue (*muazzaf*) into share of crop (*muqasema*), or *vice versa*, if the ryots desire it; otherwise not.

[*Commentary*:—The order for changing one kind of revenue into another at the wish of the ryots is for their convenience.]

Eighth.—The time for demanding fixed revenue is the harvesting of every kind of grain. Therefore, when any kind of grain reaches the stage of harvest, collect the share of revenue suited to it.

[*Commentary*:—The object is, whenever the revenue is demanded at harvest, the ryots may, without any perplexity, sell a portion of the crop sufficient to pay the revenue and thus pay the due of the State. But, if the demand is made before that time, it puts them into perplexity and anxiety. Therefore, the Emperor's order is to seek their convenience.]

Ninth.—In lands subject to fixed revenues, if any non-preventable calamity overtakes a sown field, you ought to inquire carefully, and grant remission to the extent of the calamity, as required by truth and the nature of the case. And in realising [119*b*] revenue in kind from the remnant, see that a net one-half [of the produce] is left to the ryots.

[*Commentary*, 118 *b*:—"If *Kharaj-i-muazzaf* has been fixed on a land, and a calamity befalls some crop of the land by which it is not totally destroyed, then you ought to inquire into the case, and deduct from the revenue to the extent of the injury done; and from the portion that remains safe, take so much of the produce (*mahsul*) that the ryot may have a net one-half"; *e.g.*, ten *maunds* are [usually] produced in a field; on account of the calamity six maunds only are left [safe], the net half of this is five maunds; therefore, you should take one maund only [as revenue], so that the net half (*viz.*) five maunds may be left to the ryot.]

Tenth.—*In lands with fixed revenues*: If anybody leaves his land untilled, in spite of his ability to till it and the absence of any hindrance, then take the revenue [of it] from some other* [field in his possession.] In

* *B'aze Zamin*—See Wilson, p. 69, i. "The Baze Zamin or certain lands set apart for various uses."—(*Brit. Ind.*, p. 276.)

the case of fields which have been flooded, or where the [stored] rain-water has been exhausted, or any non-preventable calamity has overtaken the crop before reaping, so that the ryot has secured nothing, nor has he time enough left for a second crop to be raised before the beginning of the next year,—consider the revenue as lost. But if the calamity happens after reaping, whether it be preventable like eating up by cattle or after the calamity sufficient time is left [for a second crop], collect the revenue.

[*Commentary*:—"If a man holds a land on which *Kharaj-i-muazzaf* has been laid, and he has the power to cultivate it, and there is no obstacle to his cultivating, and yet he leaves it untilled,—then realise the revenue of that land from any other land belonging to the man, because he left his land idle in spite of his being able to till it and there being no obstacle. If any land belonging to the man is flooded or the rain-water which had been dammed up for irrigation of crops gets exhausted, and the crop is ruined, or if any non-preventable calamity befalls his crops, before they have ripened and been harvested, so that he secures no crop nor has he any time left for raising a second crop that year,—then do not collect the revenue. But if any non-preventable calamity overtakes the crop of the man after reaping, or if the calamity takes place before the reaping but enough time is left for a second crop that year, take the revenue (*mahsul*)," because the calamity happened through his own carelessness after the reaping of the corn. And so, too, "if the calamity happens before the reaping, but time enough is left for another crop," then [as the loss] occurred through his neglect, it is proper to take revenue from him.]

Eleventh.—If the owner of a land, subject to a fixed revenue, cultivates it but dies before paying the year's revenue, and his heirs get the produce of the field [121, *a*] collect the revenue from them. But do not take anything if the aforesaid person died before cultivating and [time] enough is not left that year [for anyone else to till it].

[*Commentary,* 120, *a*:—What has been published about "the death of the owner of the land, taking the revenue from his heirs, and not demanding the revenue from the heirs if he died before tilling" is manifestly just; because the land-owner, *i.e.*, truly speaking the owner of the crop, died before cultivating, and so it is far from just to collect revenue from his heirs, even though they may have got something from him by way of bequest; for the [true] owner of the land is the king, and the owner of the crop, *i.e.*, the deceased [ryot] died before cultivating, and his heirs have not got anything or crop that may be a ground for [demanding] revenue, so, nothing should be collected from them.]

Twelfth.—Concerning fixed assessments: If the owner gives his land in lease or loan, and the lessee or borrower cultivates it, take the revenue from the owner. If the latter plants gardens, take the revenue from the latter. But if a man after getting hold of a *Kharaji* land denies it, and the owner can produce witnesses, then if the usurper has cultivated it, take the revenue from him; but if he has not done so, take the revenue from neither of them. If the usurper denies [the usurpation] and the owner cannot produce witnesses, take the revenue from the owner. In cases of mortgage (*rihan*), act according to the orders applicable to cases of unsurpation. If the mortgagee has engaged in cultivation without the permission of the mortgager, [121, *b*] [exact the revenue from the former].

[*Commentary*, 120 *b*:—This order may be construed in either of the following two ways, or it will yield no sense: "If the owner of a land under fixed revenue gives his land in lease or loan, and the lessee or borrower cultivates it, realise the revenue from the owner. If the latter has planted gardens on it, take the revenue from him, because he has planted the gardens. If a man after getting hold of a *Kharaji* land denies it, and the owner has witnesses, then, in the case of the usurper having tilled it, take the revenue from him, but if he has not done so take the revenue from neither of them. If the usurper denies [the usurpation] and (i) the owner *has no* witness, take the revenue from the owner." This is one construction. The other is (ii) "if the owner *has* witnesses, take the revenue from the owner," *i.e.*, the usurper denies [the usurpation] and the owner produces witnesses to prove his own cultivation, therefore the owner should pay the revenue.

"In cases of mortgage act according to the orders

issued for cases of usurpation. If the mortgagee has engaged in cultivation without the consent of the mortgager, [demand the revenue from the former]," because if the mortgagee engaged in cultivation *with* the consent of the mortgager, the latter ought to have paid the revenue, because the right to cultivate is [here] included in the mortgage. But if he has engaged in cultivation *without* the mortgager's consent, he ought to pay the revenue, because the land alone, and not the right to cultivate it, was mortgaged.]

Thirteenth.—About lands under fixed revenue: If a man sells his *Kharaji* land, which is cultivated, in the course of the year, then, if the land bears one crop only and the buyer, after taking possession, gets enough time during the rest of the year to cultivate it and there is none to hinder him, collect the revenue from the buyer; otherwise from the seller. If it yields two crops, and the seller has gathered in one and the buyer the other, then divide the revenue between the two. But if the land is [at the time of sale] under a ripe crop, take the revenue from the seller.

[*Commentary*, 122 *a*:—If a man wishes to sell his land, *i.e.*, the crop of his land, and the purchaser gets sufficient time during the year to cultivate it, take the revenue from the purchaser. If it bears two crops, of which the seller has gathered in one and the buyer the other, divide the revenue and collect it from the two parties. If the land be under a ripe crop, take the revenue from the seller, because as the crop is ripe and the seller has sold it with full knowledge, he must have taken the price of the ripe grain. Therefore the seller should pay the revenue.]

Fourteenth.—Concerning lands under fixed revenue: If a man builds a house on his land, he should pay the rent as fixed before; and the same thing if he plants on the land trees without fruits. If he turns an arable land, on which revenue was assessed for cultivation [123, *a*] into a garden, and plants fruit-trees on the whole tract without leaving any open spaces [fit for cultivation], take Rs. 2¾, which is the highest revenue for gardens, although the trees are not yet bearing fruit. But in the case of grape and almond trees, while they do not bear fruit take the customary revenue only, and after they have begun to bear fruit, take Rs. 2¾, provided that the produce of one canonical *bigha*, which means 45 × 45 Shah-Jahani yards, or 60 × 60 canonical yards, amounts to Rs. 5½ or more. Otherwise take half the actual produce [of the trees]. If the price of the produce amounts to less than a quarter-rupee,—as in the case when grain sells at 5 Shah-Jahani seers a rupee and the Government share of the crop amounts to one seer only (?)*—you should not take less than this [quarter-rupee].

If a Hindu sells his land to a Muhammadan, demand the revenue in spite of his being a Muslim.

[*Commentary*, 122 *b*:—If a man holds a land under

* Is not this a very round-about way of saying that when the revenue in kind is worth only 1/5 of a rupee, a quarter-rupee should be regarded as the minimum assessment?

a fixed revenue, and builds a house on it or plants a garden of trees that bear no fruit, there should be no change in its revenue, the former revenue should be taken. If a garden is planted on a land which was used for cultivation and on which the revenue of culturable land was fixed, and the fruit-trees are placed so close together that no open space is left for tillage, take Rs. 2-12, which is the due (*hasil*) of gardens, even while the trees do not bear fruit. But in the case of grape and almond trees, the [usual] revenue is taken while they have not begun to bear fruit, and afterwards the due (*hasil*) of gardens. But if this due of gardens, which is fixed at Rs. 2-12—on the ground that the total yield (? *rab'a*) of a legal *bigha* including the owner's share, may reach to Rs. 5-8—does not reach that amount, then take half the actual produce as revenue.† But if the price of this half-share of the produce be less than As. 4—as, in the case of grain, if you get one seer in five Shah-Jahani seers (?)—do not take less [than As. 4]. If an infidel sells his land to a Muhammadan, collect the revenue from the latter, because in truth it was not the latter's possession.]

Fifteenth.—If any man turns his land into a cemetery [123, *b*] or *serai* in endowment (*waqf*), regard its revenue as remitted.

[*Commentary*, 124 *a*:—As it is a pious act to endow

† In revennue by division of crops, the State took only 1/3 of the gross produce in the case of grain; but 1/4 to 1/8 in the case of opium, sugar-cane, vine plantain, and cotton. (*Brit. I d.*, p. 179.)

tombs and *serais*, therefore the Emperor forbids the collection of revenue from them, for the sake of benefiting and doing good [to the public]. Revenue ought not to be taken [from such lands].

Sixteenth.—About revenue by division of crops (kharaj-i-muqasema): If a man, whether Hindu or Muhammadan, is not the owner of a revenue-paying land, but has only bought it or holds it in pawn, he ought to enjoy the profit from whatever is produced in it. Collect from him the proper portion which has been fixed [as revenue],—provided that the share is neither more than one-half nor less than one-third [of the total crop]. If it be less than one-third, increase it, [if more than one-half, decrease it], as you consider advisable.

[*Commentary*:—If a man is not the real owner of a *muqasema* land, but holds it [by purchase or] in pawn, he ought to enjoy the gain from the land, whether he be Hindu or Muhammadan, on condition that in case of mortgage he has received permission [to till] from the mortgager. Therefore, collect from him the portion [previously] fixed as the assessment on that land. But this portion ought not to be more than one-half nor less than one-third. If more than one-half, decrease it, if less than one-third, increase it, to a proper amount.]

Seventeenth.—If the owner of a *muqasema* land dies without leaving any heir, act, in giving it in lease, direct cultivation, etc. according to the ordinances issued [above] for *muazzaf* lands.

[*Commentary*:—If the cultivator dies without heir,

the man who administers the land should act in the manner prescribed in the third clause about *kharaj-i-muazzaf*, in giving it in lease or direct cultivation.]

Eighteenth.—In *muqasema* lands, if any calamity overtakes the crop, remit the revenue to the amount of the injury. And if the calamity happens after reaping the grain or before reaping, gather revenue on the portion that remains safe.

[*Commentary*:—The Emperor seeks the happiness of the ryots. Therefore he strongly orders that no revenue should be demanded for the portion destroyed. But it should be collected for the remnant according to the share of that remnant.]

Farman of the Emperor Aurangzib-'Alamgir to Rasik-das krori in the form of a revenue-guide.

[267*a*] Rasik-das, thrifty and obedient to Islam, hope for imperial favours and know—

That, all the desires and aims of the Emperor are directed to the increase of cultivation, and the welfare of the peasantry and the people at large, who are the marvellous creation of and a trust from the Creator (glorified be His name!).

Now the agents of the imperial court have reported, after inquiry among the officers of the *parganahs* of Crown-lands and fiefs (*taiul*) of jagir-holders, that at the beginning of the current year the *amins* of the *parganahs* of the imperial dominions ascertain the revenue of many of the *mauz'as* and *parganahs* from a consideration of the produce (*hasil*) of the past year and the year preceding it, the area capable of cultivation, the condition and capability of the ryots, and other points. And if the ryots of any village do not agree to this procedure, they fix the revenue at the time of harvesting by [actual] survey or estimated valuation of crop.* And in some of the villages, where the cultivators are known to be poor and deficient in capital, they follow the practice of division of crops [*ghalla-bakhshi*] at the rate of 1/2, 1/3, 2/5, or more or less. And at the end of the year they send to the imperial record office the account-books (*tumar*)† of the cash collection of revenue, according to rule and custom, with their own verification (*tasdiq*), and the *Kroris'* acceptance, [267, *b*] and the signatures of the *chaudhuris* and *qanungoes*. But they do not send there the records of the lands of every *parganah* with description of the cultivation and details of the articles forming the autumn and spring harvest,—in such a way as to show what proportion of the crop of last year was actually realised and what proportion fell short, what difference, either increase or decrease, has occurred between the last year and the present and the number of ryots of every *mauz'a* distinguishing the lessees, cultivators, and others. [Such papers] would truly exhibit the circumstances of every *mahal*, and the work of the officers there—who, on the occurrence of a decrease in the collection of the *mahal*, after the ascertaining of the revenue had taken place, remit a large

* *Kankoot*—"Estimate of the ripened corn is called *Koot.*" (*Brit. Ind.*, p. 216.)

† *Tumar*—rent-roll.

amount from the total [standard] revenue on the plea of deficient rainfall, the calamity of chillnip, dearth of grain, or something else.

If they act with attention to minute details, after inquiring into the true state of the crops and cultivators of every village, and exert themselves to bring all the arable lands under tillage and to increase the cultivation and the total standard revenue, so that the *parganahs* may become cultivated and inhabited, the people prosperous, and the revenue increased, then, if any calamity does happen, the abundance of cultivation will prevent any great loss of revenue occurring.

THE EMPEROR ORDERS THAT—

You should inquire into the real circumstances of every village in the *parganahs* under your *diwans* and *amins*, namely, what is the extent of the arable land in it? [268*a*] what proportion of this total is actually under cultivation, and what portion not? What is the amount of the full crop every year? What is the cause of those lands lying uncultivated?

Also find out, what was the system of revenue collection in the reign of Akbar under the diwani administration of Tudar Mal? Is the amount of the *sair* cess the same as under the old regulations, or was it increased at His Majesty's accession? How many *mauz'as* are cultivated and how many desolate? What is the cause of the desolation? After inquiring into all these matters, exert yourself to bring all arable lands under tillage, by giving correct agreements (*qaul*)* and proper promises, and to increase the first-rate crops. Where there are disused wells, try to repair them, and also to dig new ones. And assess their revenue in such a way that the ryots at large may get their dues and the Government revenue may be collected at the right time and no ryot may be oppressed.

And every year after correctly preparing the papers containing the number of the cultivators of every *mauz'a*, [the extent of] the cultivated and uncultivated lands, lands irrigated by wells and by rain [respectively], the higher and lower crops, the preparations for cultivating the arable land for increasing the first-rate crops and bringing under culture the villages which had lain desolate for years,—and what else has been ordered in previous revenue-guides (*dasturu-l-'aml*),—report these details, with the amount of the money collected during the year just completed [268, *b*]. Know this regulation and procedure as established from the beginning of the autumn of the year of the Hare,† the 8th year of the reign, and act in this way, and also urge the officers of the *mahals* of the *jagirdars* to act similarly:—

First.—Do not grant private interviews to the *'amils* and *chaudhuris*, but make them attend in the [public] audience-hall. Make yourself personally familiar with the ryots and poor men, who may come to you to state their condition, by admitting them to public and private

* Tippu Sultan's order: "On the commencement of the year [the *amil*] shall give *cowle* to all the ryots...and encourage them to cultivate the lands." *British India Analysed*, I, 1 and 2.

† A Turkish year.

audiences, so that they may not need the intermediation of others in making their requirements known to you.

Second.—Order the *'amils* that (i) at the beginning of the year they should inquire, village by village, into the number of cultivators and ploughs, and the extent of the area [under tillage]. (ii) If the ryots are in their places, the *'amils* should try to make every one of them exert himself, according to his condition, to increase the sowing and to exceed last year's cultivation; and advancing from inferior to superior cereals they should, to the best of their power, leave no arable land waste. (iii) If any of the peasants runs away, they should ascertain the cause and work very hard to induce him to return to his former place. (iv) Similarly, use conciliation and reassurances in gathering together cultivators from all sides with praiseworthy diligence. (v) Devise the means by which barren (*banjar*) lands may be brought under cultivation.

Third.—Urge the amins of the *parganahs*, that at the beginning of the year, after inquiring into the agricultural assets (*maujudat-i-mazru'aat*) [269*a*] of every tenant, village by village, they should carefully settle the revenue in such a way as to benefit the Government and give ease to the ryots. And send the *daul** of revenue to the imperial record office without delay.

Fourth.—After settling the revenue, order that the collection of revenue should be begun and the payment

* *Daul*—"an account of particular agreements with the inferior farmers of the district, attested by the Canongoes; sub rent-roll." (*Brit. Ind.*, p. 222.)

demanded at the appointed time, according to the mode agreed upon in every *parganah* for the payment of the instalments of revenue. And you yourself should every week call for reports and urge them not to let any portion of the fixed instalments fall into arrears. If by chance a part of the first instalment remains unrealised, collect it at the time of the second instalment. Leave absolutely no arrears at the third instalment.

Fifth.—Having divided the outstanding arrears into suitable instalments according to the condition and capability of the ryots, urge the *kroris* to collect the instalments as promised [by the ryots], and you should keep yourself informed about the arrangements for collecting them, so that the collection may not fall into abeyance through the fraud or negligence of the *'amils*.

Sixth.—When you yourself go to a village, for learning the true condition of the *parganahs*, view the state and appearance of the crops, the capability of the ryots, and the amount of the revenue. If in apportioning [the total revenue among the villagers] justice and correctness have been observed to every individual, fair and good. But if the *chaudhuri* or *muqaddam* or *patwari* has practised oppression, conciliate the ryots [269, *b*] and give them their dues. Recover the unlawfully appropriated lands (*gunjaish*) from the hands of usurpers. In short, after engaging with honesty and minute attention in ascertaining [the state of things] in the present year and the division (? or details) of the assets, write [to the Emperor] in detail,—so that the true services of the *amins* and the admirable administration of this wazir [Rasik-das] may become known [to His Majesty].

Seventh.—Respect the rent-free tenures, *nankar*† and *in'am*, according to the practice of the department for the administration of Crown-lands. Learn what the Government *'amils* have increased (?), namely, how much of the *tankha* of *jagirs* they have left in arrears from the beginning, what portion they have deducted on the plea of shortage [of rain] and [natural] calamity. In consideration of these things resume [the unlawfully increased rent-free lands] of the past, and prohibit [them] in future, so that they may bring the *parganahs* back to their proper condition. The truth will be reported to the Emperor, and favours will be shown to all according to their devotion.

Eighth.—In the cashier's office (*fotakhana*) order the fotadars to accept only 'Alamgiri coins. But if these be not available, they should take the Shah-Jahani Rupees current in the bazar, and collect only the *sikka-i-abwab.* Do not admit into the *fotakhana* any coin of short weight which will not pass in the bazar. But when it is found that the collection would be delayed if defective coins are returned, take from the ryots the exact and true discount for changing them into current coins, and immediately so change them.

Ninth.—If, (God forbid!) any calamity [270 *a*] from earth or sky overtakes a *mahal*, strongly urge the *amins*

† *Nankar*—(*Brit. Ind.*, p. 148). *Enams*—"the meanest and more general gifts of land, bestowed on mendicants and common singers." (*Brit. Ind.*, p. 186.)

and *'amils* to watch the standing crops with great care and fidelity; and after inquiring into the sown fields, they should carefully ascertain [the loss] according to the comparative state of the present and past produce (*hast-o-bud*).* You should never admit [as valid] any *sarbasta*† calamity, the discrimination (*tafriq*) of which depends solely on the reports of the *chaudhuris, qanungoes, muqaddams*, and *patwaris*. So that all the ryots may attain to their rights and may be saved from misfortune and loss, and usurpers may not usurp [others' rights].

Tenth.—Strongly urge the *amins, 'amils, chaudhuris, qanungoes*, and *mutasaddis*, to abolish *balia* (? or *halia?*), exactions (*akhrajat*) in excess of revenue, and forbidden *abwabs*‡ (cesses),—which impair the welfare of the ryots. Take securities from them that they should never exact *balia* or collect the *abwabs* prohibited and abolished by His Majesty. And you yourself should constantly get information, and if you find anyone doing so and not heeding your prohibition and threat, report the fact to the Emperor, that he may be dismissed from service and another appointed in his place.

Eleventh.—For translating Hindi papers into Persian,

* *Hastabood jama*—"Comparative account of the former and actual sources of revenue, showing the total increased valuation of the lands, the variations produced by casualties, new appropriations &c." (p. 220).

† *Sarbasti*, exemption from payment. Hence the word in the text means entitled to remission of revenue. *Sarbasta* in the sense of secret does not yield so good a sense.

‡ *Abwabs*—"Imposts levied under the general head of Sair" (*Brit. Ind.*, p. 168); they are enumerated in pp. 164-166. "Aurangzeb abolished 70 of these *abwabs*" (p. 168).

inquire into the rateable assessment and apportionment (*bachh-o-bihri*)§ of the revenue, exactions (*akhrajat*), and customary perquisites (*rasumat*)* name by name. As for whatever is found to have been taken from the peasants on any account whatever, after taking account of the payments (*wasilat*) into the *fotakhana*, the balance should be written as appropriated by the *amin*, *'amil*, *zamindars* and others, name by name. And, as far as possible [270*b*] collect and translate the rough records (*kaghaz-i-kham*) of all the villages of the *parganah*. If owing to the absence of the *patwari* or any other cause, the papers of certain *mauz'as* cannot be got, estimate this portion from the total produce of the villages [taken collectively], and enter it in the *tumar*. After the *tumar* has been drawn up, if it has been written according to the established system, the *diwan* ought to keep it. He should demand the refunding of that portion of the total gains of *'amils*, *chaudhuris*, *qanungoes*, *muqaddams*, and *patwaris*, which they have taken in excess of their established perquisites (*rasum-i-muqarrar*).

Twelfth.—Report the names of those among the *amins* and *kroris* of the *jagirdars*, who have served with uprightness and devotion, and by following the established rules in every matter have proved themselves good officers,—so that as the result they may be rewarded according to their attention to the gain of the State and

§ *Bachh*—Distribution of an aggregate sum among a number of individuals (Wilson, p. 42*b*). *Behri*—Proportionate rate (Wilson, p. 70*b*).

* *Russooms*—"Customs or commission." (*Brit. Ind.*, p. 149).

their honesty. But if any have acted in the opposite manner, report the fact to the Emperor, that they may be dismissed from the service, put on their defence and explanation [of their conduct], and receive the punishment of their irregular acts.

Thirteenth.—With great insistence gather together the papers of the records (*sar-i-rishta*) at the right time. In the *mahal* in which you stay, every day secure from the officers the daily account of the collection of revenue and cess and prices-current, and from the other *parganahs* the daily account of the collection of revenue and cash (*maujudat*) every fortnight, and the balance [271*a*] in the treasuries of *fotadars* and the *jam'a wasil baqi* every month, and the *tumar* of the total revenue and the *jam'a bandi*† and the incomes and expenditures of the treasuries of the *fotadars* season by season. After looking through these papers demand the refunding of whatever has been spent above the amount allowed (? or spent without being accounted for), and then send them to the Imperial record office. Do not leave the papers of the spring harvest uncollected up to the autumn harvest.

[271*b*] *Fourteenth.*—When an *amin* or *amil* or *fotadar* is dismissed from service, promptly demand his papers from him and bring him to a reckoning. According to the rules of the *diwan's* department, enter as liable to recovery the *abwabs* that ought to be resumed as the result of this auditing. Send the papers with the records of the *abwabs* recovered from dismissed *'amils*, to the

† *Jamabandi*—"Annual settlement of the revenue." (*Brit. Ind.*, p. 174.)

imperial *cutchery*, in order that the auditing of the man's papers may be finished.

Fifteenth.—Draw up the *diwani* papers according to the established rules season by season, affix to them your seal [in proof] of verification, and send them to the imperial record office.

ORISSA IN THE SEVENTEENTH CENTURY.

1. Sources of Information Extant.

In his *Account of Orissa Proper or Cuttack,* writen in 1822, Alexander Stirling complains, "The slender information extant of the proceedings of the Mughal officers from the retirement of Raja Man Singh in A. D. 1604 to the dewanship of the famous Nawwab Jaffar Khan Nasiri (A.D. 1707 to 1725), has to be gleaned from a few scattered notices in Persian histories of Bengal and scarcely intelligible revenue accounts, though the century in question must be regarded as a *most important period* in the annals of the country, when we consider the deep and permanent traces impressed on the state of affairs, by the arrangements, institutions, offices, and official designations, introduced by the imperial government during that interval."

From Persian works, not indicated by Stirling, it is now possible to fill, though partially, this gap in our knowledge of Orissa during the seventeenth century, which Stirling rightly calls "a most important period in the annals of the country." Our sources of information are:—

(i) The Memoirs of Jahangir and the official annals of the reigns of Shah Jahan and Aurangzib, which throw light only on the conquests and changes of officials but not on the administration or the condition of the people. (ii) The *Muraqat-i-Hassan,* or Letters of Maulana Abul

Hassan, who served the *subahdars* of Orissa as Secretary for about 12 years (1655—1667), and put this collection together in 1080 A.H. (1669—1670). Only one manuscript of this work is known to exist, which belongs to the Nawwab of Rampur in Rohilkhand. (iii) Letters addressed by Aurangzib to Murshid Quli Khan when *diwan* of Bengal, Bihar and Orissa, about 1700—1705, included in imperial secretary Inayetullah Khan's *Ahkam-i-Alamgiri.*

By means of these sources the middle and close of the century are brightly lit up for the historian, but the other portions of it will remain dark till some other happy discovery among Persian manuscripts.

2. List of Mughal Subahdars.

Baqar Khan Najam Sani, 4th February, 1628-1632.

The order removing him from Orissa was dated 24th June, 1632, but he reached the imperial court on return on 13th January, 1633.

Mutaqad Khan (Mirza Maki), 1632-1641.

The order removing him from Orissa was issued on 9th March, 1640, but he reached the imperial court on 29th July, 1641.

Shah Nawaz Khan, 1641-1642.

Appointed to Orissa on 9th March, 1640, but went there about the middle of 1641, removed by order dated 8th March, 1642, but continued in the province till the end of the year.

Muhammad Zaman Tihrani (as agent of Prince Shuja), 1642-1645.

Order of appointment dated 8th March, 1642, removal dated 21st November, 1645.

Mutaqad Khan, 1645-1648.

Appointed 21st November, 1645. Recalled to court in the 22nd year of Shah Jahan's reign (July 1648—June 1649).

Tarbiyat Khan (Shafiullah Birlas, vilayet-za) as agent of Prince Shuja, 1655-1656.

Anarchy, 1658-1659.

Ihtisham Khan, November 1659—September, 1660.

Khan-i-Dauran, September 1660—May 1667.*

Tarbiyat Khan, June 1667—October 1669.

Safi [or Saif] Khan, October 1669—?

Rashid Khan, ?—March, 1676.

Shaista Khan, March 1676—December 1676 (?)

Nurullah (as agent of Prince Azam), June, 1678—?

Kamgar Khan, ?—1704.

Murshid Quli Khan, 1704-1725.

3. The Expansion of the Mughal Province of Orissa.

In the sixteenth century the independent Rajahs of Orissa were crushed between the upper mill-stone of the Afghans advancing southwards from Bengal and the nether mill-stone of the Qutb-Shahi power (of Golkonda) expanding northwards from the Madras side. Under Akbar the Mughals held only the northern portion of Orissa, while the central portion was ruled by native

* The *Alamgirnamah* says that the Emperor learnt of Khan-i-Dauran's death on 7th December 1667 (page 1067), but on page 1050 he is represented as dead in the preceding June. I have accepted the latter date.

princes with semi-independent powers, but bearing the title of *mansabdars* in the Mughal peerage. The Qutb-Shahis held the southern extremity of the province. In the reign of Shah Jahan the power of Golkonda was broken by the Mughals in 1636 and 1656, and Qutb Shah became a loyal feudatory of the Emperor of Delhi, paying him an annual tribute. Early in Aurangzib's reign Malud was the southernmost outpost of Mughal Orissa, and beyond it lay the Qutb-Shahi district of Chicacole, from which the Golkonda tribute "appertaining to the province of Orissa," about Rs. 20,000 a year, was sent to the Mughal Subahdar of Orissa (*Muraqat*, 51, 160).

This result, however, was achieved after much fighting. On 13th Bahman, 12th regnal year (about the end of January, 1618), Jahangir records in his Memoirs: "At this time it was reported to me that Mukarram Khan, the governor of Orissa, had conquered the country of Khurda, and that the Rajah of that place had fled and gone into Rajmahendra. Between the province of Orissa and Golkonda there are two zamindars, one the Rajah of Khurda and the second the Rajah of Rajmahendra. The province of Khurda has come into the possession of the servants of the Court. After this it is the turn of the country of Rajmahendra. My hope in the grace of Allah is that the feet of my energy may advance further. At this time a petition from Qutb-ul-mulk reached my son Shah Jahan to the effect that as the boundary of his territory had approached that of the King [*i.e.*, the Mughal Emperor], and he owed service to this Court, he hoped an order would be issued to Mukarram Khan not to stretch out his hand, and to acquire possession of his country" (Rogers and Beveridge, i, 433).

In the winter of 1629-30, Baqar Khan, the Governor of Orissa, marched to Khiraparah, 4 miles from Chattar-duar, a very narrow pass on the frontier between the Qutb-Shahi kingdom and Orissa, and 24 miles from Mahendri, and plundered and laid waste its territory. The approach of the rainy season compelled him to retire without doing anything more. In the autumn of 1630 he set out again, with friendly levies from the zamindars of Khalikot, Kudla and Ala, and on 3rd December arrived in the environs of Mansurgarh, a fort built by a Golkonda officer named Mansur, 8 miles from Khiraparah. The enemy offered battle in the plain outside the fort, but were routed, and then the commandant of the fort, a Naikwar, capitulated. Baqar Khan returned, after leaving garrisons at Khiraparah and Mansurgarh (Hamid-uddin's *Padishahnamah*, I.A., 333). The Qutbshahis assembled in force to recover the fort, but Baqar Khan on hearing of it made a forced march and defeated the Deccan army. The news of this second victory reached the Emperor on 23rd April, 1631 (*Ibid*, 373).

4. Baqar Khan's Administration.

Complaints against Baqar Khan's oppression of the peasantry and zamindars repeatedly reached Shah Jahan's ears and at last on 24th June 1632 an order was issued removing him from the post. It is said that the Governor called all the zamindars of the province together and then threw them into prison to extort revenue. By his order seven hundred of the captives were massacred, and only one escaped to carry the tale to Shah Jahan's Court. This fugitive produced a list (*tumar*, rent-roll) showing that Baqar Khan had collected forty lakhs of rupees from the province. The Khan was in consequence recalled, and ordered to account for the money (*Masir-ul-umara*, iii, 484). His successor Mutaqad Khan ruled the province long and well, and died on 17th October, 1651 in extreme old age.

5. Interregnum and Ihtisham Khan's Administration.

From September 1657, when Shah Jahan fell ill and a war of succession broke out among his sons, to 6th May 1660, when Shuja fled from Dacca and Aurangzib became the sole master of Eastern India, there was anarchy in Orissa. The troops and most of the officers were withdrawn by Prince Shuja for his two advances on Agra and latterly for his prolonged struggle with Mir Jumla in the Rajmahal and Malda Districts. Taking advantage of this state of things, all the Orissa zamindars withheld the revenue, and several of them built forts and looted their neighbourhood, for which they had afterwards to pay a heavy penalty, as we shall see in the section on Khan-i-Dauran's administration. But, by the autumn of the year 1659, Mir Jumla had established himself in Western Bengal in sufficient strength to enable him to detach from his army Ihtisham Khan to take charge of the governorless province of Orissa. Ihtisham Khan's stay there was too short to enable him to restore orderly government. That arduous task fell to the lot of Khan-i-Dauran, who in April 1660, was transferred from Allahabad to Orissa and worked there as *subahdar* till his death in May, 1667.

Ihtisham Khan's first acts were to issue a proclamation that the *khutba* should be read in all the mosques of Orissa, in the name of the new Emperor Aurangzib (*Muraqat*, 45), and to send a *parwanah* to all the *mansabdars*, *zamindars*, *chaudhuris*, *qanungoes*, etc., of the province announcing his own appointment as *subahdar* and ordering them to meet him at Narayangarh, whither he would march from Medinipur, the northern frontier of the province, some time after 14th November, 1659 (*Ibid*, 47-49).

When, less than a year afterwards, he was replaced by Khan-i-Dauran, and sent to Bengal to serve under Mir Jumla, he tried to carry away with himself as prisoners for default of revenue, the brothers of Rajah Nilkantha Dev, Gopinath, the brother of Bharat Patnayak and chief officer of Rajah Mukund Dev, and the other zamindars of the environs of Katak. As their zamindaris could not be administered nor any rent collected in the absence of these men, the Mughal faujdar of Katak secured the release of Gopinath Patnayak by himself signing a bond for Rs. 14,000 to Ihtisham Khan. And the other captives were similarly released. For this the faujdar was severely censured by Khan-i-Dauran, who insisted that they should be unconditionally delivered up to him as Ihtisham Khan's successor in office (*Muraqat*, 183-184, 156-157).

6. MUGHAL RECONQUEST OF ORISSA UNDER KHAN-I-DAURAN, 1660-1663.

The first part of Khan-i-Dauran's viceroyalty was devoted to a task that was practically equivalent to the reconquest of Orissa for the Mughal Government, as imperial authority had disappeared from the province during the late War of Succession. The state of anarchy is very graphically described in the letters of this subahdar: "All the zamindars are refractory, owing to the slack rule of my predecessors" (page 134). The "zamindars on the further side of the Katjhuri, in the jurisdiction of Sayid Sher Khan, have refused tribute and declared war against him" (page 59). "Krishna Bhanj, of Hariharpur, the leading zamindar of this province, during the interregnum spread his power over the country from Medinipur to Bhadrak, a distance of 50 or 60 *kos*, seizing the property of the inhabitants and wayfarers and severely oppressing the people" (pages 72 and 107). "The fort of Panchira was wrested from Shuja's men by Lakshmi Narayan Bhanj, the Rajah of Keonjhar, during the time of disorder" (pages 52, 58, 129). "For the last three years, the zamindars on the further side of Katak have been collecting vast forces and getting ready for war" (page 72). "Bahadur the zamindar of Hijli is in rebellion" (page 130). "Chhut Rai has dispersed the ryots of Medinipur, and is building a fort in the jungles with evil intentions" (page 190). It is useless to give a list of the names of the other rebel zamindars here, as they will be mentioned in detail in the history of Khan-i-Dauran's campaigns which follows.

The *farman* appointing Khan-i-Dauran to Orissa was sent from the Imperial Court on 3rd April, 1660 (*Alamgirnamah*, 474). He received it at Allahabad, where he was subahdar, and soon set out for his new province "in the very height of the monsoons, defying raging storms, excessive mud, and flooded rivers, which had closed the paths" (*Muraqat*, 85). On 26th September he entered Medinipur, the first town after crossing the Orissa frontier (page 130). After spending some days here to settle the district, organize the civil administration and revenue collection and station faujdars in all directions, he set out for Jaleshwar, in the meantime writing to the zamindars of northern Orissa to meet him on the way and pay their respects as loyal subjects (page 134). His intention was to "finish the Hijli business" first. Bahadur, the zamindar of that port, had rebelled, and had to be subdued before the Mughal route from Medinipur *via* Narayangarh and Jaleshwar to Baleshwar could be rendered safe. But "the other zamindars report that the country of Hijli is now covered with mud and water, and, not to speak of cavalry, even foot soldiers cannot traverse it. After a time, when the roads of the district become dry again, the campaign should be opened" (pages 132 and 134). So, Khan-i-Dauran put off the idea, and went direct to Jaleshwar, which he reached in the latter half of October (page 156).

At the news of the Governor's approach, both Bahadur and Krishna Bhanj, the Rajah of Hariharpur (*i.e.*, Mayurbhanj), wrote to him professing submission and promising to wait on him at Jaleshwar (pages 133, 136 and 181). The Mughal faujdar of Remuna, on the Mayurbhanj frontier, wrote to the new Governor that the agents (*wakils*) of these two zamindars had reached him to arrange for their masters' interview. He was ordered in reply to reassure them with kindness and send them back to their masters that they might come without fear or suspicion and see Khan-i-Dauran at Jaleshwar (page 181).

7. Hariharpur (Mayurbhanj) Affairs.

Bahadur evidently changed his mind and held off; Krishna Bhanj* came, but met with a terrible fate, which is best described in the Governor's own words: "When I reached Jaleshwar, which is near his zamindari, Krishna Bhanj saw me after wasting a month on the pretext of choosing a lucky day [for the visit], and offered false excuses [for his late disloyal conduct]. During the inquiry and discussion for settling the amount of the revenue to be paid by him, he, inspired by pride in the largeness of his force, drew his dagger and rushed towards me. His companions, too, unsheathed their swords and made repeated charges. The grace of

* His offences are thus summed up: "He kept one thousand horse and ten or twelve thousand foot soldiers, and was obeyed and helped by all the zamindars of this country. [During the anarchy] he had plundered the tract from Bhadrak to Medinipur, carried off the ryots to his own territory, increased their cultivation and ruined the Imperial dominions" (page 107).

the Emperor saved my life. We slew Krishna Bhanj and many of his men. The rest fled. Some chiefs, such as Udand, the zamindar of Narsingpur, Chhattreshwar Dhol, the zamindar of Ghatsila, and Harichandan, the zamindar of Nilgiri, threw away their weapons and delivered themselves up as prisoners" (pages 72 and 107-109).

"The relatives of the slain Rajah [of Mayurbhanj] raised disturbances, molesting the ryots. So, I started for Hariharpur to punish them and halted at Remuna on the frontier of his dominion. His brother, Jay Bhanj, submitted, begged pardon, and brought to me his mother and son and three elephants and some money as a present (*peshkash*), and begged the *tika* of the Rajahship and zamindari for the son. I agreed, and then started to punish the rebels near Katak" (page 109).

8. Khurda Raj Affairs.

When the Khan reached Katak, Rajah Mukund Dev of Khurda, "the leading zamindar of this country, whose orders are obeyed by the other zamindars"—"whom all the other zamindars of this country worship like a god* and disobedience of whose order they regard as a great sin" (pages 77 and 102)—waited on him with due humility, accompanied by the other zamindars and Khandaits [of Central Orissa] (page 110). Then, "owing

* *Cf.* Stirling: "The title of sovereignty has been always acknowledged, by the general voice and feeling of the country, to vest in the Rajahs of Khurda. Down to the present moment the Rajahs of Khurda are the sole fountain of honour in this district" (86).

to the badness of the climate, a severe malady seized the governor and he was confined to bed for two months, unable to move about." "The rustics [*i.e.*, uncultivated local zamindars] seized the opportunity and caused disorder. Rajah Mukund Dev absented himself from the force sent by me to punish the rebels, and himself caused lawlessness. The Mughal troops subdued many of the rebels and took several forts. After recovering a little I (*i.e.*, Khan-i-Dauran) on 7th February 1661 set out from Katak against the other forts which my subordinates were too weak to capture" (page 77). "On 16th February I arrived near the forts of Kaluparah, Mutri, Karkahi, Khurdiha and [three] others,—seven forts close to each other on the side of a high hill. An assault was ordered next day. When our troops appeared near the forts, the enemy in a numberless host, consisting of *paiks* and infantry, both *Khudshan* (?) and zamindars of Banki and Ranpur, and other *Bhumiahs* and *Khandaits*,—offered battle. Our men slew many of them and carried their trenches at the foot of the hill and after repeated charges entered their [main ?] lines. The enemy fought with matchlocks, arrows, *khandahs*, *sablis*, *duars*, *dhukans*, *sintis*, etc., but being unable to resist fled away with their families. A great victory—unequalled by that of any former *subahdar*—was won. The seven forts were captured. Two or three days were spent in settling the conquered district and appointing *thanahs*" (pages 99-101).

"On 20th February, 1661, I left for the conquest of Khurda, the ancestral home of Mukund Dev, situated in the midst of a dense jungle and lofty hills (page 78). On the 23rd, I encamped a mile from Khurda. The Rajah had fled from it, and we seized a vast amount of booty and many prisoners at his capital" (page 102). "During the last 50 years, no other *subahdar* had reached these places. They were all conquered by my army! and the rustics became the food of the pitiless sword. I gave Mukund Dev's throne to his younger brother Bhramarbar" (page 78). The victorious *subahdar* halted at Khurda for some days. The fate of the premier Rajah of the province struck a salutary terror in the hearts of the other evil-doers. "All lawless men are now waiting on me with every mark of abject submission. The zamindar of Banki and Khand Narendra (the zamindar of Ranpur) have sent trusty agents to arrange for their interview with me. The path for collecting the revenue has been opened in all places and mahals. Rajah Mukund Dev, who had been ill-advised enough to defy my authority and withhold tribute, finding no way of escape from our heroes, saw me penitently on 18th March. The rebel Bharat [Patnayak], too, has done the same" (pages 158-159). Mukund Dev was afterwards restored to his throne, as we know from other sources.

An interesting bit of the history of the Khurda Rajahs is furnished in a letter of Khan-i-Dauran to his agent at the Imperial Court. "Received your letter reporting that a counterfeit Gangadhar has gone to the Court and secured an interview with Kumar Ram Singh [Kachhwa, son of Mirza Rajah Jay Singh] through the mediation of Rai Brindaban-das, the *musharraf* of the elephant department, and offered to pay every year 12 lakhs of rupees as tribute if the State is given to him. When I arrived in this province, Mukund Dev was the Rajah of Khurda. As he caused disturbances, I expelled him from his zamindari and gave the *tika* of Rajahship to his younger brother and reported the case to the Emperor. I have learnt the following facts from trustworthy men:—when the late Mutaqad Khan was *subahdar*; he slew Narsingh Dev and made his nephew Gangadhar Rajah. Balabhadra Dev, the elder brother of the slain, became Rajah after killing Gangadhar with the help of the officers of the State. When he died, Mukund Dev succeeded at the age of four years only. During the administration of Muhammad Hayat, the agent of Shuja, a pretended Gangadhar appeared and created a disturbance. He was slain by a confederacy of the zamindars near Katak. After my arrival in the province, another man claiming to be the same (Rajah) appeared in Talmal (in South Orissa). Muhammad Jan, the faujdar of that district, arrested him and sent him to me, and he is still confined in the fort of Mankhandi at Katak. They say another man assuming the same name is roving in the jungles" (pages 186-187).

9. MORE CONQUESTS BY KHAN-I-DAURAN.

On 8th March 1661, the *subahdar* left Katak to chastise Lakshmi Narayan Bhanj, the Rajah of Keonjhar, who had wrested the fort of Panchira from Shuja's men (pages 58-59). His territory was ravaged and the fort in question recovered (pages 52 and 129).

At a subsequent date (probably), Bahadur, the rebel zamindar of Hijli, was captured with his family (page 116).

After Khan-i-Dauran had expelled Mukund Dev from Khurda, "Khand Narendra, the zamindar of Ranpur and the zamindars of Malhiparah and Dompara, who had never before waited on any *subahdar*," saw him and agreed to pay tribute (page 103). "The zamindars on the further side of the Katjhuri, who had withheld tribute and fought the faujdar, Sayyid Sher Khan, were defeated" (page 59).

At the same time the Mughal faujdar of Malud, on the southern frontier of Orissa, was engaged in suppressing the rebellion of Pitam, the zamindar of Andhiari, and Kumar Guru, the zamindar of Malud (page 158).

The zamindari of Kanika was conquered by Mian Muhammad Jan, and the Rajah was driven out to a fort named Rika (?) on an island in the ocean. In order to besiege him there, *chhamp* boats of the river Mahanadi and larger boats too were sent to Muhammad Jan, with the help of Gopali, the zamindar of Kujang (pages 167 and 168).

Rao Tara [or Rawat Rai],* the zamindar of Kuyilu Madhupur, was thrown into prison for heavy arrears of revenue to the imperial exchequer for the parganah of

* On page 172 the name is spelt as *Bar-avatara* ?

Awlas. Gopali of Kujang also suffered the same fate (pages 170 and 172).

Khwajah Khalid Naqshbandi laid siege to the fort of Kulrah and carried mines under its walls. Then Sri Chandan [or Harichandan ?], the *qiladar*, begged quarter. He was promised his life, but thrown into prison and the fort was taken possession of. So also was another fort named Katkal (page 176).

Chhut Rai, the zamindar of Kailikot,* evidently in the neighbourhood of Narayangarh, had dispersed the ryots of (the parganah of) Medinipur and built a fort in the jungle with evil intentions (page 190). But his sons were thrown into prison, and he seems to have submitted, for we read in another letter how a *parwanah* was sent to him to stop the horse-dealers who used to deviate from the imperial road and take their horses by way of Banpur. They were to be sent to the provincial governor in future (page 160).

Rajah Nilkantha Dev was a loyal servant of the empire and fought under the Mughal banners with his contingent (page 143). Parganah Qutbshahi was his *jagir*, which he administered through his agent Gajadhar. Rs. 4,400 were due from the Rajah as arrears of revenue (pages 145 and 165). His brothers were placed in confinement by Ihtisham Khan for default, but Khan-i-Dauran secured their release (page 156).

The result of these operations was the restoration

* I am doubtful about this locality. Page 160 seems to imply that it was in the extreme south of Orissa.

of Imperial authority in Orissa. The country again enjoyed peace and order and the imperial revenue, which had entirely dried up during the interregnum, began to be realized again. Khan-i-Dauran could legitimately boast of his military successes, which in his own words were "unrivalled by any preceding *subahdar*." As he wrote in his despatches to the Emperor Aurangzib, "I have punished all the usurpers, oppressors, and lawless men of the province and made them obedient. The revenue is being collected by our officers. The people are enjoying peace and happiness and plying their trades" (page 49). And, again, a year later, about April, 1662, he wrote, "The province is being well administered" (page 54).

10. Revenue Collection.

After taking effective possession of the province and restoring order in this way, Khan-i-Dauran, early in 1662, sent five elephants as his present to the Emperor on the occasion of the marriage of two of his (the Khan's) sons, together with two other elephants presented by the Sultan of Golkonda. (*Muraqat*, page 53.) These, as we know from the official history (*Alamgirnamah*, 751), reached the Court at the end of May. The forests of Telingana, immediately west of Orissa and lying in the Golkonda territory, were famous for elephants, and these animals formed the usual present from the governors of Orissa to the Padishah. In May, 1628, Shah Jahan received five elephants from Baqar Khan and in September

1636 eight others from Mutaqad Khan. (Abdul Hamid's *Padishahnamah*, I.A. 201 and I.B. 216.)

Elephants, however, were occasional presents. The normal revenue also began to be sent to the Imperial Court regularly from this time. Having "punished all the usurpers, oppressors, and lawless men of the province, and made them obedient," Khan-i-Dauran could report to the Emperor, "the revenue is being collected by our officers"; and, as a proof of it, he at once transmitted to the exchequer at Delhi "the accumulated revenue of 15 lakhs of rupees, kept at Katak and the parganahs, together with seven pieces of cloth (*parchah*), one piece of scarlet cloth, and two caskets of *Chhani* decorated in the Dutch style." These were escorted by his own men as far as Rajmahal,* whence they were to be sent to Court with the revenue of Bengal. (*Muraqat*, page 50.)

He next devoted himself to realizing the portion of the Golkonda tribute which "appertained to the province of Orissa," being paid from the Golkonda district of Chicacole. This money had naturally remained unpaid during the civil war between Aurangzib and his brothers. Its exact amount was also in dispute. The Qutbshahi agent at Chicacole (Haidar Khan) asserted that he had paid the fixed sums of Rs. 12,000 and Rs. 1,000 during every year of Shuja's viceroyalty. But the papers sent from Delhi put the tribute at Rs. 20,000 a year. Khan-i-Dauran

* Later, the Orissa revenue used to be delivered to the faujdar of Burdwan for transmission to Court. (Page 189.)

succeeded in collecting Rs. 80,000 out of the arrears under this head, and sent an agent to Chicacole to dun for the balance. (Page 51.)

Evidently all the financial records of Shuja's time had been lost or destroyed by dishonest officers (page 60), and this produced uncertainty about imperial dues also. For example, the Emperor knew the tribute of the zamindars of Saranghara to be Rs. 8,000 a year, but could not say what additional sum they used to pay as succession fee. Khan-i-Dauran wrote in reply, "I find from the old records of the *subah* that they used to pay Rs. 10,000 as succession fee, but then their annual tribute was nothing like what your Majesty represents it. They used to pay something as *nazar* at intervals of two or three years [but no regular tribute]. I have now laid on Purushottam Dev Rs. 10,000 as fee for succeeding his brother [in the zamindari], which has been fully realized." (Page 61.)

Severe measures had to be taken with the revenue collectors and zamindars lest they should defraud the Government of its dues. Khan-i-Dauran writes thus to Muhammad Jan, a former diwan of the province, whom he had appointed (page 196) land-steward or factor (*sahib-i-ihtamam*) for his fiefs from Bhadrak to the southern limit of Orissa:—"Balabhadra and Brajanath *qanungoes*, who have been released from prison, and Paramananda, the zamindar of Rahmachnan (?), are sent to you in chains under a bailiff (*sazawāl*) as asked for by you......If you fear that before my arrival near Katak the zamindars will carry off the crops, then write urging the *amils* to collect the dues and attach the standing crops. Appoint men to guard the grain." (Pages 163, 164.) And, again, to Man Singh, the faujdar of Remuna:—"Send select men to hasten the gathering in and guarding of the crops and the collection of the Government dues......Send them quickly that the revenue (*i.e.*, Government share) of the autumn harvest may not be removed." (Page 182.)

The inference naturally suggested by the above passages, namely, that in Mughal times the revenue of Orissa was collected in the form of rice, is definitely supported by a letter from Murshid Quli Khan to Aurangzib written about 1704: "The revenue-collection of Orissa depends on the autumn harvest, which has to be kept stored for a long time, and, in spite of all my devices, cannot be sold." To this the Emperor replied, "I have heard that traders take the crop and in return for it they bring from the ports whatsoever is in demand." (Inayetullah's *Ahkam-i-Alamgiri*, Rampur MS., 219*b*.) Khan-i-Dauran says the same thing,—"In this country the realization of the land-revenue of the whole year depends on the three months of autumn." (Page 65.) "As for the *malangi* boats for loading rice in, they have not been procured owing to the bad conduct of the darogha of the port. Get boats from the zamindars of the mahal, and send the rice to the port to be shipped in the sailing season." (Page 165, see also page 146.)

Some incidental light is thrown on the State purchase of local industries. Khan-i-Dauran writes to Muhammad Jan, "The officers of the Imperial Government have reported that 210 *kudi* of cloth, of the *sahan*, *barbarah*, *do-suti* and *thati* varieties, 20,000 maunds of rice, 300 maunds of mustard oil ('yellow oil'), 260 maunds of sesamum, and 100 maunds of *galmosafr* are required for provisioning the ships [of the State]. According to the schedule attached to this letter, urge the officers of Jajpur, Bhadrak and other mahals in your faujdari to get them ready quickly and send them before the sailing season to the port of Baleshwar to Muhammad Baqar, the darogha of ship construction." [This is evidently a reference to Shaista Khan's vigorous naval construction programme with a view to his conquest of Chittagong in 1665.] "The price of these things will be deducted from the amounts due from the *amlas*."

"The *amlas* should advance to the weavers, artisans, oil-vendors, etc., money for the things ordered. First, settle the price with the help of brokers. Then, take bonds with the attestation of the brokers for the delivery of the goods in time. Send the *do-suti* before the other articles to the darogha that he may make sails with them. All the *kalapatis* and *najars*,—master craftsmen and blacksmiths,—living at the port of Harishpur and other places, should be won over and sent to Baleshwar, to engage in shipbuilding [for the Government] there. Dated 28th December, 1664." (Pp. 173—175.)

We also learn that "Rs. 39,000 was due from the

chaudhuri and qanungo of Chakla Medinipur, on account of the *taqavi* loan and *pattan* to the peasants." (Page 189.) A much larger amount must have been granted by the State for this purpose.

11. Comparative Revenue Returns.

No useful or very reliable return of the total revenue of Orissa during the seventeenth century can be constructed, first because the area under imperial rule varied considerably from time to time, and, secondly, because the Persian statistical books (*Dastur-ul-aml*) now extant are very badly written and occasionally drop certain figures out of a sum and thus give palpably wrong amounts. In these MSS. arithmetical figures are not represented by the Arabic numerals (as in all modern countries), nor by letters of the alphabet (as in the Roman system of notation and the Arabic *abjad*), but by *raqaim* or groups of symbolic marks suggestive of Chinese writing. The slightest carelessness or indistinctness in writing these *raqaim* may turn 20 into 2,000. The following comparative study of the revenue of Mughal Orissa at different periods is placed before the reader with the warnings that (*a*) the area assessed was not always the same, (*b*) these figures give only the standard or paper assessment, while the actual collection fluctuated from year to year and was always short of these amounts, and (*c*) some of the figures quoted below are probably unreliable or incorrectly transcribed in the Persian MSS.

Revenue of Orissa.

1594 A.D.	Rs.	31,43,316	(Ain-i-Akbari ii. 141-144)
1648 „	Rs.	50,00,000	(Abdul Hamid's Padishahnamah ii. 711)
1654 „	Rs.	56,39,500	(Dastur-ul-aml used by Thomas)
1665 „	Rs.	72,70,000	(Bernier, 457)
c 1690 „	Rs.	35,70,500	(Dastur-ul-aml Br. Mus. Or. 1641 f. 5b)
c 1695-1700	Rs.	43,21,025	(Dastur-ul-aml used by Thomas)
c 1695 A.D.	Rs.	1,01,02,625	(Khulasat-ut-tawarikh, 32a)
c 1697-1707	Rs.	57,07,500	(Manucci, ii. 414)
1707 A.D.	Rs.	35,70,500	(Ramusio)
1707 „	Rs.	35,70,275	Jagjivandas, in India Office MS. 1799, p. 5.
Tieffenthaler,	Rs.	35,70,525.	

It will be seen that the 5th, 9th, 10th and 11th of the above figures are all derived from the same source, *viz.*, an official return. The amount mentioned in the *Khulasat-ut-tawarikh** is clearly wrong. The rather high figures given by Bernier and Manucci are not necessarily incorrect, but may be due to the efficient administration of Khan-i-Dauran and Murshid Quli Khan respectively.

12. THE DIWANS AND THEIR METHOD OF REVENUE ADMINISTRATION.

List of Diwans of Orissa.

Mian Muhammad Jan, ?—1657; dismissed, lived at Baleshwar, afterwards (1661) appointed land-agent of the Subahdar, Khan-i-Dauran.

* For the *Khulasat*, see my *India of Aurangzib: Statistics, Topography and Roads*, xiv, lviii, 47, 48.

Mir Ismail, ?—October, 1660.

Mirza Ibrahim, Bakhshi, officiates as diwan also, October, 1660—March, 1661, dismissed.

Muhammad Hashim, March 1661—*c.* 1663, dismissed.

Muhammad Tahir, died in the province.

Muhammad Taqi, *c.* October, 1664—1665 ?

Khwajah Muhammad Mumin, *c.* 1665—?

Owing to the political disturbances through which the province had passed at the end of Shah Jahan's reign, the loss of financial papers, and the appointment of an almost entirely new staff of officials, the revenue department was in a very unsatisfactory and confused condition during the first few years of Aurangzib's reign. Some of the provincial diwans seem to have been inefficient, slack or dishonest; otherwise we cannot account for their rapid succession and frequent dismissal. A permanent diwan arrived in March 1661 in the person of Muhammad Hashim. This man set to work with the proverbial energy of a new broom. Proud of having been appointed from the Court by the officiating Imperial Chancellor (Rajah Raghunath), and no doubt charged with a mission to reform the administration of the department and realize the State dues fully, he reached the province with a contempt for his predecessors in office and a deep-rooted suspicion that the Subahdar had been robbing the State in collusion with the local diwans.

Muhammad Hashim, diwan, started by rudely quarrelling with Khan-i-Dauran. The Subahdar wrote to him on 1st July, 1661, "Your predecessors were

Muhammad Jan and Mir Ismail. You have called for their papers. What objection can I possibly have to giving them to you? Muhammad Jan gave up his office long ago, and has since then been living at Jajpur on account of ill-health. You complain that Mir Ibrahim, Bakhshi, has usurped and appropriated to himself some villages in the parganah of Sarsatibisi. What his agents have collected from that parganah will be paid into the imperial treasury. You write that the amil of parganah Karmul has misappropriated some money collected in that mahal. I order an inquiry to be made, and in case the allegation is found true, the man will be beaten to make him disgorge the money." (Pp. 141, 142, see also 142—145.)

The new diwan seems to have set himself up as a centre of defiance to the provincial governor's authority, and introduced confusion into the executive government. As Khan-i-Dauran wrote to him, "You have summoned the employés of the Mint to Hariharpur. Have you received any order from the Emperor to set up a Mint there? If not, send the men immediately back to Katak to do their former work." [Then follows a censure of the diwan's conduct.] "The men of the imperial artillery, starving through non-payment of their salary, have come away from the outposts where they were stationed. You should come here quickly and grant them *tan* (cash pay) according to the regulations." (Pp. 146, 147.) We learn a little later that their pay had been stopped on the plea of checking the accounts!

Even in the department of revenue collection, the inconsiderate and capricious methods of Muhammad Hashim spelt ruin to the imperial administration. As Khan-i-Dauran wrote to Aurangzib:—

"The mahals of crown-land (*khalsa*) have been reduced to desolation and their affairs have fallen into confusion, by reason of the harsh assessment (*tashkhis*) of an unsuitable amount of revenue and the neglect of attention to details by Muhammad Hashim, the diwan. The villages have been ruined by his harsh exactions. He used to transact business in this way: when a candidate for revenue-collectorship (*krori*) accepted the post, Hashim Khan used to impose on him the (paper) assessment of the parganah and send him there, before he could learn about the (actual) yield of the place. After a short time, another man was secured for the same post, and Hashim Khan, taking money for himself from this man, dismissed the former collector, appointed the second man and made him promise in writing to pay a larger revenue than the first *krori* had engaged for. After a little more time, a third man appeared, offering a still higher sum to the State, and he was sent as collector to the parganah, on his giving a bribe to Hashim Khan and signing a bond (*muchalka*) for the payment of a larger revenue! The Khan never informed the zamindars, headmen (*chaudhuris*) and ryots about this assessment (*jama-bandi*), but kept them full of anxiety and distraction as to the State demand. He has thus increased the revenue [on paper] two-fold in some places and three-fold in others, while the ryots, unable to pay, have fled [from their homes] and the villages have turned into a wilderness... When Muhammad Hashim arrived in person to make a settlement (*band-o-bast*), the ryots, already brought to death's door by his oppression and harsh exactions, [mostly] fled on hearing the news of it. Some of them, unable to pay the demand, have died under blows; most others are in prison. It is impossible for me to report [fully] the grievances of the ryots, who, having sold their wives and children, have barely succeeded in keeping body and soul together." (Pages 63, 64.)

As Muhammad Hashim refused to follow the advice of Khan-i-Dauran and reform his ways, the latter wrote to the Imperial Chancellor to remove him and appoint another *diwan* (page 65). This was done, either late in 1662 or early in 1663 (as Rajah Raghunath, to whom the Governor's letter was addressed, died on 2nd June, 1663).

13. Islam in Orissa.

The pro-Islamic ordinances issued by Aurangzib early in his reign and described in my *History of Aurangzib*, Volume III, pages 89—106, were enforced in Orissa also. On page 203 of the *Muraqat-i-Hassan* is given the text of the proclamation by which "the *faujdars*, *thanahdars*, *gumashtahs* of *jagirdars*, *amils*, *kroris*, ferrymen, road-guards, *chaudhuris*, *qanungoes* and *zamindars*, of the entire *subah* of Orissa" are told that His Majesty the Emperor had abolished the duty on "the commodities mentioned in the following schedule," for the good of his subjects, and that these officers should abstain from levying the taxes and should keep the roads open for the transit of goods, on pain of imperial displeasure and chastisement. The schedule is not given in my MS., but we know from other sources what the abolished duties were. (See page 80 of my *History of Aurangzib*, Vol. III.)

The beginning of Aurangzib's reign saw the strict restoration of the offices of Canon Law Judge (*qazi*) and Censor of Public Morals (*muhtasib*) enjoyed by Islamic rule and precedent, in every province and important town. Shaikh Junaid was appointed *muhtasib* of Katak, and his duties are described on page 196. (See also *History of Aurangzib*, III, 93, 94.) Of the *qazis* of Katak we find two names: Rahmatullah, who was dismissed for misconduct and violation of canon law, and Sayyid Muhammad Ghaus, who succeeded him both as *qazi* and *mir-i-adil*, on a salary of Rs. 4 daily, in 1665. (Pages 192—195 and 125.)

At the end of the sixteenth century, Orissa, like many other parts of Eastern India, was notorious for the castration of children and their sale as eunuchs by their mercenary parents. (Jarrett's *Ain-i-Akbari*, II, 126.) In 1668 Aurangzib issued a general order forbidding this wicked practice throughout his empire. (*Masir-i-Alamgiri*, 75.) Even some years earlier he had made the Imperial Chancellor, Rajah Raghunath Khatri, write to the Governor Khan-i-Dauran, a "letter by order" telling him that in Orissa many people used to castrate their sons, that Shuja had forbidden it during his viceroyalty, and that the *subahdar* should put a stop to the practice immediately on the receipt of this imperial order. Khan-i-Dauran replied, "I have made careful inquiries, but found no trace of this practice. They say that it has never been done in this province from ancient times to this." (Pages 75, 76.)

The Muhammadan rulers of India used to make grants of rent-free land to the holy men and scholars of their faith as "help to subsistence" (*madad-i-mash*). Several instances of this system are given in the *Muraqat*. "Shaikh Abul Khair lives like a *darvish* in a monastery in the village of Qutbpur in *sarkar* Goalpar. For the last 24 years he has been enjoying as his *madad-i-mash* a village named Darbast-Jasra in parganah Kasijurah in that *sarkar*, in accordance with the *sanads* of former governors. The papers sent by the Khan-i-Khanan (*i.e.*, Mir Jumla) to the diwan of this *subah* show the village as resumed to the State. Please move the Emperor to restore this faqir's grant." (Khan-i-Dauran to the Imperial Chancellor, pages 78, 79.) "Shaikh Bar-khurdar, a member of the Naqshbandi order and a holy monk of Katak, enjoys as his *madad-i-mash* a village yielding Rs. 317 a year, named Nur-tank in parganah Karmul, in *sarkar* Katak. I recommend for him the additional grant of one Rupee daily from the income of the *chabutra* of the *mir-i-bahar* (admiral or *ghat* officer) of Katak." (Khan-i-Dauran to the Chief Sadar of the empire, page 124.) We also have a *parwanah*, dated 13th December,

1665, conferring a *madad-i-mash* village in parganah Baqarabad, *sarkar* Katak, on Hakim Muhammad Rafi. (Page 200.)

The *Muraqat* also throws light on Aurangzib's policy of temple-destruction. On page 172 the governor writes to his agent Muhammad Jan: "The destruction of the temple of Kendrapara and the building of a mosque there has greatly pleased me." Page 202 gives the following general order for the demolition of Hindu places of worship:

"To all *faujdars*, *thanahdars*, *mutasaddis*, agents of *jagirdars*, *kroris*, and *amlas* from Katak to Medinipur on the frontier of Orissa. The imperial Paymaster Asad Khan has sent a letter written by order of the Emperor, to say that the Emperor, learning from the news-letters of the province of Orissa that at the village of Tilkuti in Medinipur a temple has been [newly] built, has issued his august mandate for its destruction and the destruction of all temples built anywhere in this province by the... infidels. Therefore, you are commanded with extreme urgency that immediately on the receipt of this letter you should destroy the above-mentioned temples. Every idol-house built during the last 10 or 12 years, whether with brick or clay, should be demolished without delay. Also, do not allow the...Hindus and...infidels to repair their old temples. Reports of the destruction of temples should be sent to the Court under the seal of the *qazis* and attested by pious Shaikhs."

14. Topographical Notes.

The following *faujdaris* or subdivisions, each under a *faujdar*, are incidentally mentioned in the *Muraqat*:—

1. Chakla Medinipur, from Medinipur to Narayangarh. (Pp. 38, 188.)

2. Remuna, on the frontier of Mayurbhanj. (Pp. 181, 109.) Five miles north-west of Balasore.

3. Katak. (P. 137.)

4. Pipli Niur, beyond the Katjhuri river. (P. 52.) Twenty-two miles due north of Puri.

5. Padishahnagar, beyond the Katjhuri river. (P. 52.)

6. Pachhera (P. 62.) *Panchira*, west of the Baitarani, 24 miles west of Bhadrak and 3 miles west of Killah Amboh; it stood at the gate of the kingdom of Keonjhar when proceeding from the east.

7. Sarang-garh and Sandhahpur ['Sarangerh and Santrapur' of Stirling, page 49.] (Page 82.)

8. Talmal. (Pp. 145, 156, 163.)

9. Malud, "on the frontier facing the Deccan." (Pp. 81, 158, 160, 162.) South of Lake Chilka, 19.33N. 85.19E.

All the above are mentioned by Stirling (48, 49) as Mughal thanahs, with the exception of *Padishahnagar*, the nearest approach to which in Stirling's list is *Alemghir Shirgerh*.

We also learn that Soroh was on the frontier of Bhadrak and Lakhanpur on that of Keonjhar (*Muraqat*, pp. 41, 59.) As to *Khalikot* or *Kailikot*, Stirling (page

45) mentions the zamindari of *Kalicote* as "a Hill Estate, now under the Ganjam District. Separated from Orissa about 1730." Fifteen miles due north of Ganjam Town.

Mansurgarh.—I find a *Mansur-Kota* 12 miles south-west of Ganjam and 8 miles due east of Berhampur.

Hariharpur.—Nine miles south of Baripada (in the Mayurbhanj State.)

Narsinghpur.—North of the Mahanadi 20.27N. 85.7E.

Nilgiri.—Eleven miles south-west of Balasore.

Soroh.—On the railway line, midway between Balasore and Bhadrak.

Khurda.—The old fort stands 5½ miles west of the Khurda Road station.

Kujang.—20.14E. 86.34E. on the seacoast.

Dompara.—19 miles south-west west of Katak.

Malipara.—Eleven miles south south-east of Dompara.

Kaluparah.—"Gurr Kalloparra" of *Indian Atlas*, sheet 116, 5 miles south-east of the Khurda Road station.

Mutri.—"Mootooree" of the *Atlas*, 1 mile north-west of Kalloparra.

Khurdiha.—"Gurr gorodhea" of the *Atlas*, 2 miles south-west of Kalloparra.

Bani.—On the south bank of the Mahanadi, 23 miles south-west west of Katak.

Ranpur.—20.4N. 85.25E.

Talmal.—At the north-east corner of Lake Chilka, 15 miles north-west west of Puri.

Harishpur Garh.—On the seacoast, 20.4N. 86.29E.

Kanika.—Along the seacoast, north of Point Palmyras and south of 21N. Latitude.

Kulrah.—"Khulardah" of *Atlas*, 8 miles south south-east of Katak.

Bhanpur.—Fourteen miles north of Kalikot. (Sheet 107.)

Rawata.—There is a parganah "Raootrah" in *Atlas*, due north-east of Balasore, across the river. (Sheet 115.)

A GREAT HINDU MEMOIR-WRITER.

I. Family History.

The complete official history of the reign of the Emperor Aurangzib (1657-1707 A.D.) was written from State papers and personal recollections by Muhammad Saqi Mustaid Khan only three years after that Emperor's death. It is invaluable for dates, names of persons and places, the proper sequence of events, and official changes and administrative regulations. But it is a small volume, devoting only ten pages to the affairs of one year of the reign of a sovereign who was one of the most active and ambitious rulers of the world and effected such momentous changes in Northern India and Southern India alike. A chapter of this work is therefore usually a dry list of official appointments and changes (exactly like the Government Gazettes of the present day) and a bare summary of events following one another in rapid succession. It tells us nothing about the real circumstances under which the events took place, their true causes and effects, the condition of the people and the state of the country.

For these latter points the most valuable contemporary history of Aurangzib is the *Nuskha-i-Dilkasha* written by a Hindu named Bhimsen, who was a hereditary civil officer of the Mughal Government, passed his life in the Mughal cities and camps of the Deccan, and visited most places of India from Cape Comorin to Delhi. This work contains very important, and often unique information about many historical personages and events of the time and topographical details. The British Museum, London, has a complete manuscript of the *Dilkasha*, hastily but correctly written (*Or.* 23). The copy belonging to the India Office Library, London, is less correct and covers only the first half of the book, ending abruptly with the capture of Golkonda in 1687. (No. 94, Ethe's Catalogue 445.) The Bibliotheque Nationale, Paris, has another and a complete copy (Suppl. 259, Blochet's Catalogue 602.) No other MS. of it is known to exist. An abridged and incorrect English translation of a part of it was published under the title of *Journal of a Boondelah Officer*, in Jonathan Scott's *History of the Deccan*, (Shrewsbury, 1794.)

Bhimsen's father, Raghunandandas was one of the six sons of Jivmal, a Kayastha of the Saksena section, the other five being Bhagwandas, Shyamdas, Gokuldas, Haridas and Dharamdas. Of these Bhagwandas rose to the highest position then open to a Hindu. He was appointed *Diwan* (Chancellor) of Mughal Deccan with the title of *Dianat Ray* (=Baron Honesty) in 1657, accompanied Aurangzib from the Deccan during his march northwards to contest the throne of Delhi, and lived at that capital with the court till his death in 1664. He had every expectation of being appointed chief Diwan of the Empire, but when Aurangzib confined his old father in Agra Fort (June, 1658), Ray-i-rayan Raghunath Rai, the Assistant Diwan, who had been doing all the duties of the Imperial Diwan, deserted to the prince, and his timely treachery was rewarded by his being given the post of the chief Diwan of the Empire, though without the title. Thus Dianat Ray lost his highest hope.

Raghunandan was *musharraf* of the imperial artillery of the Deccan, a post which he resigned about 1670, in order to pass his old age in religious meditation, dying at Aurangabad in 1674.

Genealogy of the family:—

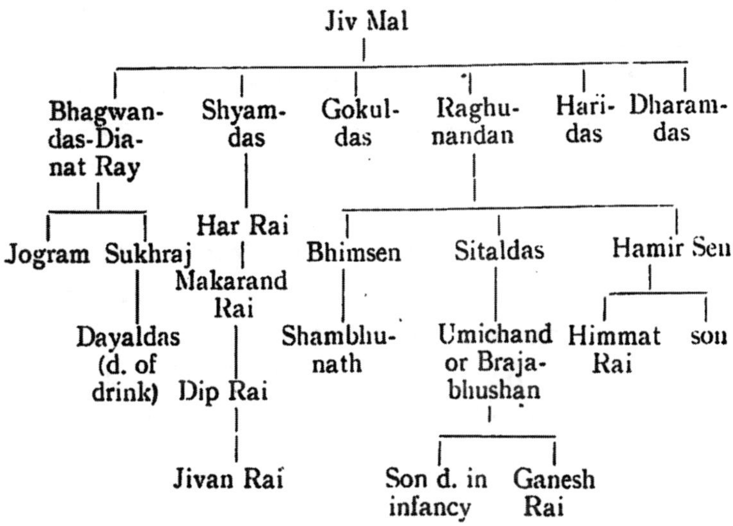

II. Early Life.

Bhimsen was born at Burhanpur on the Tapti (the capital of Khandesh) in Samvat 1705 (1649 A.D.), and at the age of eight he left this place to join his father at Aurangabad. That was an eventful year (1657). The crown of Delhi was changing hands and the boy retained a vivid recollection of the "rumours of war" in Northern

India that agitated the citizens of Aurangabad. At the age of ten he paid a visit to the Nasik caves and Trimbak fort in his father's company. The death of Dianat Ray at Delhi (1664) dashed down to the ground all the hopes of high promotion cherished by his family. His eldest son Jogram was appointed by the Emperor *musharraf* of the Elephants,—no very high post; but died in a few years. Then Sukhraj, the younger son of Dianat Ray, was appointed *musharraf* of the Imperial Drink and Betel leaf Departments.

At Aurangabad Bhimsen received his education in Persian from his ninth to his fifteenth year, under the care of his father. Then, for seven years he acted as his father's deputy. Raghunandan was growing old and weak, and felt himself unable to attend his office and do his duties as *musharraf* of Artillery. Fearing that the Emperor would be angry if he heard that Raghunandan was staying at home, while his office work was being actually done by a youth of 21, he resigned (1670).

Young Bhimsen had now to look out for some employment and turned to many patrons of his family, but in vain. At last he secured the post of *musharraf* of muster and branding of horses in the division of Daud Khan Quraishi, immediately under Mir Abdul Mabud, the Paymaster (*bakhshi*) of that general. He had to pay a large bribe to get the post and had also to run into debt to engage and equip followers in a manner worthy of his post and mansab. He started for Daud Khan's camp at Junnar, but met him on the way and returned with him to Aurangabad to the court of Prince Muazzam, the Viceroy of the Deccan. But now a bitter quarrel broke out between the Prince and his general Dilir Khan, the latter being supported by Daud Khan. Thus the projected expedition under Daud Khan was abandoned, and Bhimsen's new post was abolished. But Maharajah Jaswant Singh very kindly took him into his service, and they set off together northwards to the Tapti in pursuit of Dilir Khan. Bhimsen took this opportunity of revisiting his birthplace Burhanpur, and then returned to Aurangabad, Sept. 1670.

III. Official Employment.

A few days afterwards, Daud Khan was detached by the Prince to intercept Shivaji on his return from the second loot of Surat. Bhimsen accompanied this army as clerk (*peshdast*) to the Bakhshi in addition to his former post, and was present at the battle of Vani-Dindori in which the Mughals were defeated by Shivaji with heavy slaughter. Then he went with Daud Khan's force to Nasik and Ahmadnagar.

After some time the Khan marched to Ankai Tankai (near the Manmad junction) to check the Marathas who were active near the forts of the Chandor range, such as Dhodap. Thence he hastened into Baglana to raise the siege of Salhir. During this march our author was separated from the army and in great danger of being cut off; but he was saved by Nur Khan, a Muhammadan mercenary of the Maratha army, who had formerly been befriended by his father at Aurangabad. Daud Khan arrived too late to save Salhir from being captured by Shivaji, but continued fighting near the Chandor range for some time and took the fort of Ahivant.

A letter now arrived from the Emperor accepting the Prince's recommendation that Bhimsen should be appointed *musharraf* of *muster and branding.* Jaswant had induced the Prince to make this proposal. But through the machinations of the Hindu favourites of Mahabat Khan, the new commander-in-chief of the Deccan, the post was conferred on a son of Brindaban (the son of Dara's diwan). The cup was thus snatched away from the lips of Bhimsen and he had to pass a long time in unemployment and distress, but his high-placed friends helped him with money.

After a time Bahadur Khan, the new Viceroy of the Deccan, (1672) gave that post to Bhimsen and he held it for many years afterwards.

In the course of the pursuit of the Marathas who had raided Ramgir (110 miles north-east of Haidarabad) in November, 1672, Bhimsen had a marvellous adventure with a *darvish* which reads like a romance. For the next two years he made much money and lived in great happiness and comfort; "even great nobles could not live in that style" as he brags! But a succession of bereavements overtook him soon afterwards: he lost his uncle Gokuldas (a few years earlier), his brother Sitaldas, and his father Raghunandan, then Har Rai and Har Rai's father Shyamdas.

For a long time Bhimsen had been childless. So, he adopted as his own, a son of his younger brother Sitaldas, who was born in 1671 and named Umichand by the astrologers and Brajabhushan by our author. In 1678 this little child was married.

In 1686 Bhimsen, tired of work, left his office duties in the imperial army to be discharged by his agents (*gumashtas*) and went to live with his family at Naldurg, a fort 25 miles north-east of Sholapur. Here in 1688 a son was born to him and named Shambhunath; but Brajabhushan, whom he had adopted as his son, continued to be cherished as a member of his family, like his eldest son.

IV. Serves Dalpat Rao Bundela.

Soon afterwards, Bhimsen left Naldurg and joined the Mughal army at Sholapur. At this place he was taken into the service of Dalpat Rao, the Bundela chieftain of Datia and an important general in Aurangzib's army, as his private secretary and "man of business." Lands yielding Rs. 12,000 a year were given to him as his salary, evidently in Bundelkhand. [Bhimsen does not seem to have resigned his post in the imperial army.] The connection thus begun continued till Dalpat's death eighteen years later.

In the company of Dalpat Rao, who was lieutenant to Aurangzib's foremost general Zulfiqar Khan Bahadur Nusrat Jang (the son of Asad Khan), our author marched through jungles to Jinji (in the South Arcot District) in 1691. The siege of this fort by the Mughal army was soon abandoned (for a time), and Dalpat with Bhimsen went to Wandiwash and then to Madras for treatment under the celebrated European doctors of the place. The Rao was not cured and returned after losing much money. The Italian traveller Niccolao Manucci, who had set up as a doctor without any medical knowledge, says that Dalpat's agent was deceived by a selfish middleman and did not consult him but went to some other quack, and hence his failure! (*Storia do Mogor*, iii. 139.)

The business of Dalpat Rao brought Bhimsen from Madras to the imperial camp at Brahmapuri on the Bhima river, 18 miles south-east of Pandharpur. After finishing it, he returned quickly to Jinji, only to come to Naldurg again for the marriage of his son Shambhunath (celebrated at Haidarabad.) Soon after going back to Jinji he retraced his steps and travelled to Agra on a mission of Dalpat Rao, and on his return he stopped at Naldurg. To this district Dalpat Rao came after the fall of Jinji in 1698, and our author joined him. During the journeys of these eight years, Bhimsen visited most of the famous temples and cities of the Madras Presidency and Northern India, and he has left short but extremely valuable descriptions of them as they were two hundred and thirty years ago.

About the middle of 1698, a Mughal army was sent to besiege Panhala, a fort 10 miles north of Kolhapur. During the enforced idleness of the siege, Bhimsen began to write his History in his tent at the foot of Panhala. But the long wars of Aurangzib had made the

Deccan desolate, famine and disorder raged everywhere; the government seemed to have collapsed. It was not safe to live amidst such anarchy. Bhimsen, therefore, sent his whole family from Naldurg, at first to Aurangabad and then to Dalpat Rao's capital Datia (1706).

V. Last Years.

Next year Aurangzib died; his third son Azam crowned himself in the Deccan and set out with his army to seize Delhi and Agra. But at Jajau, 20 miles south of Agra, he was defeated and slain by his elder brother Bahadur Shah I. (8th June, 1707.) On that fatal field, a cannon ball passed through the body of Dalpat Rao killing him and wounding in the arm Bhimsen, who was sitting on the same elephant behind the Rao. Our author, though wounded, burnt his master's body at Dhamsi, 16 miles south of Agra, and then retired to Datia with all his hopes crushed. To make matters worse, a war broke out between the two sons of Dalpat for the *gadi*. Bhimsen in disgust left Datia with his family and came to Gwalior. As the right-hand man of Dalpat, who was a most influential partisan of Azam Shah, Bhimsen had been created by that prince a commander of five hundred, and he would have risen still higher if his patron had triumphed at Jajau.

But now he was thrown out of employment and put to great distress for his daily bread. After trying in vain for a post under Bahadur Shah I., he succeeded in getting his sons Brajabhushan and Shambhunath enrolled (as petty clerks) in the service of Prince Khujista Akhtar Jahan Shah, through the kind help of Ray-i-rayan Gujar Mal, and returned home to lead a life of religious meditation. We know nothing of his death, nor of the after history of his family. But the genealogical tree given above may be a means of tracing his living descendants, if my readers at Datia, Gwalior, Burhanpur and Aurangabad make inquiries and write to me.

VI. As a Writer.

The value of Bhimsen's History lies in his extensive and accurate personal observation and his position. As a clerk in the Mughal army of the Deccan and the friend of many generals and other high officers, he secured correct official information and learnt many a State secret, while his situation at a distance from the throne and the fact of his History not having been written for the Emperor's eyes placed him above the temptation to omit or disguise facts discreditable to the Government or write a fulsome eulogy on the Emperor and his courtiers. He is thus free from the worst defects of the official histories of the Mughal emperors. Bhimsen knew the truth and could afford to tell it. He has also given true sketches of the characters of the various historical personages of the time and pointed out their defects. His reflective mind and Hindu creed enabled him to look with the eyes of a neutral spectator at the events of Aurangzib's reign and to narrate their true causes and effects. Above all, his account of many incidents of the Mughal warfare in the Deccan is as valuable as the reports of the "Eye witness" in the present European war. Indeed, he is our only source of detailed information about them.

Things which the pompous official historians of the day scorned to mention,—such as the prices of food, the amusements of the people, the condition of the roads, and the social life of the official class,—are described here only. For Deccan history in the late 17th century, he is invaluable.

The character of Bhimsen as a man is unfolded in his Memoirs without any disguise. We see his weakness, but we also see his strong fidelity to friend and master, his devotion to his kith and kin, his love of children and his devout faith in Hinduism. Bhimsen was a charming character, tender, unpretentious, frank and serene, loving social gaiety but also deeply touched by sorrow. If it be true that "the style is the man," then we must highly praise this master of a simple business-like prose, in which there are no useless flowers of rhetoric, no profuse wordiness, no round-about expression, but plenty of accurate observation and concise but clear statement of all essential points. These are rare qualities in a Persian writer.

AN OLD HINDU HISTORIAN OF AURANGZIB.

There are two extremely valuable contemporary histories of Aurangzib's reign (1657-1707 A.D.), written in Persian but by Hindus. One is the *Nuskha-i-Dilkasha* by Bhimsen, a Kayasth, born at Burhanpur, and the other is the *Fatuhat-i-Alamgiri* composed by Ishwar-das of Patan in Gujrat. Of the latter only one manuscript is known to exist in the world, *viz.*, British Museum Pers. MS. Additional No. 23,884. It contains 329 pages of 11 lines each. I have made a full translation of it into English, which I intend to publish. The great importance of these two historians lies not only in their looking at the reign through the eyes of contemporary Hindus, but also in their living near enough to the great Mughal officers to learn the historical events of the time accurately, but not near enough to the throne to be lying flatterers.

Ishwar-das, a Nagar Brahman and inhabitant of the city of Patan in the *subah* of Gujrat (now in the Gaekwar's dominions), served Shaikh-ul-Islam from his youth up to his 30th year. This Shaikh, as the Chief Qazi of the Empire, used to accompany the Emperor Aurangzib in camp and court alike, and Ishwar-das in the train of his master got good opportunities of learning the true facts of Indian history directly from the chief officials of the time or their servants. We know from the official record of Aurangzib's reign (entitled the *Masir-i-Alamgiri*) that Shaikh-ul-Islam acted as

Chief Qazi in succession to his deceased father Abdul Wahhab (a Borah) from December 1675 to November 1683, when he resigned his post on account of the Emperor rejecting his advice not to fight with brother-Muslims like the sultans of Bijapur and Golkonda, as that would be a sin according to the *Quran*. In December 1684, the Shaikh set out on a pilgrimage to Mecca, and Ishwar-das now took service under Shujaet Khan who was Viceroy of Gujrat from 1684 to 1701. As he was in his 30th year at this time he must have been born in 1655 A.D., and his history was completed in 1731, when he was seventy-six years old. It is interesting to note that Khafi Khan's famous history of the Mughal Empire was also completed within four years of this date.

Shujaet Khan employed Ishwar-das as *amin* and *shiqdar* (revenue-collector) in certain *mahals* of the Jodhpur *parganah* which the Emperor had annexed on the death of Jaswant Singh in December, 1678. This position brought Ishwar-das into frequent contact with the Rathors and, as he tells us in his History, a strong friendship sprang up between him and them. From this cause came his life's chance of official reward and elevation to the rank of a *mansabdar*.

We all know, that Aurangzib's fourth son, Muhammad Akbar, rebelled in 1681, but being defeated fled to the Maratha court (and finally to Persia), leaving his infant son Buland Akhtar and daughter Safiyat-un-nissa in the hands of the Rajputs. These were tenderly brought up in a secret nook by Durgadas Rathor, the guardian and champion of Ajit Singh, the young heir to the Jodhpur throne. Aurangzib was ever eager to recover his grand-children and thus preserve his family-honour. At the same time, Durgadas was worn out by the constant war with the Mughals and the devastation of his country.

The rest of the story we shall give in the words of Ishwar-das:—

"His (*i.e.*, Durgadas's) days of suffering were over and his happy days arrived. So (in 1698) he sent a letter to the author of this book,......stating that if Shujaet Khan gave him a safe-conduct and spared his home from harm pending the Emperor's orders on his petition (for forgiveness), he would send Safiyat-un-nissa Begam to the Imperial Court. The Emperor at once acceded to the proposal......The author (*i.e.*, Ishwar-das), on the arrival of the Emperor's reply, by order of the Khan visited Durgadas, who was living in a place extremely difficult of access, persuaded him with wise advice, confirmed him in his good resolution, and returning to the Khan, took proper escort and conveyances back with him for conducting the princess to her grandfather. As the Begam had been pleased with his slave's services and arrangements, she asked him to accompany her to the Imperial Court......Arrived there, the Begam informed Aurangzib that Durgadas had been so attentive to her as to get for her a Muhammadan tutoress from Ajmir, under whose tuition she had already read the

Quran, and committed it to memory. This fact convinced the Emperor of Durgadas's devotion and induced him to forgive all his past offences. The imperial grace gushed forth and he asked, "Tell me what Durgadas wants?" The Begam answered that Ishwar-das knew it. His Majesty at once ordered me to be presented to him in his private chamber by Qazi Abdullah, the friend of Shujaet Khan. Next day, I was honoured with an audience and reported Durgadas's prayer to receive a *mansab* and allowance. It was granted; and this humble atom (*i.e.*, Ishwar-das) was also created a commander of 200 horse in rank (*zat*), invested with a robe of honour (*khilat*), and sent to bring Buland Akhtar and Durgadas to the presence......On my return to Ahmadabad I was rewarded by Shujaet Khan, too. Repeatedly visiting Durgadas, I took solemn oaths on behalf of the Khan, and reassured his mind with promises. Durgadas, on getting *parwanahs* conferring *jagirs* on himself and being put in actual possession of the *mahals* assigned to him, came with me to Ahmadabad. The Prince and Durgadas were conducted by the author to Surat, where many officers deputed by the Emperor met the Prince in advance, both to welcome him and also to teach him court-etiquette. But the Prince continued to behave like a dumb and awkward clownish lad, and the court doctors failed to remedy his defect.

When Durgadas arrived at the portico of the Audience Hall, the Emperor ordered him to be ushered unarmed (like a prisoner or suspect). Durgadas, without a moment's hesitation or objection, took his sword off. Hearing this, His Majesty ordered him to come in with his arms on! When he entered the tent, [the finance minister] Ruhullah Khan was ordered to meet him in advance and present him. The Khan conducted him to the Emperor after binding his wrists together with a handkerchief. [This was a mummery by which the offender had to beg the royal pardon, appearing like a captive of war or criminal under arrest. The reader will remember how the representatives of the citizens of Calais had to make submission to Edward III. by appearing with halters round their necks. It was, in Mughal India, a merely theatrical action, intended to soothe the imperial dignity].

His Majesty now graciously ordered Durgadas's arms to be united, promoted him to be a commander of 3,000 horse (in rank, with an actual contingent of 2,500 troopers), and gave him a jewelled dagger, a *padak* (gold pendant), and a string of pearls,—and an order on the Imperial Treasury for one *lakh* of rupees.

The author, too, was favoured by the Emperor with a robe of honour and a promotion of 50 horsemen in rank and ten troopers in his actual following, and was given a *jagir* in Mairtha (in Marwar, west of Ajmir.)"

So, Ishwar-das became a commander of 250 horse in rank, in reward of his success in diplomacy. This account of himself is also supported by the Persian history, *Mirat-i-Ahmadi*, p. 350-351. We know nothing further of our author. The colophon of his book tells us that he completed it on 21st Rabi-ul-awwal, 12th year of the reign of Muhammad Shah, 1143 A. H. (=1731 A.D.), "as a memorial of Mehta Ishwar-das of the Nagar caste,...and for the information of Lala Khush-hal." Now, a Persian work entitled *Dastur-ul-aml-i-Shahanshahi* mentions a certain Lala Sahib, the son of Braja Rai, the son of Ishwar-das. If this Lala Sahib was Lala Khush-hal, we can conclude that our author in his old age composed his reminiscences of the grand times in which he had lived, for the information of his grandson, who must have pressed him to tell the story of the famous Aurangzib's reign.

Contents of Ishwar-das's History with references to the folios of the MS. :—

Emperor treacherously destroys the eyesight of Ghaziuddin Khan Bahadur Firuz Jang with the help of the Court doctor. . . . . . . (145*a*)

Campaign against Shambhuji. . . . . (146*b*)

Capture and execution of Shambhu. . . . . . (149*b*)

Capture of many Maratha forts. . . . . (156*b*)

Flight of Rajaram, the brother of Shambhuji. . . (159*b*)

Aghar Khan slain near Agra. . . . . (164*b*)

Submission of Durgadas; Ishwar-das has audience of the Emperor and is rewarded. . . . (165*a*)

(The book ends on 169*a*.)

WILLIAM IRVINE, THE HISTORIAN OF THE LATER MUGHALS.

HIS CAREER.

William Irvine, the son of a Scotch advocate, was born in Aberdeen on 5th July, 1840. He came to London when quite a child, and after leaving school at the early age of fifteen he went into business, until he obtained an appointment in the Admiralty at nineteen. He stayed there for a year or two; but having acquired a very good knowledge of French and German, he eventually resigned, went to King's College, London, to complete his studies, and entering for the Indian Civil Service he passed very high in the examination of 1862.

Arriving in India on 12th December, 1863, he was attached to the North-Western Provinces Civil Service in the following June, as Assistant Magistrate of Saharanpur. After spending nearly a year there, he was sent to Muzaffarnagar, for four years (April 1865—July 1869.) A long furlough to Europe consumed more than two years, 1872 and 1873. He next served in Farrukhabad (June 1875—April 1879) where he rose to be Joint Magistrate. He had already begun to study Indo-Muḥammadan history with scholarly seriousness, and the first fruits of his work in this line were an accurate and luminous Account of the Bangash Nawwabs of Farrukhabad published in the *Journal of the Asiatic Society of Bengal*, 1878—79, and some valuable Chapters contributed to the *Gazetteer of the*

Farrukhabad District, edited by Mr. Atkinson and issued by Government in 1880.

But Ghazipur was the district with which he was connected longest, namely for seven years. Here he first served as Settlement Officer and then as Collector, and left a memorial of his work in a blue-book, *The Settlement Report of Ghazipur District*, 1886. His keenness in revenue work and his application to detail are evidenced by his article on *Canal Rates versus Land Revenue* published in the *Calcutta Review*, 1869, and a volume entitled *The Rent Digest or the Law of Procedure relating to Landlord and Tenant, Bengal Presidency*, 1869.

His literary attainments and painstaking exertions as a revenue officer, did not, however, bring him any of the prize posts in the Civil Service, for which an officer of his unusual parts might have reasonably hoped. So, he retired as soon as he qualified for pension, leaving the service on 27th March 1888, as Magistrate of Saharanpur,—curiously enough the same district that he had joined at the beginning of his official career. Out of his twenty-five years of service, almost exactly one-fifth was spent on leave.

LITERARY WORK IN ENGLAND.

At his retirement he was only 48, and looked forward to many years of health and leisure which could be devoted to literary work. Already while in India he had perfected his knowledge of Persian, and, what was much more difficult, he had become proficient in reading manuscripts written in that tongue. He had also begun to collect Persian historical MSS., in addition to printed and lithographed works in Urdu and Hindi having even the remotest connection with the Mughal period. During his official career many Indian gentlemen, knowing his special taste, sought to please him by presenting Persian MSS., and he also purchased them both in India and in England. Besides, he kept in his pay a Muhammadan scribe of Bhitari Sayyidpur (Ghazipur District), to hunt for and copy such Persian MSS. as could not be had for love or money. Transcripts were also made for him of those rare MSS. of the Royal Library, Berlin, which he required for his historical researches. Thus it happened that he made a collection of original MS. authorities on his special period which was unapproached by any of the public libraries of Europe.

To take only one example, he had two MSS. of the Anecdotes of Aurangzib (*Ahkam-i-Alamgiri*) ascribed to Hamiduddin Khan Nimchah, which is not to be found in any public library of India or Europe, and of whose existence historians were unaware, though it is a work extremely characteristic of the Emperor and gives information of first-rate importance concerning his life and opinions. I was happy to have been able to discover another fragment of this work and to present a transcript of it to him. Again, of the *Chahar Gulshan*, a rare 18th century volume on the topography and statistics of the Mughal Empire, I could find only one copy in India, (that belonging to the Khuda Bakhsh Library), and had to base a portion of my *India of Aurangzib* on this single manuscript. But Mr. Irvine possessed three MSS. of it,—two of them having been presented to him by Indian friends. After I had made his acquaintance, whenever I came upon any find of rare Persian MSS. on Indian history, he was sure to secure a copy of them for himself. Thus I was the means of enriching his private library with transcripts of Mirza Rajah Jai Singh's letters (*Haft Anjuman*), the orders issued by Aurangzib in his old age and collected by his secretary Inayetullah Khan (*Ahkam-i-Alamgiri*), the letters of Shah Jahan and his sons as preserved in the *Faiyaz-ul-qawanin*, and the epistles of the Persian King Shah Abbas II. As Mr. Irvine wrote to me,—

"What you tell me about your various finds of MSS. makes my mouth water, and I shall be very grateful if you can engage any one to copy for me Inayetullah Khan's *Ahkam* and the various fragments you have of Hamiduddin's collection. The *Haft Anjuman* seems to be a valuable and most unexpected discovery. I have scolded Abdul Aziz [his retained scribe]—whose special hunting ground is Benares,—for not having discovered it !!" (*Letter*, 13 Nov., 1918.)

His *Later Mughals*.

With such a wealth of original Persian sources in his possession and his knowledge of continental tongues opening to him the East Indian records of the Dutch, French and Portuguese Governments, as well as those of the Christian missions to the East (especially the letters of the Society of Jesus), Mr. Irvine planned an original history of the decline of the Mughal Empire. It was entitled *The Later Mughals* and intended to cover the century from the death of Aurangzib in 1707 to the capture of Delhi by the English in 1803. As he wrote to me on 23rd February, 1902:

"I have first to finish the History from 1707 to 1803 which I began twelve years ago. At present I have not got beyond 1738, in my draft, though I have materials collected up to 1759 or even later."

But the work grew in his hands, and so conscientious a workman was he, so many sources of information did he consult, and so often did he verify his references, that his progress was slow and he lived to complete the narrative of only fourteen years out of the century he intended to embrace in his work. Chapters of *The Later Mughals* appeared from time to time in the *Indian Antiquary*, and the *Asiatic Quarterly Review*, but mainly in the *Journal of the Asiatic Society of Bengal*. Five years after writing the above to me, he thus speaks of the state of his undertaking in the *L'envoi* to its last published chapter (*J. A. S. B.*, November, 1908):

"With the disappearance of the Sayyid brothers the story attains a sort of dramatic completeness; and I decide to suspend at this point my contributions on the history of the Later Mughals. There is reason to believe that a completion of my original intention is beyond my remaining strength. I planned on too large a scale, and it is hardly likely now that I shall be able to do much more...The first draft for the years 1721 to 1738 is written. I hope soon to undertake the narrative of 1739, ncluding the invasion of Nadir Shah. It remains to be seen whether I shall be able to continue the story for the years which follow Nadir Shah's departure. But I have read and translated and made notes for another twenty years ending about 1759 or 1760."

These words were written in October 1907, and they show that the work had not grown at all during the preceding five years. What lured Mr. Irvine from the *Later Mughals* was his monumental edition of Niccolao Manucci's Travels in the Mughal Empire, the *Storia do Mogor*,—a work which entailed seven years of hard labour and about which I shall speak later. Another but lesser source of distraction was his monograph *The Army of the Indian Mughals*,—a thoroughly sound and scholarly work, which will long endure as an indispensable dictionary of Persian, Turki and Hindi military technical terms. He hurriedly brought together in it the fruits of long years of study, lest he should be anticipated by Dr. Paul Horn, an eminent German Orientalist, who had published a similar work on an earlier period of Muhammadan India. Chips from Mr. Irvine's workshop were also published in the *Indian Antiquary*, the *Indian Magazine* (1903), the *Journal of the Moslem Institute* (Calcutta), and the *Journal of the Asiatic Society of Bengal*. Thorough in everything that he undertook, his careful editing and annotation cost him an immense amount of time even in the case of these bye-products of his historical factory.

Left a Fragment.

But the students of Indian history must lament that

Mr. Irvine ever set his hand to the *Storia* and the *Army of the Indian Mughals;* these books prevented the continuation of *The Later Mughals* to the date, 1756, after which the Persian records cease to be of first-rate value and we get fuller light from the documents in the European tongues. In these Persian records lay the special strength of Mr. Irvine. He had spent a life in collecting, mastering and arranging them; and his death robbed the world of all his garnered knowledge. His successor in the same field will have to begin at the very beginning and to spend years in going over the same materials, and can arrive at Mr. Irvine's position only after twenty years of preliminary study. If Mr. Irvine had rigorously shunned all such diversions of his attention and pushed on with his grand work, he could in his remaining years have placed on record his life's accumulation of information and reflection on the decline and fall of the Mughal Empire, and completed its history at least up to its practical extinction about the middle of the 18th century. But he has not done it; and for probably 30 years to come we have little chance of his unfinished task being carried to completion with anything approaching the high standard of fulness and accuracy he attained in the portion he lived to write. In this respect the world is distinctly the poorer for his having undertaken to edit Manucci.

For the last eight years of his life Mr. Irvine was haunted by a sad foreboding that his days on earth were numbered and that the chosen work of his life was destined to remain a fragment. In letter after letter he urged me to hurry on with my own historical work if I wished him to see it.

"At my age I cannot afford to lose any time, as I fear not surviving to finish the long and heavy tasks I have on hand." (18th March, 1904).

"I see every reason to believe that your edition of the Alamgir letters will be a thorough, good piece of work,—but I trust it will not be too long delayed,—for I am getting old and shall not last very much longer." (16 Jan. 1906).

"I hope that your first volume of *Aurangzib* may appear before I leave the scene." (29 Jan. 1909).

At last in October, 1907 he mournfully admitted that he had not enough strength left to complete his original plan, and that he was not likelv to write much more of *The Later Mughals* than the portion already sent to the press. Things looked a little more hopefully for him in the warm weather of 1910. As he wrote on 8th July—

"Thanks for your enquiries about my health. Decay has not come on so rapidly as I thought it would. The complain I suffer from is under control and apparently no worse than was five years ago,—and considering I was 70 three days ago, I have a fair amount of activity, bodily and mental, left to me In fact I am contemplating this next winter writing out my Bahadur Shah chapter (1707—1712) and sending it to the Asiatic Society of Bengal."

But unfortunately the hope was delusive. On the last day of the year he was taken very ill. For some time it was expected that he might recover a certain amount of health and strength. In the summer of 1911 he was a little better and appeared to be getting stronger. On 31st August he wrote to me,

"I am coming downstairs once a day for 4 or 5 hours . . . . . I am working on quietly and happily. My upper part—heart, lungs and liver, are declared by the specialist to be quite clear and likely to go on [doing their] work so long well that I may reasonably [hope for] a continued life of five to ten years. So it is worth while going on as I shall be able to finish one thing or [another.]"

The improvement, however, was temporary. Since the autumn set in, he began to fail rapidly and it was realised that he could not last the winter. He bore his long and trying illness with admirable patience and fortitude, and passed away quietly at last on Friday, 3rd November, 1911.

Since S. R. Gardiner died with the cry "My history! Oh, my history!" there has been no such sad case of a monumental work undertaken with the fulness of knowledge but cut short by the cruel hand of death. For Gardiner, however, there was the consolation that he had arrived almost within sight of his goal, the Restoration, and was leaving a not unworthy disciple and continuer in Prof. Firth. This consolation was denied to the closing years of William Irvine.

His edition of Manucci's Travels.

Of all Mr. Irvine's works the *Travels of Manucci* (*Storia do Mogor*) is most appreciated by the European public, and with them, strangely enough, it is his chief title to fame as a scholar. This attitude is well represented by the *Pioneer* (18th November, 1911), which thus notices his death:—

"At Home Mr. Irvine's name outside a small circle of students must have been as nearly as possible unknown when the first two volumes of his Manucci appeared in 1907 and were at once recognised as the most valuable and important work of the kind that had seen the light since the publication of Col. Yule's Marco Polo. . . . His reputation as a scholar had been already established, and it stands on an enduring basis. . . . It is not likely that any other English edition of Manucci's work will ever be forthcoming to supersede that of Mr. Irvine."

The editor's work is a marvel of industry and accurate scholarship. It seems incredible that one man could have done it all, and a reviewer has well remarked, "The notes appear to have been written by *a syndicate of scholars* instead of by one man only." Mr. Irvine's notes and appendices are often of more value than Manucci's text, as they contain the fullest and most accurate information available in any European tongue, about the details of the reign of Shah Jahan, Aurangzib and Shah Alam, with exact dates and references to authorities. Every person who crossed the orbit of Manucci or Manucci's acquaintances even for a moment, has his life unfolded here with a wealth of accurate detail. Indeed, it may be rightly said of William Irvine that he left no part of Indian history from 1650 to 1750 untouched, and touched nothing that he did not illumine. Writers on Indian history who are ignorant of Persian would do well to study the notes in the *Storia* and the *Later Mughals* and carefully correct their own statements in the light of the information there collected.

History of Manucci's MSS.

Before Mr. Irvine rediscovered Manucci's MSS. at Berlin and Venice, that Italian traveller had been known to the world only through the pirated and incorrect French version made by Catrou, and scholars had been sighing for the recovery of the original text as a thing hardly to be hoped for. The history of Manucci's book reads like a romance.

Niccolao Manucci had left Venice in November, 1653 at the age of fourteen as a stowaway. Reaching India in January 1656, he took service under prince Dara Shukoh and latterly under Shah Alam. At intervals he set up practice as a doctor without any medical training, travelled all over India, went through various adventures and changes of fortune, and passed his old age at Madras and Pondicherry, dying in 1717. Thus his life in India covered more than sixty years.

At different times he wrote his history of the Mughals (*Storia do Mogor*) in Portuguese, French and Italian,—about one-third of the whole work having been drawn up originally in his mother tongue Italian, and nearly the whole being rewritten in Portuguese mixed with French. It consists of five Parts, dealing with

(i) the author's journey from Venice to Delhi and a short chronicle of the Mughal emperors down to the accession of Aurangzib,

(ii) the reign of Aurangzib, with the author's personal history,

(iii) the Mughal court, its system of government and revenue, much mixed up with digressions on European companies, the Hindu religion, Indian animals, the Catholics in India, &c.,

(iv) current events in the Mughal camp in the Deccan from 1701, with long accounts of the doings of the Jesuits and other Catholics,

(v) events in 1705 and in 1706, with many stories of earlier years interspersed.

The first three Parts he sent to Paris in 1701 by the hand of M. Boureau Deslandes, an officer of the French East India Company, "evidently in the hope that the *Storia* would be published at the expense of Louis XIV." Deslandes lent the MS. to Father Francis Catrou, a Jesuit, who in 1705 published an incomplete, garbled and grossly incorrect French version of it, with interpolations from other sources. This work ends with 1658 and has been translated into English, two reprints of the English version having been issued in Calcutta since 1900. In 1715 Catrou published a continuation, which is almost entirely taken from Part II of Manucci's MS. and covers the reign of Aurangzib. It has not been translated into English.

This Manucci MS.,—*i.e.*, the version of the *Storia* which was first sent to Europe,—lay in the library of the Jesuits in Paris till 1763 when it was sold with other works of that collection and passed through successive hands into the Royal Library of Berlin (1887.) It is described at the *Berlin Codex* Phillipps 1945, as consisting of three volumes written in Portuguese with three gaps subsequently filled up in French, and it forms the text translated by Mr. Irvine.

When Manucci in India learnt of the audacious plagiarism of Catrou, he sent (1706) the original Italian draft of his *Storia*, Parts I, II, and III, (which he had always kept by himself), as well as the only extant MS. of Parts IV (French) and V (French and Portuguese), to the Senate of Venice begging that august body "to order the publication of this little work which is likely to be of the greatest use to travellers, missionaries, and merchants, etc." This MS. is styled *Venice Codex XLIV* of Zanetti's catalogue. The only complete and consecutive text of Part V is an Italian version in manuscript made by Count Cardeira out of Portuguese in 1712, (*Venice Codex XLV*).

For a long time it was believed that the MS. which Manucci had presented to the Venetian Senate was mislaid during Napoleon's invasion of the Republic. But what Napoleon I. took away in 1797 was only a volume of 56 contemporary portraits of the princes and other celebrities of the Mughal court drawn at Manucci's instance by Mir Muhammad, an artist in the household of Shah Alam before 1686, and presented by Manucci to the Senate. (It is now *O. D.* No. 45 of the National Library, Paris). These portraits are of surpassing value and have been reproduced in Mr. Irvine's edition. Another volume of 66 drawings of Hindu gods, religious ceremonies, etc., sent by Manucci to Venice at the same time, is still there.

While scholars were for nearly a century mourning the disappearance of Manucci's original MSS., they had been quietly reposing in the Library of Saint Mark, Venice, their original destination! In 1899 Mr. Irvine rediscovered them there, and three years afterwards had them copied for his use. The Government of India lent him generous aid, and his translation was published in four sumptuous volumes in the "Indian Texts Series" in 1907 and 1908. Manucci in his original and undistorted form has at last been placed within the reach of readers, and the confusion, error, and obscurity which hung over his work for more than two centuries have at last been dispelled. This is Irvine's achievement.

IRVINE AS A MAN.

The most charming feature of Mr. Irvine's character was his spirit of unfailing and eager help and appreciation extended to younger men engaged in researches connected with his own subject. In this respect he presents a notable contrast to most other Orientalists whose mutual jealousies and acrimonious criticisms of each other darken their fame. I am only one out of the many students of Indian history who were indebted to him for help, guidance and light on obscure points. But for his assistance in securing for me loans or transcripts of rare Persian MSS. from England, France, and Germany, my *History of Aurangzib* could hardly have come into being. He also freely lent me MSS. from his own collection, and beat down the rates demanded by photographers in London and Paris for mechanically reproducing Persian MSS. for me by a process called rotary bromide print, in which the writing appears as white and the paper as black. In every difficulty and doubt that I have appealed to him, he has given me prompt advice and assistance. A certain Indian Nawwab has a rare collection of Persian historical letters. I secured his permission to take a copy of it at my expense and engaged a scribe. But for more than a year the Nawwab's officers under various pretexts refused my man access to the MS. At last, in despair I wrote to Mr. Irvine about the case. He wrote to one of his friends high in the Civil Service of Allahabad, and this gentleman communicated with the Nawwab. The owner of the MS. now had it copied *at his own expense*, bound the transcript in silk and morocco, and presented it to Mr. Irvine, who lent it to me soon after receiving it! Mr. Irvine also criticised and emended the first five chapters of my *History* as freely and carefully as if it were his own work.

Indeed, he rendered literary assistance in such profusion and at so much expense of his own time, that I was at times ashamed of having sought his aid and thus interrupted his own work. In connection with the statistical accounts of the Mughal empire, I had complained that ancient India, like ancient Egypt, can be better studied in the great European capitals than in the country itself, and Mr. Irvine's reply was to send me unsolicited his three MSS. of the *Chahar Gulshan*, a valuable work on Indian statistics and topography in the early 18th century, of which I had found only one and incorrect copy in India. Similar instances might be easily multiplied.

And yet so scrupulously honest was he that the most trivial assistance rendered by others to *him* was fully acknowledged in his works, as can be seen from the notes and addenda of his *Storia do Mogor.* He overwhelmed me with assistance while he lived, and yet his last letter written only two months before his death closes with the words, "Thanks for all the help of many sorts I have received from *you*!"

As a Historian.

As a historian, Mr. Irvine's most striking characteristics were a thoroughness and an accuracy unsurpassed even by the Germans. His ideal was the highest imaginable: "A historian ought to know *everything*, and, though that is an impossibility, he should never despise any branch of learning to which he has access." (*Letter to me*, 2nd October, 1910).

He brought light to bear on his subject from every possible angle; Persian, English, Dutch and Portuguese records, the correspondence of the Jesuit missionaries in India, books of travel, and parallel literatures, were all ransacked by him. The bibliography at the end of the *Storia* or the *Army of the Indian Mughals* is itself a source of instruction. A conscientious workman, he gave exact reference for every statement, and only those who carry on research know how very laborious and time-absorbing this seemingly small matter is. For these reasons I wish that our Indian writers in particular should study and imitate *The Later Mughals* as a model of historical method and a means of intellectual discipline.

Some are inclined to deny Mr. Irvine the title of the Gibbon of India, on the ground that he wrote a mere narrative of events, without giving those reflections and generalisations that raise the *Decline and Fall* to the rank of a philosophical treatise and a classic in literature. But they forget that Indian historical studies are at a much more primitive stage than Roman history was when Gibbon began to write. We have yet to collect and edit our materials, and to construct the necessary foundation,—the bed-rock of ascertained and unassailable *facts*,—on which alone the superstructure of a philosophy of history can be raised by our happier successors. Premature philosophising, based on unsifted facts and untrustworthy chronicles, will only yield a crop of wild theories and fanciful reconstructions of the past like those which J. T. Wheeler garnered in his now forgotten *History of India*, as the futile result of years of toil.

His Humour.

As a writer, Mr. Irvine was a vigorous controversialist. His article on *Canal Rent vs. Land Revenue* makes a trenchant attack on Mr. A. O. Hume's proposal to exclude the profits due to canal irrigation when fixing the assessment of land revenue and to fix the former on purely commercial principles. He had also a happy vein of humour which appears now and then in his writings, but oftener in his letters. Thus to his remark in the above article that "such a haphazard application of his great doctrine (of the greatest happiness of the greatest number) might well make old Jeremy Bentham shudder in his grave," he adds the foot-note "That is, if he ever got there. We believe his body was embalmed and kept in a glass case!"

In his *Army of the Indian Mughals*, p. 110, after asserting that the strange word *janjal* is a corruption of the known word *jazail*, and tracing the supposed steps of the corruption, he adds 'Q. E. D.' !

Again, he urged me to settle our difference as to the date of Shah Alam's confinement on the ground "If doctors disagree, what will laymen think of it?" In another letter he wrote:—

"I suppose man has still enough of the brute in him to have remained a fighting animal,—and the 'drum and trumpet school [of historians] seem just as popular as ever. . . . . The losing side [*e. g.* Dara Shukoh's] always get scant justice in histories." (13 Aug. 1905.)

"So far the Berlin Librarian has taken no notice of my communication [asking to be put in relations with a photographer there.] But I suppose one must have patience and wait the pleasure of these Great Men!" (10 Oct. 1905.)

"I have seen no mention of Bhimsen, [the Hindu author of a most valuable Persian history of Aurangzib's reign], or his sons. Historians are rarely mentioned (in other histories);—*not much hope for us!*"

EDITING HIS HISTORY.

The section of the *Later Mughals* covering the period from the death of Bahadur Shah I. to the accession of Muhammad Shah and the fall of the Sayyid Brothers (1712-1719), was printed under Mr. Irvine's eyes in the *Journal of the Asiatic Society of Bengal.* The portion immediately before this, *viz.*, that dealing with the reign of Bahadur Shah (1707-1712), is in MS., and will require minute and careful editing before it can be prepared for the press, as he left several gaps, queries, and pencil-notes in the margin for verification of references, consultation of authorities, and reconsideration of statements and views. The chapters on the origin and early history of the Sikhs, for example, were marked by him for revision after the expected publication of Macauliffe's *Sikh Religion* in 6 volumes. This section, however, attained to completeness of literary form in his hands, and requires correction or change in individual points and matters of detail only.

The last section, namely the narrative of events from 1720 to 1738, has been left in the form of rough drafts and detached notes. But even these "studies" of a master craftsman like him have a high value for students of history, in spite of their not having been retouched and given finality of form by him.

His daughter Mrs. Margaret L. Seymour has very kindly sent me the MS. portion of the *Later Mughals* to be revised completed and published; and I have, for the last two years, been collecting Persian MSS. dealing with the period 1720-1738, to enable me to edit and complete Mr. Irvine's work in a manner that will not be hopelessly below the high standard of all his published writings. If my calculations are not upset, the first volume (Bahadur Shah) will be sent to the press about the middle of 1920.

KHUDA BAKHSH, THE INDIAN BODLEY.

LIFE AND CHARACTER.

Khan Bahadur Khuda Bakhsh, C.I.E., was born at Chapra in North Bihar, on Tuesday, 2nd August, 1842, (23rd Jamadi-us-sani, 1258 of the Hijera era). His family was distinguished for scholarship if not for wealth, and one of his clansmen, Qazi Haibatullah, took part in compiling the Institutes of Aurangzib (*Fatawa-i-Alamgiri.*) Muhammad Bakhsh, the father of our hero, was a lawyer at Bankipur. Though not a rich man, he had a passion for Persian and Arabic books and succeeded in adding 1,200 manuscripts to the 300 which he had received by inheritance. On his death-bed he charged young Khuda Bakhsh to complete the collection in every branch of Oriental learning and build a library-hall for the use of the public. The family was then in hard straits; there was no patrimony for Khuda Bakhsh, and the future seemed cheerless. But without a moment's hesitation or fear, he accepted his father's command, and right nobly did he fulfil it. The 1,500 volumes left behind by Muhammad Bakhsh increased during the lifetime of his son to about 5,000, and their value in 1891, when they numbered only 3,000, was estimated by an expert under Sir Alfred Croft at two and a half lakhs of Rupees (£16,666). An English collection, worth nearly a lakh of Rupees, has been added; and the whole has been housed in a splendid edifice costing Rs. 80,000. All these represent the life's work of one man, Khuda Bakhsh.

Young Khuda Bakhsh read in Calcutta for some time under the care of Nawwab Amir Ali Khan Bahadur, a pleader of the Sadar court, who helped to maintain the English administration at Patna during the Mutiny. Bad news from home recalled the young student to Bankipur; his father was stricken with palsy, unable to earn anything, and the family was in great distress. Khuda Bakhsh was called upon to support them. He applied for a *Naib*-ship under a *Munsif*, but without success. Appointed *Peshkar* of the District Judge, he soon disagreed with his chief, Mr. Latour, and resigned. We next see him serving as a Deputy Inspector of Schools for 15 months. But in January, 1868, he passed the Higher grade Pleadership examination held at Patna, threw up his post, joined the local bar at the age of 25, and followed a career of striking brilliancy and success from the outset. On the very day that he began his practice, he signed 101 *wakalat-namahs*. Of no other lawyer has such phenomenal success been recorded.

His memory was wonderful; and numerous as his cases were, he required only a rapid view to master his briefs. Sir Louis Jackson, a Judge of the Calcutta High Court, while on a visit to Patna was struck by Khuda Bakhsh's advocacy, and was pleased to learn that he was the son of Muhammad Bakhsh whom he had known well during his District Judgeship of Patna. Sir Louis visited the bed-ridden Muhammad Bakhsh and offered Khuda Bakhsh a Sub-Judgeship with hopes of promotion to the

Statutory Civil Service. But he had a roaring practice and declined to enter the public service.

Public honours, however, came thick upon him. Like a true citizen he cheerfully gave his time freely to many a public cause. For his work on the School Committee he got a Certificate of Honour at the Delhi Darbar of 1877. He was the first Vice-chairman of the Patna Municipality and of the Patna District Board, when these self-governing bodies were created by Lord Ripon. His forensic ability found recognition in his appointment as Government Pleader; and he received the highest honour of his profession when, in 1894, he was appointed Chief Justice of the High Court of the Nizam. A Khan Bahadurship was conferred on him in January, 1883, and a C.I.E. in 1903. He was also a Fellow of the Calcutta University.

Returning from Haidarabad in 1898, he again joined the Bankipur bar. But his health was already on the decline, and the toils of his profession were too much for him. Latterly his mental powers gave way, and finally at 1 P.M., August 3rd, 1908, he breathed his last, after having completed his 66th year the day before. His younger brother, Mr. Abul Hassan, Bar-at-law, was for some time Chief Judge of the Calcutta Small Cause Court. Of Khuda Bakhsh's sons, the eldest, Mr. Salih-ud-din, M.A., B.C.L. (Oxford), Bar-at-law, has already made his mark as an Orientalist; the second, Mr. Shihabuddin, is a Deputy Superintendent of police and possesses a rare knowledge of Persian MSS.; the third died in early youth; and the fourth is a lawyer.

HIS SCHOLARSHIP.

Khuda Bakhsh was one of the greatest authorities on Islamic bibliography. An article from his pen on this subject appeared in the *Nineteenth Century*. But it represents only a small part of his knowledge. I remember how one day he poured out of the copious store of his memory, a full list of Arabic biographers and critics from the first century of the Hijera to the eighth, with running comments on the value of each. Most of their works he had himself collected. But alas! Arabic has long been a dead language in India. He also compiled a descriptive catalogue of many of his manuscripts, (the *Mahbub-ul-albab*, written in Persian and lithographed at Haidarabad in 1314 A.H.) Next to the acquisition of a rare MS. what gave him most delight was to see anybody using his library in carrying on research.

THE LIBRARY BUILDINGS.

Khuda Bakhsh had promised to his dying father to erect a house for the library, but the way in which he carried out his promise must have delighted Muhammad Bakhsh's soul in Paradise. This middle-class lawyer,—there are two or three such men in many District Courts of Bengal,—spent Rs. 80,000 on the library buildings. It is a two-storied structure with a spacious hall and two side-rooms on the first floor and a wide shady verandah going all around it. The two staircases, the west verandahs and most of the lower rooms are paved with marble or stone mosaics; in the other verandahs and rooms the floor is covered with encaustic tiles. The whole library with its buildings and grounds was made over to the public by a trust-deed, on 29th October 1891, one of the conditions being that the MSS. should not be removed from Patna. The donor in his unselfishness did not even give his own name to his gift, but called it the Oriental Public Library. The public, however, do not accept this self-effacement, and the Khuda Bakhsh Library is the only name by which it is known in India.

HIS DEVOTION TO THE LIBRARY.

But Khuda Bakhsh's devotion to the library is not to be measured by the money he spent on it, practically all his earnings. His whole heart was set on it. The library was the subject of his thoughts in waking and sleep alike. His very dreams centred round it. Two of them are here given from his narration; "At first MSS. came in very slowly. But one night a stranger came to me in my dream and said, 'If you want books, come with me?' I followed him to a grand building like the Lucknow Imambara, and waited at the gate while my guide entered it. After a while he came out, and took me inside to a vast hall in which a veiled being sat surrounded by his friends. My guide said, 'This man has come for the manuscripts.' The veiled one replied, 'Let them be given to him.' Shortly after this, MSS. began to pour into my library from various places." (This was a vision of the Prophet Muhammad and his *Ashab* or companions.)

"One night I dreamt that the lane near the library was filled with a dense crowd of people. When I came out of my house, they cried out, 'The Prophet is on a visit to your library, and you are not there to show him round!' I hastened to the manuscript-room, and found him gone. But there were two manuscripts of the *Hadis* (Traditions) lying open on the table. These, the people said, had been read by the Prophet." [Both these volumes now contain a note by Khuda Bakhsh, stating that they are never to be allowed to go out of the library; but no reason is given for the prohibition.]

So keen was his love for the library, that in his last year, when age had brought in its train a weakening of the intellect, he constantly thought of it and conjured up imaginary dangers to it. The position of every book in it was fixed in his memory. Only two days before his death he accurately described the case and shelf in which a copy of Abu Daud's work is kept.

I can still picture to my eyes the venerable founder as he sat near the library porch, his *huqqa* resting on a tripod, his grey hair and beard and plain white dress conspicuous from a distance. There were usually one or two visitors with him, or he was sedately turning over the leaves of some manuscript.

THE NATIONAL IMPORTANCE OF HIS LIBRARY.

He is buried in the place which he loved so well,

and to which he gave his all. A low unpretentious tomb, between the library buildings and the reading room, marks the last resting-place of the greatest benefactor and first citizen of Patna, a man sprung from the middle class who has left the country richer by a treasure surpassing the gifts of princes and millionaires. He was the Indian Bodley, and unborn generations of Indian scholars and readers will bless his memory and say that he was rightly named *Khuda Bakhsh*, 'the gift of God.'

For, the value of his gift and its full significance in the growth of our nation will be realised more and more as time passes. At present the Indian Orientalists are a small body, and few of them have taken to Persian, almost none to Arabic. A European scholar, after inspecting this library and noticing its lack of readers, remarked to Khuda Bakhsh, "What a fine cemetery for books have you built! In Europe such a library would have been daily thronged with a hundred students busy in research; but I see none such here." But it will not be so with us for ever; already a new era of research has dawned among us. In the meantime the Khuda Bakhsh Library forms a nucleus round which Indian manuscripts are gathering, sometimes by purchase, but mainly by gift. A most admirable feature of the European character is that wherever they go they collect MSS., antiques, and specimens for presentation to their national museums. In the Bodleian, the British Museum, and the India Office Library, there are many precious Oriental MSS. bearing the signatures of historical Anglo-

Indians of the 18th century,—Kirkpatrick, Gladwin, Fitzpatrick, Jonathan Scott, etc. Even in those early days of British power, while they were conquering and settling the land, they eagerly hunted for MSS. and bequeathed them to their country's use. Many rare and even unique works have thus disappeared from India, and now adorn the libraries of European capitals. European *savants* use them; to the Indian scholar, unless he is rich enough to visit Europe, they are sealed books. The Khuda Bakhsh Library, by offering a well-known and secure home for books and ensuring their public use, is tempting private owners all over India to send their collections to it and thus save them from being dispersed or lost to the country. This has been strikingly seen in some recent valuable gifts of Persian MSS. to this library by generous Muhammadan gentlemen. Jahangir's book of fortune-telling, *i.e.*, a copy of Hafiz's *Odes*, which he used to open at random to learn the future, (just as people took *sortes* from Virgil's poems in mediæval Europe),—has been presented by M. Subhanullah Khan of Gorakhpur. It contains marginal notes in the Emperor's own hand, stating when and with what result he consulted his oracle. Then again, Secretary Inayetullah Khan's *Ahkam-i-Alamgiri*, giving the Emperor Aurangzib's letters in his last years and graphically describing the break-down of the imperial authority, was formerly known by name only; no public library in Europe or India had a copy of it. In October, 1907 I discovered an old Padshahi MS. of it in the Rampur

(Rohilkhand) State Library and got the Nawwab's kind permission to take a copy of it. On my return to Bankipur, what was my surprise and pleasure to see that another MS. of it, (once belonging to some noble of the Court, and supplying many differences of reading),—had been shortly before presented to the O.P.L. by Safdar Nawwab! These are only two examples out of many which show how this library has been the means of keeping in our land India's literary treasures.

ITS PAINTINGS AND SPECIMENS OF CALIGRAPHY.

The specimens of Eastern painting,—Chinese, Central Asian, Persian and Indian,—collected here are invaluable to the student of Oriental Art, and have gained the warmest praise from a critic of Mr. Havell's ability. Many of them are illuminations of manuscripts from the Mughal Imperial library, some from Ranjit Singh's collection, most others from the picture-albums of the nobles of the Courts of Delhi and Lucknow, or scrap-books completed piecemeal after years of waiting and search by the untiring and single-minded founder. Most of the portraits of bygone celebrities are unique. The very papers on which the manuscripts are written are of such varied description and represent so many countries and periods of the paper-making art, that a special treatise may be written on them. The finest and most numerous specimens of Persian penmanship are to be found here, of any country in Asia.

ITS ENGLISH BOOKS.

Great as are the value and celebrity of its Persian and

Arabic manuscripts, its English books are of no mean importance even by their side. There are standard works on every subject,—poetry, philosophy, history, fiction, essays, etc.—and costly and very complete collections of dictionaries, English translations of Oriental works, and rare books on Indian history. Alibone's *Dictionary of English Literature* (with the supplement), the *Dictionary of National Biography*, 63 vols., the *Sacred Books of the East*, Burton's *Arabian Nights*, and many other works are to be found here only in all Bihar. There is a set of the very first edition of the *Waverley Novels*. Admirers of Scott will be delighted to see the once famous small volumes, printed at Edinburgh by Scott's friend and ruinator Ballantyne, and bearing on the title-page the words "By the author of Waverley" and not Scott's name,—for he was still the "Great Unknown," "the Wizard of the North."

Of the illustrated English books the total price runs up to several thousands of Rupees. There are Griffiths's *Ajanta Caves*, Maisey's *Sanchi*, Cunningham's *Bharhut*, Fergusson and Taylor's *Bijapur* and *Dharwar and Mysore*, Finden's *Byron* and many more. Khuda Bakhsh purchased an entire library in England by auction for £4,000 (Rs. 60,000). Hence the beautiful leather binding of most of his English volumes.

THE ROMANCE OF HIS BOOK COLLECTION.

There are many romances connected with the history and growth of the library. The most precious MSS. in

India were undoubtedly those of the Mughal library of Delhi. Thither, through the 16th and 17th centuries, came all rare and fine examples of caligraphy and illumination in the East. Some were purchased, others were executed by artists retained in the Imperial service, some were secured by conquest (as of Haidarabad and Bijapur in Aurangzib's reign), and many by the confiscation of the goods of great nobles on their death. Thus was formed the largest library in the East in that period; for, while Central Asia, Persia and Arabia were torn by incessant war, India enjoyed peace under the Great Mughals. In the 18th century many of these MSS. found their way to the library of the Nawwabs of Oudh. But the Sepoy Mutiny of 1857 brought about the fall of Delhi and Lucknow. The Imperial and Nawwabi treasures were dispersed. The Nawwab of Rampur (Rohilkhand), who had joined the English, got the best of the loot, as he had proclaimed among the victorious loyal sepoys that he would pay one rupee for every MS. brought to him. Khuda Bakhsh began his collection much later; but there was the greatest rivalry between him and the Nawwab. At last Khuda Bakhsh won over from the Nawwab's side that jewel of a book-hunter, an Arab named Muhammad Makki, paid him a regular salary of Rs. 50 a month (besides commission) for 18 years, and employed him in searching for rare MSS. (mostly Arabic) in Syria, Arabia, Egypt, and Persia, (especially at Beirut and Cairo). It was Khuda Bakhsh's invariable practice to pay the double railway fare to every manuscript-seller who visited

Bankipur, whether he bought anything from him or not. Thus his fame spread throughout India, and he was given the first choice of every MS. on sale in any part of the country.

Curiously enough, one year the library was broken into by a former book-binder and some of the best MSS. stolen. The thief sent them for sale to a broker or merchant at Lahore, and the latter unsuspectingly offered them to Khuda Bakhsh as the likeliest person to buy them. So, in the end the honest man came by his own and the thief was punished.

In another case divine justice asserted itself by a similar roundabout process. Mr. J. B. Eliot, Provincial Judge of Patna, (a great MS.-collector and donor to the Bodleian), borrowed a unique MS. of the Odes of Kamal-uddin Ismail Isfahani from Muhammad Bakhsh and afterwards refused to return it, offering a large price for it. The owner indignantly declined the proposal, but held his peace. When Mr. Eliot retired, he packed his choicest MSS. in some cases and shipped them to England, while his worthless books were put in another case and left at Patna to be sold by auction. But by the irony of fate or of the hand of God, call it what you will,—not only the extorted volume of Odes but some other rare MSS. (such as the *Majalis-i-Khamsa* bearing Shah Jahan's autograph), had got into the wrong case, and Muhammad Bakhsh bought them! On reaching England Mr. Eliot discovered his mistake, but only to fret and fume in vain.

One day when Khuda Bakhsh was driving back from the High Court at Haidarabad, his eyes, ever on the look out for MSS., discovered a bundle of volumes on a sack of flour in a grocer's shop. He stopped, turned the books over, and asked about the price. The owner shrewdly answered, "To any other man I should have sold this heap of old and rotten papers for Rs. 3. But as your lordship is interested in them, they must contain something of value. I want Rs. 20 for them." A true guess, for along with some worthless things the bundle contained an old work on Arabic bibliography not to be found elsewhere. Immediately after Khuda Bakhsh's purchase, Rs. 400 were offered for it by the Nizam, but in vain.

ITS TREASURES.

One of his literary treasures, Jahangir's Book of Fate, has been already described. Another is an autograph copy of the *Shahanshah-namah,* an epic poem celebrating the victories of Sultan Muhammad II. (the conqueror of Constantinople in 1453), written by the author in 1594 and presented to Sultan Muhammad III. Many bold and striking battle-pieces illuminate the volume, which reached India in Shah Jahan's reign, and either that Emperor or some later owner paid Rs. 750 for it. Jami's poem *Yusuf wa Zulaikha,* copied by the greatest of Persian caligraphists, Mir Ali, for which Jahangir paid 1,000 gold mohars, now adorns this library. There are two of Shah Jahan's Commonplace Books, one of them containing his signature at the age of 14,—Dara Shukoh's autograph copy of his work, the Lives of Saints (*Safinat-ul-awliya*), —the *Odes* of Hafiz belonging to the king of Golkonda and brought away to Delhi as a spoil of war,—Amir Khasrau's *Masnavi* copied for Sultan Abdul Aziz of Bukhara by Nur Ali (who was kept in confinement for 3 years to finish it,)—Ranjit Singh's military account book, with entries in Persian and Gurmukhi,—the richly illuminated copy of Firdausi's *Shahnamah* which Ali Mardan Khan presented to Shah Jahan at his first audience (1640),—the works of Khasrau containing the seal of Akbar's mother Hamida Banu Begam,—Hatifi's romance *Shirin wa Khasrau* written for Ibrahim Adil Shah, king of Bijapur, in a fine small hand, and Jahangir's *Autobiography* presented by himself to the king of Golkonda and brought back by Aurangzib's son after the conquest of that kingdom. Among the best illuminated MSS. are (1) a *History of Timur's dynasty* down to the 22nd year of Akbar's reign, rich in pictures, some of which have been reproduced but very imperfectly in Mrs. Beveridge's *Memoirs of Gulbadan Begam*, (2) the *Padishahnamah* or History of Shah Jahan with illustrations of the finest execution, detail and ornamentation, and (3) a *History of India* written for Ranjit Singh. Most sacred in the eyes of Persian students is the first half of Mulla Jami's autograph works, of which the second half is in the St. Petersburg Imperial library. The gifted poet's signature and handwriting agree exactly with those reproduced in the St. Petersburg Catalogue from the last page of his second volume.

Among the Arabic works, we have the *Tafsir-i-kabir*, three gigantic volumes written in an uniformly small, fine and distinct hand. It is a monument of incredible human patience and industry. There is a very old MS. on botany, the *Kitab-ul-Hashaish* (full of coloured illustrations), translated from the Greek of Dioscorides into Arabic by Stephen, the son of Basil, (who died in 240 A. H.), in the reign of the Khalif Mamun. Another equally old MS. is an Arabic treatise on surgical instruments (all illustrated), composed by Zahrabi in Granada. Another volume of Zahrabi's works bears traces of fire on many pages. Could it have been a survival from the Moorish library burnt by Ximenes? There is a piece of parchment with Cufic characters ascribed to Ali's hand! Another wonder is a complete *Quran* on a single fine film-like parchment roll of great length, written in a minute but distinct hand. A second copy of the *Quran* belongs to the age before diacritical marks came into use in writing Arabic.

A historic curiosity of great interest is the "Story of Christ" (*Dastan-i-Masih*), translated from the Bible into Persian at Akbar's request by the Portuguese missionary Jeronimo Xavier. This copy was transcribed by Abdur Razzaq Qandahari in 1013 A.H. (1604 A.D.)

In short, if I go on describing the riches of the Khuda Bakhsh library I shall never end. He who would know them should see them. In January 1903, Lord Curzon, fresh from the Delhi Darbar and with his head full of visions of Mughal grandeur, hummed when he entered this library,—

'*Agar firdaus bar ru-i-zamin ast*
Hamin ast, wa hamin ast, wa hamin ast.
If there be on earth an elysium of bliss,
It is this, it is this, and Oh ! it is this.'

That is the best description of it to a scholar.

ART IN MUSLIM INDIA.

I. ARCHITECTURE.

Pathan architecture, especially in Upper India, the land of stone, has a certain gloomy massiveness and solidity, but in general it lacks the elegance of finish, delicacy and wealth of decoration of the buildings of the Mughal period. The *brick* palaces and mosques of the Bengal sultans (at Gaur), however, form a class apart from the stone edifices of that age found in other parts of India, and indicate a higher level of design and decoration, and on the whole give one the impression of having been more influenced by local genius and local art traditions, while the other Muslim buildings of India clearly suggest a foreign origin.

It has been supposed that the radiating arch was introduced into India by the Muhammadans, because the Hindu arch follows the cantilever principle and is made up of horizontal stones laid in overlapping layers. We find one example of it in the huge arch of Altamash in the enclosure of the Qutb mosque. Early Pathan architecture is represented by mosques, tombs, minars and arched gateways. Its later representatives are the Sharqi buildings of Jaunpur and the fine brick palaces and mosques of the Bengal sultans at Gaur. Some of the buildings of the Tughlaq period suggest the ancient Egyptian style by their sloping walls and general heavy and dark appearance; but no connection between ancient

Egypt and Pathan India has been historically established. Nor do we find any Hindu influence in the Pathan buildings.

Mughal builders, especially in the age of Akbar, show a decided Hindu influence in respect of narrow columns, pilasters, corbel brackets and some other ornamental features; but their essential type and architectural principles are purely Muhammadan. The distinctive features of the Mughal architecture are—

(i) the pronounced dome like an inverted bell,

(ii) long slender turrets at the corners,

(iii) palace halls supported on pillars or following the *Baradari* (12 doors) principle, that is, combining a room and four corridors in one,

(iv) the distinctly Indo-Saracen gate, which takes the form of a huge semi-dome sunk in the front wall and bearing an admirable proportion to the building, while the actual entrance is a small rectangular opening under this arch.

Fergusson gives the highest praise to this style of gateway, and places it far above the Greek and Gothic conceptions of the door in respect of propriety and grandeur. The best example of it is the *Buland Darwaza* of Fathpur Sikri.

Many of the ornamental pillars of Akbar's buildings at Fathpur Sikri and the Jahangiri Mahal in Agra Fort are thin and tapering like those of Hindu temples, while the corbel brackets (especially in the tomb of Shaikh Salim Chishti and the hall of private audience at Fathpur

Sikri) are exact copies of the brackets of many a Hindu temple like that of Dilwara on Mount Abu. The decorative detail of a bell hanging from a chain in relief, which is found in one of the Muhammadan tombs of Ahmadabad and a few North Indian buildings, is also of Hindu origin.

The conspicuous Mughal dome, which is larger than an exact hemisphere, has been supposed by one school to be a copy of the bell-shaped tents of the Turkomans of Central Asia, because there was nothing like it in Pathan or Hindu architecture; but a pre-Mughal temple in Central India is said to have this sort of dome. Mr. Havell holds that the Mughal dome is really of Hindu origin and represents an attempt to translate into stone or brick the figure of a drop of water resting on a leaf, which in Sanskrit literature is the emblem of the shortness of human life and the uncertainty of all earthly things. This theory seems to be far-fetched.

Akbar was a builder in red sand-stone and Shah Jahan in white marble; in both we have plenty of carvings and relief work and perforated stone lattices; but Shah Jahan's buildings were also grander, larger, more delicately decorated, and far more costly. Akbar's chief edifices are the Akbari Mahal in Agra Fort and much of the fortifications of that place, the buildings at Sikandra, Fathpur Sikri, the fort of Attock, etc. Shah Jahan built the Jama Masjid of Delhi, all the fort palaces of new Delhi or Shahjahanabad (except the little Pearl Mosque there, which was built by Aurangzib), the great Pearl

Mosque of Agra, and many of the marble palaces and mosques within Agra fort, the Taj Mahal, Itimad-ud-daula's tomb, the marble pavilions on the Anna Sagar at Ajmir, and many others. Aurangzib built only the small Pearl Mosque in Delhi Fort and the tomb of his wife at Aurangabad; but some grand mosques were built by other persons in his reign, such as Wazir Khan's mosque at Lahore, Zinat-un-nissa's mosque in Delhi, etc.

II. Painting.

Painting received a great stimulus at the Court of Akbar and continued to improve till the fall of Shah Jahan. The Quranic law forbids man to reproduce the form of any living being, and hence orthodox Muhammadans* cannot draw anything except plants, flowers and geometrical designs (arabesques). Akbar was not an orthodox Muhammadan, and he engaged many painters and patronised their art.

On account of the Quranic prohibition, rich Muhammadans (especially in Central Asia) used to employ Chinese painters whose name (*nakkash-i-Chini*) became proverbial in Persian literature for excellence of workmanship. In the earliest paintings of Khurasan, Bukhara, etc., we see complete Chinese influence, especially in the faces, and the representation of rocks, sheets of water, fire and dragons. There are some dated manuscripts in the Khuda Bakhsh Library, Patna, the illuminations of

* I knew a Muhammadan hawker of Agra who refused to deal in marble mosaics representing even parrots!

which enable us to trace the history of Saracen art in India step by step with absolute certainty. The sumptuous *Shahnamah* presented by Ali Mardan Khan to the Emperor Shah Jahan in 1639 A.D. (though executed much earlier) represents the pure Chinese art of Central Asia. Specimens of this school must have reached India early in Akbar's reign and even before.

In the Court of our truly national king Akbar, this Chinese (or extra-Indian Muslim) art mingled with pure Hindu art—whose traditions had been handed down unchanged since the days of the Ajanta frescoes and the Bharhut and Ellora reliefs.† Thus Muslim art in India underwent its first transformation.

The rigidity of the Chinese outline was softened. The conventionality of Chinese art was discarded. We note a new method of representing rocks, water and fire, which is no doubt suggestive of the Chinese School, but it is clearly the Chinese School in a process of dissolution and making a nearer approach to Nature. The scenery and features are distinctly Indian. In short, the new element in the old is unmistakable even to a casual beholder. The Khuda Bakhsh copy of the *Tarikh-i-Khandan-i-Timuria* is the best contemporary example of this change that we possess in any public library in India. Readers in England have a slightly later and more developed example (though of Akbar's life-time) in the

† An *ivory* relief representing pastoral scenes of Krishna's life, done at Murshidabad about a century ago and now in Mr. P. C. Manuk's possession, looks exactly like a twin brother of the *stone* reliefs of Bharhut illustrating rural life in ancient India.

illuminated *Razm-namah* (Persian translation of the *Mahabharat*) preserved in the South Kensington Museum.

This process of the Indianisation of Saracen art continued after Akbar's time, till at last in the reign of Shah Jahan the Chinese influence entirely disappeared, the Indian style became predominant, and the highest development was reached (as we see in the Khuda Bakhsh copy of the *Padishahnamah*) in delicacy of features and colouring, minuteness of detail, wealth and variety of ornamentation and approximation to Nature (but without attaining either to true perspective or to light and shade).

This Indo-Saracen art was entirely developed in the courts of the Mughal Emperors. The subjects chosen were portraits of living men, scenes from the Persian epics, like the *Shahnamah,* fancy portraits of saints and *darvishes*, pictures of historic scenes, landscapes, imaginary female figures especially at the toilet, hunting scenes, episodes from the popular Persian love-poems, and also scenes of the Hindu epics to illustrate the Persian translations of the *Ramayan* and *Mahabharat* made by order of Akbar, or detached scenes of Hindu mythology.

Portrait painting reached its perfection about the middle of the 17th century (under Shah Jahan). True, expression was not studied, but so far as we can judge fidelity to the living original was secured in a high degree, and the colouring and drapery reached the perfection of delicacy. The master secrets of these craftsmen were their indigo and gold colours, which three centuries (often of neglect and rough handling) have failed to weaken, fade, or cause to cake off. Their night scenes and fire-works were a speciality, skill in which has been lost by their unworthy grand-children.

III. The so-called Rajput School of Indian Painting.

What Dr. Coomaraswami calls the Rajput School of painting is not an indigenous Hindu product, nor has it any natural connection with Rajputana. The vassal Rajahs of the Mughal Empire used to enlist painters trained in the imperial Court and employ them in representing scenes from the Hindu epics and romances and other subjects of a purely Hindu character, but the style and art-ideas of these painters are exactly the same as those of the painters employed by the Mughal Court. So thoroughly were the painters of Hindu subjects imbued with the spirit of their masters who drew Muslim or Mughal Court pictures that the result is often comic to a modern critic. I have seen some beautiful and genuinely old Indo-Saracen Hindu pictures which represent the elders of Mathura, dressed and armed like Mughal courtiers, going out to meet Krishna; and Ram advancing to the conquest of Lanka with his army marching in exact divisions, with all the arms, equipment and transport of the Mughal imperial army, *artillery not left out*! The *kamarbands* bristle with daggers. A few strokes with a brush can turn him into Akbar. Radha is only a Mughal noble lady at her toilet, with fewer ornaments.

There is a certain crudeness,—the use of

staring colours, a return to rigidity of outline, and a certain bareness or poverty of environment,—in the Rajput School, because it falls short of the perfection of detail, delicacy of touch and elaboration of ornament which marked the climax of Mughal art in the age of Shah Jahan. The Rajput Princes who patronised these painters were less rich and civilized than the Emperors of Delhi, and hence their painters represent a comparatively primitive school, or more correctly, suggest the idea of their being the work of the immature pupils of the old masters of the Mughal Court working in a less cultured atmosphere and for poorer patrons. The art traditions of this so-called Rajput School have continued with little change or development at Jaipur till to-day. Catering for the modern European market has effectually destroyed all hope of its rising above old conventions or showing a life of its own.

Indo-Saracen painting rapidly declined after the death of Shah Jahan. Aurangzib's puritanical simplicity and miserliness, the imperial bankruptcy caused by his many wars, and the disorder and impoverishment which seized the Mughal Empire under his successors, led to the starvation of artists and the disappearance of all genius in this line. Cheap inferior pictures continued to be drawn and the life of the artist in India became miserable in the 18th century, except under a rare Rajah or Nawwab here and there, till the invasion of Nadir Shah (1739), which left chaos behind it. In the last quarter of the 18th century there was a revival of art under the patronage of the Nawwabs of Oudh. But European art now began to exercise a fatal and dominating influence upon Indo-Saracen art. The result was the bastard Lucknow School of Painting,—a contemptible half-breed product without any of the good features of either the Indian or the European style. Taste, conception and execution alike are vulgar and affected;* and none of these works is enlivened by a single spark of genius. In the 20th century there has been a revival of interest in the old Indian paintings, thanks to the teachings of Mr. Havell, Dr. Coomaraswami and Sister Nivedita. The price of genuine old Indian pictures has been greatly raised by European and American collectors, and there is at present a considerable trade in faked old Indian pictures, that is, modern copies made from a few genuine old originals but artificially treated to look old and passed off on unsuspecting European buyers, as genuinely antique art works.

The new school of Indian painting which is represented by Abanindranath Tagore and his best pupil Nanda Lal Bose, deliberately imitates the Ajanta style. The Mughal school has also found a few modern imitators; but these are all artificial products, and not works of a living inspiration or genius; hence they cannot possibly cause a new birth or development of a living *growing* Indo-Saracen art. They lack the "divine madness" of

* The so-called old portrait of Akbar fondling his Christian wife, described by Father Hosten, is only a specimen of the Lucknow school, probably done after 1825.

the true creative spirit. Whom did the Ajanta painters consciously *imitate* ?

The so-called Kangra School represents a belated but pure survival of Indo-Saracen art dealing with Hindu subjects. Its chief master was Molaram, who lived in the Garhawal hills at the end of the 18th century. These hill tracts had escaped the anarchy which ruined the Mughal Empire in the 18th century and also the influence of European art, which began to move up the Gangetic valley after 1765. Therefore, the Kangra School retained well into the 19th century, the unadulterated form of an art which had been completely modified or disappeared in its cradle-lands of Agra, Delhi, etc. Molaram's colouring is extremely beautiful and his representation of animals, plants, etc., has remarkable delicacy of touch and charm, in spite of their palpable conventionality. His night-pieces are of special excellence.

The last attempt to revive Indo-Saracen painting was made by Ranjit Singh (about 1825-40), but the result, in spite of its elaborate prettiness, is only suggestive of the last gasp of an old and discarded horse, suddenly flogged into life.

There was no development of art during the Maratha predominance (1750-1800). But Hingane, the Maratha envoy at Delhi, and other officers of his race collected many old Mughal paintings and Sanskrit manuscripts illuminated with very fine miniatures at Delhi and the Rajput courts, and sent them to the Deccan for the Rajahs of Satara and the Peshwas of Puna. The decadence of the Mughal royalty and nobility as the result of Nadir's invasion gave the Marathas a rare opportunity to collect the richest art treasures of an *older* generation, and several of these still survive in the Bombay Presidency, as I discovered during my tours in Maharashtra.

In one branch of sculpture, namely, ivory carving (often in miniature) perfection was reached in the Mughal period, and the art has continued with hardly any decay to almost our own day, when it is fast dying out for want of patronage.

IV. The Textile Art.

India has been famous from very ancient times for her cotton cloth. The hot damp climate of the plains promoted the manufacture of *thin* muslins for the use of kings and nobles. Silk rearing and silk weaving were also a highly developed and flourishing art even before the Muhammadan period. Velvet and scarlet cloth were never indigenous in the country but were imported from abroad, (usually Europe), and these were special favourites of our Muhammadan rulers. A rich trade in them was carried on by foreigners, especially European merchants, throughout the Mughal period.

It is difficult to speak with certainty on the subject, but the Muhammadans seem to have introduced or at least to have greatly developed the variety and richness of embroidery. Large numbers of skilled artisans were maintained by our Muhammadan rulers to work figures with coloured cotton thread or silk thread or metallic thread on cloth of various kinds. There was immense variety in the designs, classes of fabrics and the nature of the material used (see *Ain-i-Akbari*, Vol. I). The shawl industry of Kashmir and the Panjab was distinctly the creation of the Mughal Emperors. The *kinkhab* and other kinds of embroidery work which they required for themselves and their courtiers, made them maintain large State-factories of weavers and embroiderers in many towns, besides patronising private artisans. Ahmadabad in Gujrat, Masulipatam and a few other towns were the most famous among the seats of the cloth industry. Carpets for the floor and hangings for the walls were most likely introduced into India by Muhammadan rulers, and the perfection of ornamentation, floral decoration and artistic harmony of colours in these was reached in the reign of Shah Jahan, when extremely costly carpets were manufactured for the court. Cloth canopies of state were exclusively used and these were also manufactured at great cost and in a sumptuous style, usually at Ahmadabad and in Kashmir. (They were known in the Hindu period, too.)

The court was the chief purchaser of these things, but a certain quantity was also produced for exportation abroad by private traders. Silk embroidery was carried to a high artistic level and the muslin industry of Dacca flourished greatly as the result of royal patronage during the Muhammadan period.

V. The Jeweller's and Goldsmith's Art

These were, no doubt, highly developed in the Hindu

period, but they received a great impetus under the Mughals, who lavished large sums on them, partly from their natural love of luxury and partly from the political necessity of giving costly ornaments in return for presents received from others or as gifts of honour to foreign rulers and their own sons and officers.

VI. Pottery and Metal Work.

Ornamental pottery and metal work were also very highly developed. The Hindu kings of old are not very likely to have used porcelain or any kind of costly earthenware, as their religious prejudices confined them to stone vessels and cheap clay pots and pans which could be thrown away after one use. As the metal vessels in Hindu houses have to be daily scrubbed, there was no room for ornamental brass or silver vessels for show or metal vessels with inlaid work, (*koft-gari*) in a Hindu household. Hence, inlaid metal vessels, porcelains, Bidri pots and even sumptuously decorated brass and silver vessels were characteristic of the Muhammadan period of India and not of the Hindu.

EDUCATION IN MUHAMMADAN INDIA.

Education was a purely private matter and a hand-maid of religion in Muhammadan times as well as Hindu. The duty of the State to educate its future citizens was not recognised even in Europe till near the end of the 19th century, (because there was no citizen), and a higher political conscience could not be expected in Mughal India. It was the Hindu king's duty to make gifts to pious men and Brahman scholars, and several of the latter kept pupils.

These pupils received their board and teaching gratis from their *Guru*, who met the cost from the gifts which he received from kings and rich house-holders at marriages, funerals and religious ceremonies. But the teaching of pupils was not a condition of these gifts. Nor had the Hindu State any officer or department of its own for public instruction even on a limited scale.

In Muhammadan times also, the State had no department of education. The Sultan or Padishah made large grants of lands or money to mosques, monasteries and individual saints and scholars. This, however, was recognised as a religious and not a political duty, nor were the recipients of these favours bound to maintain schools with the money. But in actual practice a primary school (*maktab*) was attached to almost every mosque. Here the Mullah of the mosque used to assemble the Muhammadan boys and girls of the neighbourhood and teach them to write the alphabet and commit the *Quran* to memory. The education imparted, therefore, was of the most elementary character. Some of the monasteries (*khankas*) contained scholars and theologians, but the lazy illiterate darvishes outnumbered them; hence the monasteries of Mughal India were not, as a rule, seats of learning like the monasteries of Christian Europe. There were, however, families of hereditary Muslim scholars living in certain towns, (*e.g.*, Tatta, Ajodhan, Sialkot, Sarhind, Kanauj, Nagor, Ahmadabad, Pattan, Jaunpur, etc.) whose reputation attracted pupils from all parts of the country and who practically maintained high schools or colleges, imparting the highest instruction in their special subjects. Though the Muhammadan kings rewarded these scholars in the course of their gifts to pious men in general, yet, these private town-colleges were without any endowment or permanent source of income and stability. Their life depended entirely upon the capacity of the individual teacher, his power to secure gifts in adequate quantity and his reputation for scholarship. They were purely family affairs, and naturally broke up when the family ceased to produce scholars.

Though Arabic became a dead language in India, even as early as the 13th century, yet the highest Muhammadan education was imparted through the medium of this language. All books of Science, Philosophy, Grammar and Mathematics, not to speak of Theology, were written in Arabic. Persian was studied only as an accomplishment necessary for cultivated society, like French in Europe, and not as the key to serious knowledge. It was the ambition of the most advanced Muslim students of India to visit Mecca, stay there for some years, and give the finishing touch to their education. A Mecca degree commanded the highest respect in India, and was often considered as the necessary qualification for the chief Qaziship. Khurasani, Turani and Arab scholars who came to India were highly welcomed as men of superior attainments and were promptly installed in high offices of the State or the Church. The tutors of the princes were chosen from this class, wherever possible.

FEMALE EDUCATION.

The Mughal Emperors used to employ learned women, usually Persians, to teach their daughters. The ladies studied the humanities in preference to theology, and Persian rather than Arabic. But every one of them who made some progress in her studies had to commit the *Quran* to memory. Some of these princesses even distinguished themselves in literature, the best examples being a wife of Akbar surnamed *Makhfi* (the 'veiled one'), Zeb-un-nissa the daughter of Aurangzib, and Nur-un-nissa, a wife of Shah Alam I. Noblemen also engaged lady private tutors for their daughters, but progress in letters was less often achieved in their families. Noble girls were married between the ages of 15 and 18 years as a rule. Middle class people usually kept their daughters in ignorance, except in the very rare cases where the fathers acted as teachers at home. In Persia and Arabia little girls attended the same primary school under the Mullah with the boys, but in Mughal India, so far as we can judge, such mixed classes of both sexes even for very small children were not held and the girls of the poor were left in absolute illiteracy. Sometimes the Mullah of a mosque gave instruction to a group of little girls from the neighbourhood whose parents greater them to be educated, but their knowledge did not go very far, and such female classes were the exception and not the rule. On the whole the disparity in education and even in literacy between our males and females was even greater in the Muhammadan period than it is in British India. To the highest department of thought no woman, Hindu or Muhammadan, of mediaeval India made the least contribution.

SUFISM.

Sufism played a very important part in the history of Indian culture in the Mughal period. Sufism as known in the western lands of Islam such as Syria or Egypt, was different in its character, principles and origin from the sufism of the middle East. The former was influenced by the Greek philosophers especially Plato and the Neo-platonists; the latter, though originating in Islam, was completely transformed by the pantheism of the Vedanta, (*hama oo-st*, He is in all things.) In fact, it was the Hindu form of devotion (*bhakti*) in Islam. Sufism afforded a common meeting ground for the higher Hindu and Muhammadan minds that were free from bigotry and susceptible of emotional appeals. Akbar and Dara Shukoh delighted in the company of Sufis, and came to be regarded as Sufis themselves; they haunted the society of liberal-minded saints of all creeds, and took the best elements of their teaching to form an eclectic religion of their own. The Indian Sufi brotherhood included not only ordained monks and faqirs, but also busy professional men, officers of the State, etc., who in their leisure hours, especially on moonlit nights, cultivated the poetry of sufism and met each other for religious discussions, devotional songs and ecstatic dances. The noted Sufi poets, such as Jalaluddin Rumi and Hafiz, were widely read by Hindus and Muhammadans alike. In addition, throughout the 17th and 18th centuries the more spiritually-minded among the men of the world in northern India, especially members of the writer-class (Kayeths), devoted themselves to the composition of Sufi verses of their own in Persian (and in the middle 19th century in Urdu). The number of such Indian Sufi poets must have totalled over three thousand, though the quality of their poetry was usually beneath contempt.

ORIENTAL MONARCHIES.

I.

What is the essential difference between the ancient and the modern State (no matter on which side of the Ural mountain)? Between the Athenian democracy and an ancient Indian tribal republic (*gana*)? Or between a Hindu empire and say, the French monarchy under Louis XIV?

When our new "national" school of writers on Hindu polity say that in ancient India there were republics, the king regarded himself as merely exercising a trust, a cabinet of ministers was held to be necessary, or that the people enjoyed self-government,—they may be literally correct; but we feel that this is not the whole truth, that there are certain qualifications which have been withheld from us. In the mind of a twentieth century reader, the above statements imply the direct influence of the people on the foreign policy of the State, the responsibility of the executive to the governed, the reign of a law which emanates from a legislature representing the citizens,—in short the control of the administrative machinery not by one man's will but by the will of Society. And yet, every one of these latter connotations is untrue and should have been expressly contradicted by the writer in order to guard against our forming a misconception of ancient Indian polity as it really was. The comparative method is of supreme necessity here, if we want to reach the truth.

A modern State is a compact thing in which the central authority and the individuals are organically connected. The ancient Indian State (leaving out of our consideration petty principalities and tribal groups)—was very loosely knit; in it the "Sovereign" had no means of making his will effective on the governed; his resources were poorer, his instruments could touch but a few, and the agents, mechanical appliances, and social organisation at his disposal were very much more limited and imperfect. He could crush an *individual* enemy or elevate an *individual* favourite, but he could neither grind down nor uplift the mass of his subjects by a fiat of his will or any action of his government. A vast State of the ancient type, like the Chinese empire, was held together only by granting the fullest local self-government to the village communes and even to the provinces, and letting the people alone, so long as they paid their proportion of the revenue and supplied their quota of soldiers. Any attempt at *general* oppression or general reform would fail through the Sovereign's impotence and the lack of a nexus between him and his subjects.

But local autonomy in parochial matters did not mean lack possession of representative government or popular would over the executive and national diplomacy. We of lack lect our "presidents of village panchayets" and and the ment of local boards; but that would not take panchayets making the Viceroy accept a universal edu- not mean or boycot of anti-Asiatic colonies, or the mean universal an Indian national militia, or war with any foreign State at the bidding of the representatives of the Indian people. The ancient Hindu king was similarly absolute,—so long as the people chose to obey him.

The modern State, on the other hand, is omnipotent for good and evil alike. It can reach its hand out to every citizen and to every corner of the realm; it crushes the individual under its excessive organisation and socialistic regulation. A single decree of the National Assembly swept away every trace of Feudalism from France and established social equality. A single *ukase* of Tsar Alexander I. emancipated the serfs throughout the continent called Russia, while another of Nicholas II. abolished vodka drinking throughout that boundless empire. A vote in the British Parliament introduced compulsory primary education for a population of more than 30 millions. A telegram from Wilhelm II. hurled a nation in arms into Russian Poland or neutral Belgium. A word from Catherine de Medici organised the massacre of Huguenots throughout the realm of France in a single day.

But in the ancient State the case was different. No edict of Asoka or Samudragupta could have abolished caste distinctions or introduced compulsory mass education, just as they could not have successfully carried or a general massacre or spoliation of their people. rescript of the Dowager Empress could have ancient a the cultivation of opium in China; no fiat of massacre Kai could create a truly national army of introduced men.

In the antique world, not the State but Society was omnipotent. And from the tyranny of Society the only refuge was the freedom of the homeless man, the *sannyasi.* An ancient Greek would have preferred ten years' rigorous imprisonment in his own city to even a year's exile among non-Hellens, however civilised.

But at the same time that the Hindu "Sovereign" was impotent, the people were equally powerless and devoid of any apparatus for enforcing their will on the government. They could frustrate the royal mandate by passive disobedience; but the will of the people could no more compel the king to adopt any desired line of policy than an unanimous resolution of the Indian National Congress can compel the Anglo-Indian government. The ancient State was weak,—both people and king, the king more than the people,—because the population was not homogeneous, there was no *organic* connection between the king and his subjects and between the subjects in one province and another, between one caste or clan and another. A "hero as king" like Samudragupta could sweep with his victorious legions from one end of India to another; but it was a temporary raid, not the *normal* condition of any Hindu empire. For deliberate national improvement or sustained struggle with foreign invaders the State under him and his successors was extremely weak, because unorganised, loosely knit,—a chance combination of provinces and tribes, in short, a mere "geographical expression."

Within a small tribal republic or principality,

however, the dominant populace were the rulers and the State had homogeneity (if we shut our eyes to the depressed indigenous races, like the Minas in Jaipur, the Parihars in Jodhpur and the Bhils in Udaipur). But it was the homogeneity of a Highland clan, as graphically described by Macaulay in his *History of England*, ch. XIII. Its efficiency was social, not political. Here, too, Society and not the State was omnipotent and in organic touch with the individual.

The people had no control over the State, except as a matter of fear or favour on the part of the "Sovereign" now and then. A licentious Baji Rao II., or an imbecile Daulat Rao Sindhia could wreck his army and State by his individual caprice. There was no internal check on him, no means of preventing such action on his part except the dagger or the poison cup. But these things are not matters of *polity*. In this sense the term "oriental despotism" is as applicable to the ancient Hindu State as to the empire of the Cæsars. In the ancient East and West alike, the people accepted the rule of the *Imperator*, the victorious general who had repelled foreign foes, who had saved them from *matsya-nyaya*, or who led them on to a career of lucrative conquest, and they gave him a *carte blanche*. In monarchies of this type polity had pretty nearly the same efficacy as a Parliament during "a state of siege." But disregard of the popular sentiment for ever cannot, in the nature of things, but be fatal to the military type of State in the end. That is the reason why so many ancient Hindu thinkers were busy devising rules for the guidance of kings and the organisation of the administration on some basis broader than one man's will. Their failure to achieve this end is proved by the rapid changes of dynasties and paramount States in the East.

When a Bengali writer tells us that as early as the 9th century A. D., the Bengali people elected their king, we are apt to exult and cry 'Hurrah for Popular Self-government in Ancient India!' We only forget that from the moment when Gopal, the son of a successful soldier of fortune, was crowned by the people of Gaur to save them from the anarchy of the smaller fry being eaten up by the bigger (*matsya-nyaya*), he became as absolute and as independent of any normal constitutional control on his actions by the people, as the Roman general who had saved Italy from the fear of an African invasion on the waters of Actium, who had freed the Western Mediterranean from the pirate galleys of Pompey, and whose victorious brows his devoted soldiery had crowned with laurel amidst shouts of *Ave imperator*! Nay, Gopal became even more absolute than Augustus, as the latter had to go through the formality of consulting the Roman Senate and the Roman populace, while the former's authority was unlimited in theory as much as in practice.

The Vedic kingship was, no doubt, responsible to the popular assembly of freemen, like the kingship of the ancient Gothic Mark. But such kingdoms were exceedingly small and primitive. When our kingdoms grew into large States, *i.e.*, throughout our recorded history, the royal power was unlimited by any constitutional machinery of popular or ministerial control—because there was no constitution but plenty of pious wishes and counsels embodied in *Niti-Shastras.*

II.

In strict theory, the Muslim State is a pure theocracy; its true sovereign is God, and the human ruler is merely God's agent on earth, bound to carry out the divine will as manifested in the Revealed Book and subject to the interpreters of the Quranic Law. The State is, in its essence, a military democracy, the Sultan or Padishah is only the elected commander of the faithful. He reigns not under any divine sanction, nor by hereditary right, but simply as the first servant of the realm, holding his office like a trust subject to certain conditions.

Logically there can be only one legitimate ruler of the entire Muslim world, just as there can be only one spiritual head of the Catholic Church. To the people of a Muhammadan kingdom their own ruler is the Khalifa of the age, the legitimate successor of the Prophet in the command of the faithful, and therefore entitled to the obedience of *all* the faithful wherever they might live. All other Muslim rulers are usurpers, who have kept this Khalifa out of his just rights. Every Muslim ruler, therefore, styles himself the Vicegerent of God, the Present-day Khalifa, the Suzerain of the Age. To his subjects, nobody else can be Khalifa; and

Muslim subjects of non-Muslim States are bound in conscience to rebel against their infidel rulers if they accept the theory of a universal Khalifate.

This theory makes it as imperative on the part of one Muslim State to annex *other Muslim* States as to conquer and convert all *infidel* lands (*dar-ul-harb.*) Considerations of expediency and social feelings have always made a large number of thoughtful Muhammadans averse to "wars between Muslims"; but such wars are logically as necessary as the irreconcilable feud between the Pope and the Anti-Pope. Indeed, the more orthodox and the more zealous for the glory of Islam a ruler is, the more is he morally bound to assert his own claim to be regarded as the only Khalifa in the world. The Emperor Aurangzib completely subordinated the State to the Church and sought to follow the Quranic law in every act of his life. He had diplomatic intercourse with the Sultan of Turkey, but always styled him "the Cæsar of Rome" (*i.e.*, of the Eastern Roman Empire) and not the Khalifa,—though Turkey was then as much in possession of the holy places of Islam as to-day. We have the full text of Shah Jahan's letter to the Sultan of Turkey, but through the five long lines of titles the latter is never once called Khalifa or the vicegerent of God. In short, the theory that the Muslim ruler of Turkey is the *spiritual* head of *all* Muhammadans wherever they may live, is a creation of the late 19th century and merely a result of the growth of a *political* pan-Islamic movement as a natural reaction against the steady absorption of all sovereign Islamic States by the Christians.

The Muslim State being a theocracy and its ruler the mere servant of the holy Law and elected captain of the free and equal faithful citizens,—the sovereign is liable to dismissal for any violation of the Quranic Law. No type of monarchy can be more limited *in theory*. But *in practice* the Muhammadan monarch was even more absolute than the Roman Imperator. There was no constitutional agency, no organised well-known body for judging his acts and passing sentence on him as a servant. In theory the theologians (*ulema*) were the repositories of the Quranic Law and its vindicators when it was violated. But they did not form any chamber, and even the membership of the body of the *ulema* was a matter of uncertainty, being entirely dependent on the readiness of the lay public to accept a particular scholar. A nebulous court with shadowy members cannot bring the master of legions to trial; and the *ulema* failed to supply the least practical check on the Muslim king's autocracy, if he happened to be a strong man of action with the army at his back.

Aurangzib got the *ulema* to justify his forcible deposition of his father (as well as the murder of his eldest brother) by charging them with the violation of the Quranic Law; and his own son Akbar induced four theologians to issue a similar bull of deposition against Aurangzib himself on the same ground! Aurangzib succeeded because he had a conquering army behind him, Akbar failed because he had not.

The hypocrisy of appealing to the Quranic Law against a political rival was, however, the homage which force paid to public opinion. The irresistible conqueror acknowledged, in theory at least, a higher authority than the swords of his legions. General Bonaparte, no doubt, purged the Assembly by means of his grenadiers, but even he went through the form of getting his military dictatorship validated by the rump of the Legislature. In Islam, however, there was no such legislative body. Everything was left to public opinion and the limit of public endurance. Hence, there was no constitutionalism in Oriental monarchies.

Works of JADUNATH SARKAR, M.A.

Shivaji and His Times.

528 pages, Rs. 4.

A comprehensive and critical study of Shivaji's life (1627-1680), policy, achievements and aims, and history of the Deccani Powers in his time, based upon all the available sources (both printed and MS.) in Marathi, English, Dutch, Persian and Hindi. (See descriptive *Bibliography* of nine pages at the end.)

Corrects Grant Duff's numerous errors and supplies much additional infomation from *contemporary* authorities unknown to him. The chronology is the most detailed and accurate possible at present. Reconstructs the life and reign of Shivaji from year to year in ample detail as known to the men of his time.

Among the contents are—Maharashtra: the land and its crops; the people and their character—Boyhood and education of Shivaji—A minute study of the Afzal Khan affair—wars with Shaista Khan and Jai Singh—Shivaji's visit to Aurangzib and romantic escape—His long wars with Bijapur and the Mughal empire—Grand coronation fully described—Invasion of Tanjore—Conquests in Kanara—Maratha Navy and naval wars with the English and the Siddis—Relations with the English factories—Shivaji's system of administration, institutions, policy, actual achievement and place in history—Was he a mere robber?

History of Aurangzib. *Rs. 3-8 each volume.*

Based entirely upon original sources, *viz.*, Persian State-papers, memoirs of contemporary Indians, more than 5,000 Persian and Marathi letters of the leading historic characters of the age, Marathi *bakhars* travels of Seventeenth century European visitors to India, and revenue returns and official hand-books of the Mughal empire.

Vol. I. Reign of Shah Jahan.

Lessons of Aurangzib's reign—materials—Aurangzib's boyhood and education—early viceroyalties—marriages and family—war in Central Asia—sieges of Qandahar—viceroyalty of the Deccan—invasions of Golkonda and Bijapur—Rise of

Shivaji and his early conflict with Aurangzib—illness of Shah Jahan—Aurangzib's preparations for contesting the throne.

Vol. II. War of Succession.

Defeat of Jaswant Singh—defeat of Dara—pursuit, capture and execution of Dara—capture of Dara's eldest son—struggle with Shuja—war in Bengal—tragic end of Shuja—captivity and execution of Murad—grand coronation of Aurangzib—long and critical bibliography of authorities in Persian.

Vol. III, Northern India during 1658-1681.

Aurangazib's sons, sisters, and chief ministers—relations with the outer Muslim world—strict moral and religious regulations—"burial of Music"—captivity, sufferings and death of Shah Jahan—conquests of Kuch Bihar, Assam, Chittagong, &c.—rebellions of frontier Afghans—persecution of the Hindus, temple destruction—Jaziya tax fully discussed—war with the Rajputs—Maharana Raj Singh—Durgadas and Ajit Singh—Hindu reaction—Satnamis—Sikh gurus Tegh Bahadur and Guru Govind Singh—Shivaji's letter on religious toleration—Tod's *Rajasthan* criticised—correct chronology of Aurangzib's reign, 1st half—second Persian bibliography.

Vol. IV. Southern India, 1644-1689.

Keynote of Deccan history in 17th century—Decline of Bijapur and Golkonda—Jai Singh and Shivaji invade Bijapur—internal anarchy at Bijapur—siege and fall of Bijapur—fall of Golkonda—Maharashtra : character of the land and the people—**Shivaji**—his rise—his wars with Bijapur and Jai Singh—his visit to Aurangzib and romantic escape—his struggle with the Mughals—his conquests—coronation—death and character—Shambhuji's reign, capture and execution—Prince Akbar in the Deccan.

Anecdotes of Aurangzib.

(Persian text with English translation) Rs. 1½.

The Anecdotes, 72 in number, have been translated from a Ms. Persian work (the *Ahkam-i-Alamgiri*, ascribed to Aurangzib's favourite officer, Hamiduddin Khan Nimcha), which no other historian has yet used.

The work is exceedingly interesting and valuable, as it throws much new light on Aurangzib and exhibits many unknown traits of his character, his pithy sayings, and his principles of government;—his treatment of his sons and officers, his policy towards the Hindus and the Shias, curious episodes of his early life (such as "the Puritan in love") and his last will and testament.

Chaitanya's Pilgrimages and Teachings

With a portrait, 338 pp., Rs. 2.

Chaitanya, (1485-1533), the greatest saint of Bengal, caused a complete moral revolution in Eastern India by preaching the creed of *bhakti* or devotion to God as incarnate in Krishna. His faith conquered Bengal, Orissa, and Assam, and also established its strongholds at several other places, notably Brindaban.

Economics of British India

Fourth ed., thoroughly revised and enlarged. Rs. 3.

A complete account of India's physical features, economic products and resources, transport, currency, public finance, labour laws, land tenure systems and legislation, &c. The handiest and most accurate description of India's economic condition and problems, and an indispensable guide to a right understanding of the country. Statistics brought up to 1916 and 1917. A chapter on *The Economic Effects of the War on India* added.